D0918466

Ancient Egyptian Literature

VOLUME I: THE OLD AND MIDDLE KINGDOMS

Published under the auspices of the
Near Eastern Center
University of California, Los Angeles

Ancient Egyptian Literature
A Book of Readings

by
Miriam Lichtheim

VOLUME I: THE OLD AND MIDDLE KINGDOMS

UNIVERSITY OF CALIFORNIA PRESS
Berkeley Los Angeles London

UNIVERSITY OF CALIFORNIA PRESS
BERKELEY AND LOS ANGELES, CALIFORNIA
UNIVERSITY OF CALIFORNIA PRESS, LTD·
LONDON, ENGLAND
PAPERBACK EDITION 1975
ISBN: 0-520-02899-6
LIBRARY OF CONGRESS CATALOG CARD NUMBER: 75-189225

Preface

When Harper Torchbooks reissued Adolf Erman's *Literatur der Ägypter* in the English translation of A. M. Blackman,* it rendered a service of a peculiar kind, for it brought back into print a once famous anthology which, though quite obsolete, had not been superseded. Obsolete, because egyptology, being a young science, is in a state of rapid growth and change. Hence translations published in the 1920s, even if from the pen of the outstanding scholars of the time, do not reflect our current improved understanding. Yet Erman's *Literatur* had not been superseded because no other anthology of comparable scope had appeared.

Apart from some compilations done by amateurs, which merely reproduce older translations in modernized language, two types of anthologies have appeared in recent decades. Firstly, there are the scholarly anthologies focusing on one particular type of Egyptian literary works within the narrow confines of belles-lettres. Here we may mention such distinguished works as G. Lefèbvre's *Romans et contes égyptiens* (1949), S. Schott's *Altägyptische Liebeslieder* (2d ed.; 1950), and E. Brunner-Traut's *Altägyptische Märchen* (2d ed.; 1965.) In Italian there is now the sizable anthology of E. Bresciani, *Letteratura e poesia dell'antico Egitto* (Turin, 1969). And, as this volume went to press, there appeared *The Literature of Ancient Egypt; an Anthology of Stories, Instructions, and Poetry*, by W. K. Simpson, R. O. Faulkner, and E. F. Wente, Jr. (New Haven, 1972). It offers a small selection of belles-lettres from the Old, Middle, and New Kingdoms. Second, there are the translations of Egyptian texts included in the large, eminently useful, and expensive, volume known as *Ancient Near Eastern Texts Relating to the Old Testament*, ed. J. B. Pritchard (2d ed.; 1955; 3d ed.; 1969). This has become an indispensable handbook for those who work in the fields of ancient

---

* A. Erman, *The Ancient Egyptians: A Sourcebook of their Writings*; trans. A. M. Blackman (New York, 1966); orig. English ed., *The Literature of the Ancient Egyptians* (London, 1927; German orig., 1923).

99205

Near Eastern histories and literatures. It brings together literary works drawn from half a dozen different civilizations; its emphasis is historical; the arrangement is topical, hence non-chronological; and the texts are frequently abridged. That is to say, its purpose and scope are so different from that of an anthology of Egyptian literature that it did not replace Erman's work, nor is it replaced by the anthology presented here.

The aim of the present volume is to provide, in up-to-date translations, a representative selection of ancient Egyptian literature in a chronological arrangement designed to bring out the evolution of literary forms; and to do this in a convenient and inexpensive format. It is meant to serve several kinds of readers: those who pursue studies within the broad spectrum of ancient Near Eastern civilizations; scholars in other humanistic fields and other readers for whom an acquaintance with ancient Egyptian literature is meaningful; and those who read ancient Egyptian. Translations serve two purposes. They substitute—inadequately—for the original works; and they aid in the study of the originals. It is my hope that this book of readings will be useful on both counts.

In dealing with ancient literatures it is both customary and appropriate to define literature broadly, so as to include more than belles-lettres. For the most part, ancient literatures are purposeful: they commemorate, instruct, exhort, celebrate, and lament. To define literature narrowly as non-functional works of the imagination would eliminate the bulk of ancient works and would introduce a criterion quite alien to the ancient writers. In fact, the reduction of the term literature to the concept of belles-lettres did not occur before the nineteenth century. Egyptian literature, then, means all compositions other than the merely practical (such as lists, contracts, lawsuits, and letters). Given this broad definition, it is naturally impossible to encompass their bulk in one or several volumes. Hence certain principles of selection have been applied. First, except for a few very fragmentary works, all works that fall under the narrow definition of belles-lettres have been included, provided that they were composed during the Old and Middle Kingdoms—since this volume is limited to the early periods. Written on fragile papyrus, and owing their survival and their recovery to chance, these works of the imagination are the scant survivors of a prolific literary production. Second, in choosing from the vast numbers of monumental inscriptions, carved on stone, which constitute the bulk of Egyptian literature in the wider sense, the focus of this selection has been on compositions that are representative of the major genres: biographical inscriptions, historical inscriptions, and that broad class of texts known as mortuary literature.

The medical texts, written on papyrus, which may well deserve a place within the definition of Egyptian literature, have been omitted out of practical considerations, having to do with their bulk and with their very specialized character.

In preparing the translations I have of course made full use of existing translations and studies, especially the more recent ones, which are scattered throughout the scholarly literature. Evidently a book of readings is up to date only if it reflects the present state of the discipline. Those who are familiar with the texts, however, are aware of the limitations of our understanding, of the conjectural nature of much that is passed off as a translation, and of the considerable differences between the several translations of one and the same text. Hence the "present state" of the discipline is an intricate web of consensus and controversy. Agreeing sometimes with one, sometimes with another, interpretation of a difficult passage, I have frequently agreed with none and sought my own solutions. Only in certain cases are these departures from existing translations discussed in the annotations, for to discuss them all would have resulted in an all too heavy philological apparatus, which would not have been in keeping with the major aims of the work. The annotations thus combine explanations addressed to the general reader with philological remarks addressed to colleagues; and they represent a compromise in being not as ample as is customary in a specialized publication, and more numerous and detailed than is usual in a book of readings intended for a wider audience. If this calls for an apology, I offer the observation that the present state of academic learning is characterized by a vast expansion in the numbers of those participating in it, and hence calls for publications that attempt to reach beyond the confines of professional specialization while at the same time making a contribution to the specialized discipline.

M. L.

Santa Monica, California
September 12, 1971

Contents

Chronological Table

Twelfth Dynasty	1990-1785
Sehetepibre Amenemhet I	
Kheperkare Sesostris I	
Khakheperre Sesostris II	
Khakaure Sesostris III	
Nimaatre Amenemhet III	
The Hyksos Period: Dynasties 15-17	ca. 1650-1550
The New Kingdom: Dynasties 18-20	ca. 1550-1080
Eighteenth Dynasty	ca. 1550-1305
Nineteenth and Twentieth Dynasties (Ramesside)	ca. 1305-1080
The Late Period: Dynasties 21-31	1080-332
The Ptolemaic Period	323-30
The Roman Period	30 B.C.–A.D. 395

Note: Only kings mentioned in the texts have been listed here.

Abbreviations and Symbols

Abusir Papyri	*Hieratic Papyri in the British Museum*; 5th series: *The Abu Sir Papyri*, ed. P. Posener-Kriéger and J. L. de Cenival. London, 1968.
Acta Or.	*Acta Orientalia.*
AEO	A. H. Gardiner. *Ancient Egyptian Onomastica.* 3 vols. Oxford, 1947.
Ägyptische Inschriften	*Ägyptische Inschriften aus den königlichen Museen zu Berlin.* 2 vols. Leipzig, 1913-1924.
Ägyptologische Studien	*Ägyptologische Studien*, ed. O. Firchow. Akademie der Wissenschaften, Berlin. Institut für Orientforschung. Veröffentlichung, 29. Berlin, 1955.
AJSL	*American Journal of Semitic Languages and Literatures.*
ANET	*Ancient Near Eastern Texts Relating to the Old Testament*, ed. J. B. Pritchard. Princeton, 1950; 2d ed., 1955; 3d ed., 1969.
Annuaire	*Annuaire du Collège de France.*
AOAW	Anzeiger der Österreichischen Akademie der Wissenschaften.
APAW	Abhandlungen der Preussischen Akademie der Wissenschaften.
Arch. Or.	*Archiv Orientalni.*
ASAE	*Annales du Service des Antiquités de l'Égypte.*
BAR	J. H. Breasted. *Ancient Records of Egypt.* 5 vols. Chicago, 1906-1907.
Barns, *AO*	J. W. B. Barns. *The Ashmolean Ostracon of Sinuhe.* London, 1952.
Barta, *Selbstzeugnis*	W. Barta. *Das Selbstzeugnis eines altägyptischen Künstlers (Stele Louvre C 14).* Münchner Ägyptologische Studien, 22. Berlin, 1970.
Bibliothèque d'étude	Institut Français d'Archéologie Orientale. *Bibliothèque d'étude.*
BIFAO	*Bulletin de l'Institut Français d'Archéologie Orientale.*
BiOr	*Bibliotheca Orientalis.*

Bissing, *Lebens- weisheit*	F. W. von Bissing. *Altägyptische Lebensweisheit.* Zurich, 1955.
BM	British Museum
Borchardt, *Denkmäler*	L. Borchardt. *Denkmäler des alten Reiches.* Vol. I. Catalogue général ... du Musée du Caire. Berlin, 1937.
Brunner, *Erziehung*	H. Brunner. *Altägyptische Erziehung.* Wiesbaden, 1957.
Brunner- Traut, *Märchen*	E. Brunner-Traut. *Altägyptische Märchen.* Dussel- dorf-Cologne, 1963; 2d ed., 1965.
Bruxelles Annuaire	Université Libre de Bruxelles. *Annuaire de l'Institut de Philologie et d'Histoire Orientale et Slave.*
de Buck, *Coffin Texts*	A. de Buck. *The Egyptian Coffin Texts,* ed. A. de Buck and A. H. Gardiner. 7 vols. Chicago, 1935-1961.
de Buck, *Readingbook*	A. de Buck. *Egyptian Readingbook.* Leiden, 1948.
Budge, *Facsimiles*	E. A. Wallis Budge. *Facsimiles of Egyptian Hieratic Papyri in the British Museum.* London, 1910.
Capart, *Rue de tombeaux*	J. Capart. *Une rue de tombeaux à Saqqarah.* Brussels, 1907.
CdE	*Chronique d'Égypte.*
Cemeteries of Abydos	E. Naville and T. E. Peet. *Cemeteries of Abydos.* 3 vols. London, 1913-1914.
Couyat- Montet, *Hammâmât*	J. Couyat and P. Montet. *Les inscriptions hiéro- glyphiques et hiératiques du Ouadi Hammâmât.* 2 vols. Cairo, 1912-1913.
CT	Coffin Texts
Edel, *Altäg, Gr.*	E. Edel. *Altägyptische Grammatik.* 2 vols. Analecta Orientalia, 34/39. Rome, 1955-1964.
Edel, *Inschriften*	E. Edel. *Zu den Inschriften auf den Jahreszeitenreliefs der "Weltkammer" aus dem Sonnenheiligtum des Niuserre.* Nachrichten der Akademie der Wissen- schaften in Göttingen. Phil.-hist. Kl., 1961 no. 8 and 1963 nos. 4-5. Göttingen, 1961-1964.
Erman, *Literature*	A. Erman. *The Literature of the Ancient Egyptians,* trans. into English By A. M. Blackman. London, 1927. Reprint New York, 1966 under title: *The Ancient Egyptians; A Sourcebook of Their Writings.*

Introduction by William Kelly Simpson. German
original: *Die Literatur der Aegypter*. Leipzig, 1923.

Erman,   A. Erman. *Die Märchen des Papyrus Westcar*. Mit-
Papyrus   teilungen aus den orientalischen Sammlungen, 5-6.
Westcar   Berlin, 1890.

Faulkner,   R. O. Faulkner. *A Concise Dictionary of Middle*
Dict.   *Egyptian*. Oxford, 1962.

Faulkner,   R. O. Faulkner. *The Ancient Egyptian Pyramid Texts*.
Pyramid   2 vols. Oxford, 1969.
Texts

Fecht, *Literar-*   G. Fecht. *Literarische Zeugnisse zur "persönlichen*
ische   *Frömmigkeit" in Ägypten*. Abhandlungen der Heidel-
Zeugnisse   berger Akademie der Wissenschaften. Phil.-hist.
Kl., 1965 no. 1. Heidelberg, 1965.

Fischer,   H. G. Fischer. *Inscriptions from the Coptite Nome*,
Inscriptions   *Dynasties VI-XI*. Analecta Orientalia, 40. Rome,
1964.

Frankfort,   H. Frankfort. *Ancient Egyptian Religion: An Inter-*
Religion   *pretation*. New York, 1948.

Gardiner,   A. H. Gardiner. *The Admonitions of an Egyptian*
Admonitions   *Sage*. Leipzig, 1909. Reprint Hildesheim, 1969.

Gardiner,   A. H. Gardiner. *Egypt of the Pharaohs*. Oxford, 1961.
Egypt

Gardiner,   A. H. Gardiner. *Egyptian Grammar*. Oxford, 1927;
Grammar   3d ed. 1957.

Gardiner,   A. H. Gardiner. *Hieratic Papyri in the British Museum*;
Hieratic   *Third series: Chester Beatty Gift*. 2 vols. London, 1935.
Papyri

Gardiner,   A. H. Gardiner. *Notes on the Story of Sinuhe*. Paris,
Sinuhe   1916.

Gauthier, *DG*   H. Gauthier. *Dictionnaire des noms géographiques*...
7 vols. Cairo, 1925-1931.

Goedicke,   H. Goedicke. *Königliche Dokumente aus dem alten*
Königliche   *Reich*. Ägyptologische Abhandlungen, 14. Wiesbaden,
Dokumente   1967.

Golenischeff,   W. Golenischeff. *Les papyrus hiératiques nos. 1115,*
Papyrus   *1116A et 1116B de l'Ermitage impérial à St-Peters-*
hiératiques   *bourg*. St. Petersburg, 1916.

Griffith   *Studies Presented to F. Ll. Griffith*. London, 1932.
Studies

Gunn, *Ptah-Hotep and Ke'gemni* B. Gunn. *The Instruction of Ptah-Hotep and the Instruction of Ke'gemni: The Oldest Books in the World.* London-New York, 1909; 2d ed., 1912.

Gunn, *Studies* B. Gunn. *Studies in Egyptian Syntax.* Paris, 1924.

Hatnub R. Anthes. *Die Felseninschriften von Hatnub.* Untersuchungen, 9. Leipzig, 1928. Reprint Hildesheim, 1964.

Hayes, *Scepter of Egypt* W. C. Hayes. *The Scepter of Egypt.* 2 vols. New York, 1953-1959.

Helck, *Beamtentitel* W. Helck. *Untersuchungen zu den Beamtentiteln des ägyptischen alten Reiches.* Ägyptologische Forschungen, 18. Glückstadt, 1954.

Helck, *Materialien* W. Helck. *Materialien zur Wirtschaftsgeschichte des neuen Reiches.* Teil 1-6 and Indices. Akademie der Wissenschaften und der Literatur, Mainz. Abhandlungen der geistes- und sozialwissenschaftlichen Klasse, 1960 nos. 10-11; 1963 nos. 2-3; 1964 no. 4; 1969 no. 4; 1969 no. 13. Mainz, 1961-1970.

Hermann, *Liebesdichtung* A. Hermann. *Altägyptische Liebesdichtung.* Wiesbaden, 1959.

Herrmann, *Untersuchungen* S. Herrmann. *Untersuchungen zur Überlieferungsgestalt mittelägyptischer Literaturwerke.* Berlin, 1957.

Holwerda-Boeser, *Beschreibung* Leiden. Rijksmuseum van Oudheden. *Beschreibung der aegyptischen Sammlung ... in Leiden,* by A. Holwerda and P. Boeser. 14 vols. The Hague, 1905-1932.

Intellectual Adventure H. Frankfort, H. A. Frankfort, J. A. Wilson, T. Jacobsen, and W. A. Irwin. *The Intellectual Adventure of Ancient Man.* Chicago, 1946.

JAOS *Journal of the American Oriental Society.*

JARCE *Journal of the American Research Center in Egypt.*

JEA *Journal of Egyptian Archaeology.*

JNES *Journal of Near Eastern Studies.*

Junker, *Gîza* H. Junker. *Bericht über die von der Akademie der Wissenschaften in Wien ... unternommenen Grabungen auf dem Friedhof des alten Reiches bei den Pyramiden*

	von Giza. 12 vols. Vols. 1, 4-12 issued as Denkschriften der Österreichischen Akademie der Wissenschaften, vols. 69 no. 1, 71 nos. 1-2, 72 nos. 1 and 3, 73 nos. 1-2, 74 nos. 1-2, 75 no. 2. Vienna, 1929-1955.
Lange-Schäfer, *Grabsteine*	H. O. Lange and H. Schäfer. *Grab- und Denksteine des mittleren Reiches.* 4 vols. Catalogue général ... du Musée du Caire. Cairo, 1902-1925.
Lefebvre, *Romans*	G. Lefebvre. *Romans et contes égyptiens de l'époque pharaonique.* Paris, 1949.
Lüddeckens, *Totenklagen*	E. Lüddeckens. *Untersuchungen über religiösen Gehalt, Sprache und Form der ägyptischen Totenklagen. MDIK,* 11. Berlin, 1943.
Mariette, *Abydos*	A. Mariette. *Abydos.* 2 vols. Paris, 1869-1880.
Mariette, *Mastabas*	A. Mariette. *Les mastabas de l'ancien empire.* Paris, 1889.
Maspero, *Hymne au Nil*	G. Maspero. *Hymne au Nil.* Bibliothèque d'étude, 5. Cairo, 1912.
MDIK	*Mitteilungen des deutschen archäologischen Instituts,* Abteilung Kairo.
Mélanges Dussaud	*Mélanges syriens offerts à Monsieur René Dussaud.* 2 vols. Paris, 1939.
Mélanges Maspero I	*Orient Ancien.* Institut Français d'Archéologie Orientale. Mémoires, 66. Cairo, 1934-1961.
Mélanges Michałowski	*Mélanges offerts à Kazimierz Michałowski.* Warsaw, 1966.
Mercer, *Pyramid Texts*	S. A. B. Mercer. *The Pyramid Texts in Translation and Commentary.* 4 vols. New York, 1952.
MIO	Akademie der Wissenschaften, Berlin. *Mitteilungen des Instituts für Orientforschung.*
Miscellanea Gregoriana	*Miscellanea Gregoriana:* Raccolta di scritti pubblicati nel i centenario dalla fondazione del Pont. Museo Egizio. Rome, 1941.
Möller, *Lesestücke*	G. Möller. *Hieratische Lesestücke für den akademischen Gebrauch.* 3 fascicles. Berlin, 1927. Reprint Berlin, 1961.
Müller, *Liebespoesie*	W. M. Müller. *Die Liebespoesie der alten Ägypter.* Leipzig, 1899.

ODM	Ostraca from Deir el-Medineh
OLZ	*Orientalistische Literaturzeitung.*
PJ	*Palästina-Jahrbuch.*
Posener, *Littérature*	G. Posener. *Littérature et politique dans l'Égypte de la xiie dynastie.* Bibliothèque de l'École des Hautes Études, 307. Paris, 1956.
Posener, *Ostr. hiér.*	G. Posener. *Catalogue des ostraca hiératiques littéraires de Deir el Medineh.* 2 vols. Institut Français d'Archéologie Orientale. Documents de fouilles, 1 and 18. Cairo, 1935–1972.
PSBA	*Proceedings of the Society of Biblical Archaeology.*
PT	Pyramid Texts
RdE	*Revue d'Égyptologie.*
Roeder, *Kulte*	G. Roeder. *Kulte, Orakel und Naturverehrung im alten Ägypten.* Die ägyptische Religion in Texten und Bildern, 3. Zurich, 1960.
RT	*Recueil de travaux relatifs à la philologie et à l'archéologie égyptiennes et assyriennes.*
SBAW	Sitzungsberichte der Bayerischen Akademie der Wissenschaften.
Schenkel, *FmäS*	W. Schenkel. *Frühmittelägyptische Studien.* Bonner orientalistische Studien, n.s., 13. Bonn, 1962.
Schenkel, *Memphis*	W. Schenkel. *Memphis, Herakleopolis, Theben.* Ägyptologische Abhandlungen, 12. Wiesbaden, 1965.
Schott Festschrift	*Festschrift für Siegfried Schott zu seinem 70. Geburtstag,* ed. W. Schenkel. Wiesbaden, 1968.
Schott *Liebeslieder*	S. Schott. *Altägyptische Liebeslieder.* Zurich, 1950.
Seibert, *Charakteristik*	P. Seibert. *Die Charakteristik.* Vol. I. Ägyptologische Abhandlungen, 17. Wiesbaden, 1967.
Sethe, *Erl.*	K. Sethe. *Erläuterungen zu den ägyptischen Lesestücken.* Leipzig, 1927.
Sethe, *Kommentar*	*See* Sethe, *Übersetzung*
Sethe, *Lesestücke*	K. Sethe. *Ägyptische Lesestücke.* Leipzig, 1924.
Sethe, *Pyramidentexte*	K. Sethe. *Die altägyptischen Pyramidentexte.* 4 vols. Leipzig, 1908–1922. Reprint Hildesheim, 1969.

Sethe,   K. Sethe. *Übersetzung und Kommentar zu den alt-*
Übersetzung *ägyptischen Pyramidentexten.* 6 vols. Glückstadt,
     1935-1962.

Sethe,   See *Urk. I* and *IV*
Urkunden I

Siut   H. Brunner. *Die Texte aus den Gräbern der Herakle-*
     opolitenzeit von Siut. Ägyptologische Forschungen, 5.
     Glückstadt, 1937.

SPAW   Sitzungsberichte der Preussischen Akademie der
     Wissenschaften.

Spiegel,   J. Spiegel. *Das Werden der altägyptischen Hochkultur.*
Hochkultur Heidelberg, 1953.

Studi   *Studi in memoria di Ippolito Rosellini.* 2 vols. Pisa,
Rosellini 1949-1955.

TPPI   J. Clère and J. Vandier. *Textes de la première période*
     intermédiaire et de la xième dynastie. Vol. I. Bibliotheca
     Aegyptiaca, 10. Brussels, 1948.

Unter-   Untersuchungen zur Geschichte und Altertumskunde
suchungen Ägyptens.

Urk. I and *IV* *Urkunden des ägyptischen Altertums.*
     Abt. I, *Urkunden des alten Reiches.* 2d ed. Leipzig,
     1932-1933.
     Abt. IV, *Urkunden der 18. Dynastie.* Fasc. 1-22.
     Leipzig and Berlin, 1906-1958.

Van de Walle, B. van de Walle. *La transmission des textes littéraires*
Transmission *égyptiens.* Brussels, 1948.

Vandier,   J. Vandier. *La famine dans l'Égypte ancienne.* Institut
Famine Français d'Archéologie Orientale. Recherches d'ar-
     chéologie, de philologie et d'histoire, 7. Cairo, 1936.

Vandier,   J. Vandier. *Mo'alla: La tombe d'Ankhtifi et la tombe*
Mo'alla *de Sebekhotep,* Bibliothèque d'étude, 18. Cairo, 1950.

Volten,   A. Volten. *Zwei altägyptische politische Schriften.*
Politische Analecta Aegyptiaca, 4. Copenhagen, 1945.
Schriften

Wb.   *Wörterbuch der ägyptischen Sprache,* ed. A. Erman
     and H. Grapow. 7 vols. Leipzig, 1926-1963.

Weill, *Décrets* R. Weill. *Les décrets royaux de l'ancien empire égyptien.*
royaux Paris, 1912.

Wilson   *Studies in Honor of John A. Wilson.* Studies in Ancient
Festschrift Oriental Civilization, 35. Chicago, 1969.

WZKM   *Wiener Zeitschrift für die Kunde des Morgenlandes.*
ZÄS   *Zeitschrift für ägyptische Sprache und Altertumskunde.*

Half brackets ⌐ ⌐ are used instead of question marks to signify doubt.

Square brackets [ ] enclose restorations.

Angle brackets ⟨ ⟩ enclose words omitted by the scribe.

Parentheses ( ) enclose additions in the English translations.

A row of three dots ... indicates the omission in the English translation of one or two words. A row of six dots ...... indicates a longer omission.

A row of three dashes – – – indicates a short lacuna in the text.

A row of six dashes – – – – – – indicates a lengthy lacuna.

Introduction

Literary Genres and Literary Styles

When writing first appeared in Egypt, at the very beginning of the dynastic age, its use was limited to the briefest notations designed to identify a person or a place, an event or a possession. An aura of magic surrounded the art which was said to derive from the gods. As its use slowly grew, its first major application (if we judge by the evidence of what has survived) took the form of an *Offering List*, a long list of fabrics, foods, and ointments, carved on the walls of private tombs.

The dogma of the divinity of kingship led to a marked different-iation between the royal and the non-royal, that is, private, spheres. Increasingly, what was proper for the life and death of a king differed from the usages of the private person. There was, of course, common ground, and interchange and adaptation of practices. But it was the differences between the two spheres which placed their stamp on writing, as on all aspects of cultural life.

It was in the context of the private tomb that writing took its first steps toward literature. The tombs belonged to high officials who had grown wealthy in the service of the king, and who applied a significant part of their wealth—in addition to outright royal gifts—to the construction and equipment of their "house of eternity." On the walls of the tomb, the written word gave specific identity to the pictorial representations. It named the tomb-owner and his family; it listed his ranks and titles, and the offerings he was to receive.

The *Offering List* grew to enormous length, till the day on which an inventive mind realized that a short *Prayer for Offerings* would be an effective substitute for the unwieldy list. Once the prayer, which may already have existed in spoken form, was put into writing, it became the basic element around which tomb-texts and representations were organized.

Similarly, the ever lenghthening lists of an official's ranks and titles were infused with life when the imagination began to flesh them out with narration, and the *Autobiography* was born.

During the Fifth Dynasty, both genres, the *prayer* and the *auto-*

3

biography acquired their essential features. The prayers focused on two themes: the request for offerings, and the request for a good reception in the West, the land of the dead. The *prayer for offerings* became standardized to a basic formula, subject to variation and expansion. It invoked the king and the god Anubis, the guardian of the dead, as the powers from whom the desired bounty would come.

Though capable of considerable literary elaboration, the prayer was essentially a function of the cult of the dead and hence not literary in the full sense. The autobiography, on the other hand, unfettered by cultic requirements, became a truly literary product. During the Sixth Dynasty it attained great length, and for the next two millennia it remained in use.

The basic aim of the autobiography—the self-portrait in words— was the same as that of the self-portrait in sculpture and relief: to sum up the characteristic features of the individual person in terms of his positive worth and in the face of eternity. His person should live forever, in the transfigured form of the resurrected dead, and his name should last forever in the memory of people. With eternity the ever-present goal, it followed that neither a person's shortcomings, nor the ephemera of his life, were suitable matter for the auto- biography. Hence the blending of the real with the ideal which underlies the autobiography as it does the portrait sculpture.

On first acquaintance, Egyptian autobiographies strike the modern reader as excessively self-laudatory, until he realizes that the auto- biography grew up in the shape of an epitaph and in the quest for immortality. The epitaph is not a suitable vehicle for the confession of sins. And the image designed for everlastingness had to be stripped of the faulty and the ephemeral.

The quest for immortality had a magical as well as a moral side. Statues, food offerings, and other rituals would magically ensure revivification and eternal life. But a good moral character, a life lived in harmony with the divine order *(maat)* was equally essential. Thus the affirmation of moral worth, in the shape of a catalogue of virtues practiced and wrongs not committed, became an integral part of the autobiography. In the Egyptian's relation to the gods morality and magic were ever intertwined. The catalogue of virtues was both a serious commitment to ethical values and a magical means for winning entry into the beyond.

The Sixth Dynasty is the period in which the autobiography, framed by the prayer for offerings, attained its full length. The terse and hesitant use of words which characterizes inscriptions till the end of the Fifth Dynasty, gave way to a loquacity that bespoke the new ability to capture the formless experiences of life in the enduring formulations of the written word. Hand in hand with the expansion of the narrative autobiography went the expansion of the catalogue of virtues. Where the former expressed the specific achievements of the individual life, the latter became increasingly formulaic. The resulting differentiation is one of content as well as of form. The narrative autobiography is told in the free flow of prose. The catalogue of virtues is recited in formalized, symmetrically structured sentences which yield a style of writing that stands midway between prose and poetry.

Two things make the catalogue of virtues significant: first, that it reflected the ethical standards of the society; second, that it affirmed, in the form of a monumental inscription, to have practiced the precepts that the Instructions, written as literary works on papyrus, preached.

These *Instructions in Wisdom*, as they are often called (the Egyptians themselves called them simply Instructions) are the second major literary genre created in the Old Kingdom. Working in the frame of a hierarchic society, the thinkers of the Old Kingdom envisaged the order of human society as the mirror image of the order that governed the universe. As the sun-god through his never failing daily circuit ruled the world, so the divine king guaranteed the human order. Within this framework, pragmatic thought working upon experience, and religious feeling and speculation combined to form convictions that were formulated as brief teachings or maxims. Through the joining of a number of such maxims there resulted the composition of an Instruction. The stylistic device by which maxims were strung together and shaped into a more or less unified work was the narrative frame: a father instructs his son.

In the earliest surviving Instruction, that of *Hardjedef*, the introductory part of the frame consists of the single-sentence statement that the Instruction was made by Prince Hardjedef for his son Au-ib-re. In later Instructions the frame was expanded until it reached the great length of the Prologue and Epilogue that surround the thirty-seven maxims of the *Instruction of Ptahhotep*.

The Instruction proved an immensely fruitful and popular genre. It was useful, enlightening, and entertaining. It lent itself to emulation and variation, and each new age filled it with new content. Though it included popular and proverbial wisdom, it was primarily aristocratic, until the New Kingdom when it became "middle class." At all times it was inspired by the optimistic belief in the teachability and perfectibility of man; and it was the repository of the nation's distilled wisdom.

Contrary to all other literary works, whose authors remained anonymous, the Instruction was always transmitted in the name of a famous sage. There is today no consensus among scholars about the nature of these attributions: whether they are to be taken as genuine or as pseudepigraphic. Many scholars have upheld the genuineness of the attributions of the *Instructions of Hardjedef* and *Ptahhotep* to Old Kingdom sages of that name—Prince Hardjedef, the son of King Khufu of the Fourth Dynasty, and a vizier Ptahhotep, not otherwise known, who according to the Instruction lived under King Isesi of the Fifth Dynasty. Of the *Instruction to Kagemni* only the final portion is preserved, according to which the instruction was addressed to a vizier Kagemni who served kings Huni and Snefru, the last king of the Third Dynasty and the first king of the Fourth, respectively.

When upholding the genuineness of the attributions, scholars are compelled to assume that two of the three works, *Kagemni* and *Ptahhotep*, were largely rewritten before they attained the forms in which they were copied in the Middle Kingdom papyri that preserved them, for the language of *Kagemni* and *Ptahhotep* is Middle Egyptian, the language of the Middle Kingdom. Only the language of *Hardjedef* is sufficiently archaic to make it appear as an Old Kingdom work not subjected to major alteration. The assumption of major alterations in the course of the transmission of the works is, however, a difficult one. There is nothing in our experience with the transmission of Egyptian texts which parallels the assumed translation of Old Egyptian works into Middle Egyptian. Furthermore, the attribution at the end of *Kagemni* is palpably fictional, for the character of the work is so much more evolved than that of the *Instruction of Hardjedef* that an attribution that makes it precede *Hardjedef* by two generations is impossible.

Given the tangibly fictional nature of this attribution, and the difficulty in the assumption of large-scale alterations, given also the parallels with biblical Wisdom Literature (e.g., the attribution of *Proverbs* to King Solomon), I personally am convinced that all three Instructions should be classed as pseudepigrapha. Once freed from the need to see in them compositions of the Fourth and Fifth Dynasties greatly altered by succeeding generations, one can inquire into the probable dates of their composition through the examination of all their aspects: language, style, method of composition, and the kind of thinking they reveal. In my opinion, such an examination makes it probable that the oldest of the three, *Hardjedef*, is a work of the Fifth Dynasty rather than the Fourth, for it is more evolved than the very brief and sparse monumental inscriptions produced in the Fourth Dynasty. *Kagemni* and *Ptahhotep*, which stylistically belong closely together, have the loquacity of Sixth Dynasty monumental inscriptions, and in all respects fit into the ambiance of the late Old Kingdom. They reflect a kingship which, whether or not still all powerful, is still serene, and a society that is orderly and optimistic. The nation is in harmony with itself and with the universe; and the moral values taught are the very same that are claimed in the autobiographies. It is also noteworthy that of the thirty-seven maxims with which Ptahhotep instructs his son, the future vizier, not one has any bearing on the vizierate—a strange situation if the work were the genuine legacy of a vizier who is introducing his son to the highest office of the land. In fact, the maxims embody the pragmatic wisdom of the upper-class Egyptian, and formulate a code of behavior befitting the gentleman of the Old Kingdom.

If seen as belonging to a time near the end of the Old Kingdom, the Middle Egyptian of *Ptahhotep* and *Kagemni* is explained as resulting from only minor alterations, for the end of the Sixth Dynasty and the beginning of the Eleventh are only a hundred years apart; and many of the forms characteristic of Middle Egyptian are found in the biographical inscriptions from Sixth Dynasty tombs.

Though the picture is incomplete, owing to the accidents of survival, it looks as if the monumental inscriptions that come from the royal sphere developed more slowly than their private counterparts. The reticence may have resulted from the sacral character of the monarchy. In any event, kings had no autobiographies. Their lives were wholly stylized, and at once more public and more remote than those of their subjects. By the end of the Old Kingdom three types of royal inscriptions had appeared in rudimentary form: the brief recording of a single event, the annalistic record, and the decree. These genres were as yet wholly functional and left no room to the literary imagination.

Only in the mortuary sphere, in the vast display of ceremonies devoted to the king's burial and resurrection, did the poetic imagination take wing. In the large body of inscriptions known as *Pyramid*

Texts, theological speculations, mythological allusions, and the formulae that served in the performance of a complex ritual were blended into incantations of great verbal force. Their central purpose was to achieve the resurrection of the dead king and his ascent to the sky. While trusting in the magical potency of words, the authors of these incantations often achieved the heightened intensity of formulation which is poetry.

The biographical inscriptions of the First Intermediate Period, that brief interlude of divided power that separates the Old from the Middle Kingdom, are characterized by a proud individualism, displayed alike by nobles and commoners. The society remained hierarchic, but the leaders were now the local chiefs, the rulers of the country's ancient districts *(nomes)*. Soon two families of nomarchs, at Heracleopolis and at Thebes, had amassed sufficient power to claim the kingship; and after the final victory of the Theban dynasty over the Heracleopolitan, the united monarchy was restored. This brief period has been much misunderstood. It was neither anarchic nor decadent. The quantities of crude artwork which it produced resulted not from any overall decline, but from the fact that quite ordinary people now made funerary monuments for themselves, while in the Old Kingdom only the wealthy high officials had done so. All that we have of Old Kingdom art is court art, done by the best craftsmen in the service of the king and the nobility. Now, all over the country, in addition to examples of first-rate work, we find that common people constructed simple monuments, done by minor local craftsmen and sometimes perhaps by their owners themselves. What has survived of these are mostly the stelae, made of hard stone, while the rest of the tomb has crumbled.

In the First Intermediate Period and thereafter the stela became the carrier of a short autobiography; and equipped with an offering prayer and an offering scene it was a self-contained memorial. The relatively small surface of the stela, as compared to the tomb-wall, led to the composition of a succinct summary of life. And when it became customary to transport a memorial stela to the holy city of Abydos, so as to bring its owner close to Osiris, the stela as a self-contained monument proved the most successful repository of the autobiography.

The second major literary legacy of this transitional period is the composition known as the *Instruction to King Merikare*. Standing in the tradition of the Instructions, it added a new dimension: it was a royal instruction; the testament of a departing king to his son and successor, and as such it embodied a treatise on kingship. Like all other Instructions, it is preserved in papyrus copies of later times, and its date must be guessed from internal evidence. The currently prevailing view, which I share, is that the work was composed not by its alleged author, the father of Merikare, but by a court scribe on orders of King Merikare. In other words, that it is pseudepigraphic as far as authorship is concerned but genuine as a work contemporary with the events to which it refers. Its historical content is usually taken seriously. Apart from its historical significance, the work is famous for its lofty morality which goes much beyond the pragmatic wisdom of Ptahhotep. It is also far more ambitious as a literary composition.

By the time Mentuhotep II had reunited the country and inaugurated the Middle Kingdom, the apprenticeship period of Egyptian literature lay behind. The Middle Kingdom produced a vast number of literary works in a variety of genres and with a complete mastery of forms. Thereby it became Egypt's classical age.

Using stelae of considerable size, the private autobiographies of officials, and artists as well, were now major works. They combined narration with catalogues of virtues and elaborate prayers. And often they contained elements not hitherto used: hymns to the gods and praises of the king.

The royal monumental inscriptions of a historical character now came into their own. They gave full and ornate expression to the dogma of the king's divinity, and to his role as leader of the nation in war and in the service of the gods.

The royal testament reappears dramatically in the *Instruction of Amenemhet I*, in which the old king—who was assassinated—warns his successor against trusting his subjects.

Otherwise, the traditional Instructions appear in a new form: the admonitory or prophetic speech of a sage who laments the evil condition into which the country has fallen. This variation on the theme of Instructions can only have resulted from the growing recognition of the problematic nature of human life. All was not well on earth. Men frequently acted from evil impulses; the nation was often rent by civil war. The seemingly permanent order could be destroyed—and yet the gods did not intervene. Thus the Egyptian began to grapple with the problem of evil.

The *Prophecies of Neferti* and the *Admonitions of Ipuwer* treat of evil as a social phenomenon, and their solution is the traditional one: a strong king is the guarantor of harmony.

To these ancient authors of around 2000 B.C. goes the credit of having formulated the problem of evil in at least one of its aspects. Their limitations in handling it are quite apparent. Painting in strong colors they reduced the problem to the dichotomy: order versus chaos. And in their efforts to describe a largely imaginary chaos, they employed an overwrought and repetitious pairing of opposites. Their principal rhetorical device was the reversal of a situation into its opposite: what was great has become small; the high has been laid low; the slaves have become masters; the masters are slaves; the riverbed is dry; the dry land is under water; and so on. These conceptual cliches, for which exact parallels exist in other literatures, have unfortunately often been taken for indicators of revolutionary upheavals. There is, however, no historical evidence whatever to warrant the conclusion that at one time or another a social revolution took place in ancient Egypt. Warfare at the time of a king's death appears to have been common. But at no time was the hierarchic order of the society abrogated or endangered. Eventually, the literary working of the theme "order versus chaos" spent itself. It had no sequel in the literature of the New Kingdom.

Egypt's high regard for the art of using words, a valuation of rhetoric comparable to that which was to prevail in Greece and Rome, found conscious expression in the composition known as the *Eloquent Peasant*. Here the art of fine speaking was made to serve the defense of justice. To the Egyptians eloquence came from straight thinking. It was left to the Greeks to discover that rhetoric could also promote an unworthy cause. In its display of fine speech this work, more than any other, made extensive and successful use of metaphors and other poetic imagery.

Hymns to the gods, close relations to the biblical psalms, appear on stone and on papyrus; and hymns to the king are elaborated into artfully constructed poems.

Brief snatches of song sung to the accompaniment of a harp grow into poetic works, some of which once again give expression to the reflective and troubled moods which inform so much Middle Kingdom literature. In lamenting the passing of life they sound a note of skepticism which was to become a continuous, if subdued, melody.

In the *Prose Tales* the art of fiction can be seen to grow in refinement, from the simply told tale of the shipwrecked sailor to the complex artistry of the *Story of Sinuhe*. All Egyptian narratives have an effective directness. They sketch a situation by a few strokes; there is no description for the sake of description. But there is a liking for the mixing of styles, a technique that culminates in the *Story of Sinuhe*, where the narration is interspersed with three poems and with an exchange of correspondence. Each poem is an example of a genre: the encomium of the king, the personal lyric, and the sacral song. The stylistic richness and refinement of *Sinuhe* cannot be adequately reproduced in translation. But the story's extraordinary vividness, its ability to convey the moods and feelings of its hero, and the excellence of its overall construction, can still fascinate. It is the crown jewel of Middle Kingdom literature.

Egyptian literature employs three styles. Prose, poetry, and a style that stands midway between the two. The hallmark of all prose is the linear forward movement of thought by means of variously structured sentences which, because they are deliberately varied, prevent the emergence of a regular sentence rhythm and of a predictable form. The intermediate style, on the other hand, is characterized by symmetrically structured sentences. It was employed exclusively in direct speech. Hence I call it "symmetrically structured speech," or, the "orational style." It has an exact counterpart in the intermediate style employed in a number of biblical books, notably Proverbs and Job, and a more distant parallel in the intermediate style of classical Arabic known as *saj'*. If prose is to poetry as walking is to dancing, the intermediate style may be compared to the formal parade step.

In Egyptian as in biblical literature, the principal device that activates the orational style is the *parallelism of members*. In Egyptian poetry, on the other hand, parallelism of members is only one among a number of stylistic means. Poetry defies a single definition. Yet most people recognize it when they see it. In formal structure Egyptian poetry was sometimes indistinguishable from the orational style. The difference then is one of content and mood, of feelings conveyed and feelings aroused in the reader or listener. All Instructions were composed in the orational style, and so were the catalogs of virtues in the autobiographies. But when in the *Instruction to Merikare* the king crowns his exhortations with a hymn to the creator, the oration rises into poetry.

By and large, Egyptian poetry used devices that underlined its distance from prose and from the orational style. A major device was the repetition of one line at regular intervals; this created stanzas.

In its simplest form the device already occurs in the song of victory which Weni inserted into his autobiography. There the repetition occurs in alternate lines; hence the poem consists of distichs. In the poems that conclude the *Dispute between a Man and His Ba*, the stanzas formed by repetition of lines are tristichs.

The orational style, and all forms of Egyptian poetry, point to a system of metrics which consisted in the accentuation of units of meaning—words, groups of words, and sentences. Whether the metrics entailed a fixed number of stresses in any given line is not known; and efforts to solve this question are stymied, just as they are in the study of biblical metrics, by the absence of all visible indications. But what can be clearly seen in Egyptian, and in biblical, poetic, and orational works is the metrical line as a whole and the principles by which it was constituted. The unit of a line was a unit of meaning, be it a whole sentence or a part of a sentence sufficiently self-contained to allow a pause before and after it. Whether in translations two clauses are gathered into a single line with a caesura, or are printed as two lines, is immaterial as long as the pauses can be observed. In Egyptian and in biblical literature, the metrical line is made apparent through parallelism of members and through more specialized devices, such as the repetition of one line or part of a line. Given the fact that biblical and Egyptian poetry operated with units of meaning, and given the overwhelming importance of parallelism and other devices making for symmetry, there can be no doubt that the metrical line was always an end-stopped line. Enjambment could not occur.

Egyptian grammar is synthetic, expressions are compact, and sentences are short. Analytic English grammar requires more words and builds longer sentences. Thus, in order to come within hailing distance of the Egyptian, it is necessary to pare the English sentences to the bone and to shun all paraphrastic additions. When this principle is adopted, and when the rule that all Egyptian metrical lines are end-stopped lines is observed, it is possible to translate Egyptian literary works with some degree of accuracy, that is to say, to imitate the Egyptian lines by comparable English lines. The resulting rhythms will roughly approximate the rhythmic beat of the original texts, even though we cannot know what particular methods of accentuation, or cantilation, the Egyptians may have employed when they read, chanted, or sang the dancing words.

PART ONE

The Old Kingdom

I. Monumental Inscriptions from Private Tombs

The six texts in this section illustrate the principal themes in the repertoire of tomb inscriptions.

The texts in the mastaba of princess *Ni-sedjer-kai* are limited to prayers for offerings and for a good reception in the West, the land of the dead. The official *Hetep-her-akhet* sounds the theme that in building his tomb he chose an empty spot and did not damage another man's tomb. He also addresses a warning to future generations of visitors not to enter the tomb with evil intentions.

Moving into the time of the Sixth Dynasty, we sample the declaration of innocence of *Nefer-seshem-re*, which embodies the principal elements in the catalogue of virtues which was being elaborated in this period. *Ni-hebsed-Pepi* has summarized his prayers for offerings and for a good reception in the West in the capsuled, self-contained form of the stela which, now still a part of the tomb, was destined to become an independent monument. Lastly, the two long inscriptions of *Weni* and *Harkhuf* are the two most important autobiographical inscriptions of Old Kingdom officials and show the growth of the autobiography into a major literary genre.

INSCRIPTIONS OF PRINCESS NI-SEDJER-KAI

In her Mastaba at Giza
Early Fifth Dynasty

The inscriptions in this fine, large tomb consist entirely of funerary prayers and of the names and titles of the princess and her father. They are carved on two architraves, two false-doors, and on the two pillars of the pillared hall. The relief figure of the princess, shown standing or seated at the offering table, concludes the texts. The two principal inscriptions are on the two architraves.

Tomb publication: Junker, *Gîza*, II, 97-121.
The two inscriptions: *Ibid.*, p. 115.

On the architrave over the entrance to the pillared hall
(Two horizontal lines:)

(1) An offering which the king gives and Anubis, lord of the necropolis, first of the god's hall: May she be buried in the western necropolis in great old age. May she travel on the good ways on which a revered one travels well.

(2) May offerings be given her on the New Year's feast, the Thoth feast, the First-of-the-Year feast, the *wag*-feast, the Sokar feast, the Great Flame feast, the Brazier feast, the Procession-of-Min feast, the monthly *sadj*-feast, the Beginning-of-the-Month feast, the Beginning-of-the-Half-Month feast, every feast, every day, to the royal daughter, the royal ornament, Ni-sedjer-kai.

On the architrave over the entrance to the inner chamber
(Four lines:)

(1) An offering which the king gives and Anubis, first of the god's hall: May she be buried in the western necropolis in great old age before the great god.

(2) May offerings be given her on the New Year's feast, the Thoth feast, the First-of-the-Year feast, the *wag*-feast, and every feast: to the royal daughter, the royal ornament, Ni-sedjer-kai.

(3) The royal daughter, royal ornament, priestess of Hathor,

(4) priestess of King Khufu, Ni-sedjer-kai.

INSCRIPTION OF HETEP-HER-AKHET

Leiden Museum
Fifth Dynasty

This is one of two inscriptions carved in vertical columns on the two sides of the entrance leading into the tomb-chapel. Behind the text columns is the standing relief figure of the tomb-owner.

Publication: Mariette, *Mastabas*, p. 342.   Holwerda-Boeser, *Beschreibung*, I, pl. v.   Sethe, *Urkunden*, I, 50-51.   H. T. Mohr, *The Mastaba of Hetep-her-akhti*. Mededeelingen en Verhandelingen van het Vooraziatisch-Egyptisch Gezelschap "Ex Oriente Lux," no. 5 (Leiden, 1943), p. 35.

Translation: BAR, I, § 253.

Right side of entrance
(Four columns:)

(1) The elder Judge of the Hall, Hetep-her-akhet, says: I made this tomb on the west side in a pure place, in which there was no (2) tomb of anyone, in order to protect the possession of one who has gone to his *ka*. As for any people who would enter (3) this tomb unclean and do something evil to it, there will be judgment against them (4) by the great god. I made this tomb because I was honored by the king, who brought me a sarcophagus.

INSCRIPTION OF NEFER-SESHEM-RE CALLED SHESHI

On the False-Door of his Tomb at Saqqara
Sixth Dynasty

As the focal point of the tomb, the false-door carried the offering-table scene and the name and titles of the tomb-owner. In addition, it came to be used for brief autobiographical statements, especially those which affirmed the deceased's moral worth. These affirmations became increasingly formulaic, and the limited space of the false-door lent itself to capsuled formulations. The stylization of these catalogs of virtues also meant that they were not told in the prose of the narrative autobiography, but were recited in the symmetrically patterned phrases of the orational style.

Publication: Capart, *Rue de Tombeaux*, pl. 11 (photograph).   Sethe, *Urkunden*, I, 198-200.

The text is written twice, in three columns on each side of the door, and ends with a short horizontal line containing the deceased's name whose relief figure stands below it:

(1) I have come from my town,
I have descended from my nome,
I have done justice for its lord,
I have satisfied him with what he loves.
I spoke truly, I did right,
I spoke fairly, I repeated fairly,
I seized the right moment,
So as to stand well with people.
(2) I judged between two so as to content them,
I rescued the weak from one stronger than he
As much as was in my power.
I gave bread to the hungry, clothes ⟨to the naked⟩,
I brought the boatless to land.
I buried him who had no son,
I made a boat for him who lacked one.
I respected my father, I pleased my mother,
I raised their children.
So says he (4) whose nickname is Sheshi.

STELA OF NI-HEBSED-PEPI FROM NAQADA

Kunsthistorisches Museum, Vienna
Sixth Dynasty

A painted slab stela ca. 34 × 61 cm. On the left, facing right, are the standing figures of the deceased and his wife. The inscription consists

of seven horizontal lines which fill the right side and one short vertical column in front of the man's legs.
Publication: Fischer, *Inscriptions*, no. 5, pp. 24-26 and pl. viii.

(1) An offering which the king gives and Anubis, who is upon his mountain and in the place of embalming, the lord of the necropolis. Buried be the Royal Seal-bearer, Sole Companion, Chief Scribe of boat crews, (3) Judge, Chief Scribe, Ni-hebsed-Pepi in his tomb which is in the good Western Desert. (5) She has taken his hand, he has joined land, he has crossed the firmament. May the Western Desert give her hands to him in peace, in peace before the great god. (7) An offering which the king gives and Anubis, so that funerary offerings be given to the Royal Seal-bearer, Sole Companion, honored by Osiris, Ni-hebsed-Pepi. *Above the woman's head*: His wife, his beloved, the Royal Ornament, Priestess of Hathor, Sepi.

THE AUTOBIOGRAPHY OF WENI

From Abydos
Cairo Museum No. 1435
Sixth Dynasty

The inscription is carved on a monolithic slab of limestone which formed one wall of the single-room tomb-chapel. The structure may have been a cenotaph rather than a tomb. The text consists of fifty-one vertical columns of finely carved hieroglyphs, preceded by one horizontal line which contains a prayer for offerings. Since some scholars include the first line in their numbering while others omit it, I have given double numbers. The stone has suffered considerable damage, resulting in a number of lacunae.

Weni's exceptionally long career spanned the reigns of Teti, Pepi I, and Mernere.

Publication: Mariette, *Abydos*, II, pls. 44-45.   P. Tresson, *L'inscription d'Ouni*, Bibliothèque d'étude, 8 (Cairo, 1919).   Borchardt, *Denkmäler*, I, 118 ff. and pls. 29-30.   Sethe, *Urkunden*, I, 98-110.

Translation: *BAR*, I, §§ 292-294, 306-315, 319-324.   M. Stracmans, *Bruxelles Annuaire*, III (1935), 509-544.   J. A. Wilson in *ANET*, pp. 227-228 (excerpts).

Additional references may be found in the works of Tresson and Borchardt.

(1/2) [The Count, Governor of Upper Egypt, Chamberlain], Warden of Nekhen, Mayor of Nekheb, Sole Companion, honored by Osiris Foremost-of-the-Westerners, Weni [says]: [I was] a fillet-wearing [youth] under the majesty of King Teti, my office being that of custodian of the storehouse, when I became inspector of [tenants] of the palace ――――. [When I had become] overseer of the robing-room under the majesty of King Pepi, his majesty gave me the rank of companion and inspector of priests of his pyramidtown.

While my office was that of ——— his majesty made me senior warden of Nekhen, his heart being filled with me beyond any other servant of his. I heard cases alone with the chief judge and vizier, concerning all kinds of secrets. [I acted] in the name of the king for the royal harem and for the six great houses, because his majesty's heart was filled with me beyond any official of his, any noble of his, any servant of his.

(5/6) When I begged of the majesty of my lord that there be brought for me a sarcophagus of white stone from Tura, his majesty had a royal seal-bearer cross over with a company of sailors under his command, to bring me this sarcophagus from Tura. It cam with him in a great barge of the court, together with its lid, a doorw y, lintel, two doorjambs and a libation-table. Never before had the like been done for any servant—but I was excellent in his majesty's heart; I was rooted in his majesty's heart; his majesty's heart was filled with me.

While I was senior warden of Nekhen, his majesty made me a sole companion and overseer of the ⌜royal tenants⌝.[1] I replaced four overseers of ⌜royal tenants⌝ who were there. I acted for his majesty's praise in guarding, escorting the king, and attending.[2] I acted throughout (10/11) so that his majesty praised me for it exceedingly.

When there was a secret charge in the royal harem against Queen Weret-yamtes, his majesty made me go in to hear (it) alone. No chief judge and vizier, no official was there, only I alone; because I was worthy, because I was rooted in his majesty's heart; because his majesty had filled his heart with me. Only I put (it) in writing together with one other senior warden of Nekhen, while my rank was (only) that of overseer of ⌜royal tenants⌝. Never before had one like me heard a secret of the king's harem; but his majesty made me hear it, because I was worthy in his majesty's heart beyond any official of his, beyond any noble of his, beyond any servant of his.

When his majesty took action against the Asiatic Sand-dwellers, his majesty made an army of many tens of thousands from all of Upper Egypt: from Yebu in the south to Medenyt in the north; from Lower Egypt: from all of the Two-Sides-of-the-House[3] (15/16) and from Sedjer and Khen-sedjru; and from Irtjet-Nubians, Medja-Nubians, Yam-Nubians, Wawat-Nubians, Kaau-Nubians; and from Tjemeh-land.

His majesty sent me at the head of this army, there being counts, royal seal-bearers, sole companions of the palace, chieftains and mayors of towns of Upper and Lower Egypt, companions, scout-leaders,[4] chief priests of Upper and Lower Egypt, and chief district officials at the head of the troops of Upper and Lower Egypt, from the villages and towns that they governed and from the Nubians of those foreign lands. I was the one who commanded them—while my rank was that of overseer of ⌐royal tenants⌐—because of my rectitude, so that no one attacked his fellow, (20/21) so that no one seized a loaf or sandals from a traveler, so that no one took a cloth from any town, so that no one took a goat from anyone.

I led them from Northern Isle ⌐and⌐ Gate of Iyhotep ⌐in⌐ the district of Horus-lord-of-truth[5] while being in this rank. ——————. I determined the number of these troops. It had never been determined by any servant.[6]

> This army returned in safety,
>   It had ravaged the Sand-dwellers' land.
> This army returned in safety,
>   It had flattened the sand-dwellers' land.
> This army returned in safety,
>   It had sacked its strongholds.
> This army returned in safety,
>   It had cut down its figs, its vines.
> This army returned in safety,
>   It had thrown fire in all its [mansions].
> This army returned in safety,
>   It had slain its troops by many ten-thousands.
> This army returned in safety,
>   [It had carried] off many [troops] as captives.

His majesty praised me for it beyond anything. His majesty sent me to lead this army five times, to attack the land of the Sand-dwellers as often as they rebelled, with these troops. I acted so that his majesty praised me [for it beyond anything].

Told there were ⌐marauders⌐ among these foreigners at the nose of Gazelle's-head,[7] I crossed (30/31) in ships with these troops. I made a landing in the back of the height of the mountain range, to the north of the land of the Sand-dwellers, while half of this army was on the road. I came and caught them all and slew every marauder among them.

Weni Becomes Governor of Upper Egypt

When I was chamberlain of the palace and sandal-bearer, King Mernere, my lord who lives forever, made me Count and Governor of Upper Egypt, from Yebu in the south to Medenyt in the north, because I was worthy in his majesty's heart, because I was rooted in his majesty's heart, because his majesty's heart was filled with me. When I was chamberlain and sandal-bearer, his majesty praised me for the watch and guard duty which I did at court, more than any official of his, more than any noble of his, (35/36) more than any servant of his. Never before had this office been held by any servant.[8]

I governed Upper Egypt for him in peace, so that no one attacked his fellow. I did every task. I counted everything that is countable for the residence in this Upper Egypt two times, and every service that is countable for the residence in this Upper Egypt two times.[9] I did a perfect job in this Upper Egypt. Never before had the like been done in this Upper Egypt. I acted throughout so that his majesty praised me for it.

His majesty sent me to Ibhat to bring the sarcophagus "chest of the living" together with its lid, and the costly august pyramidion for the pyramid "Mernere-appears-in-splendor," my mistress.[10] His majesty sent me to Yebu to bring a granite false-door and its libation stone and granite lintels, (40/41) and to bring granite portals and libation stones for the upper chamber of the pyramid "Mernere-appears-in-splendor," my mistress. I traveled north with (them) to the pyramid "Mernere-appears-in-splendor" in six barges and three tow-boats of eight ribs in a single expedition. Never had Yebu and Ibhat been done[11] in a single expedition under any king. Thus everything his majesty commanded was done entirely as his majesty commanded.

His majesty sent me to Hatnub to bring a great altar of alabaster' of Hatnub. I brought this altar down for him in seventeen days. After it was quarried at Hatnub, I had it go downstream in this barge I had built for it, a barge of acacia wood of sixty cubits in length and thirty cubits in width. Assembled in seventeen days, in the third month of summer, when there was no (45/46) water on the sandbanks, it landed at the pyramid "Mernere-appears-in-splendor" in safety. It came about through me entirely in accordance with the ordinance commanded by my lord.

His majesty sent me to dig five canals in Upper Egypt, and to build three barges and four tow-boats of acacia wood of Wawat.

Then the foreign chiefs[12] of Irtjet, Wawat, Yam, and Medja cut the timber for them. I did it all in one year. Floated, they were loaded with very large granite blocks for the pyramid "Mernere-appears-in-splendor." Indeed I made a ⌐saving⌐ for the palace with all these five canals. As King Mernere who lives forever is august, exalted, and mighty more than any god, so everything came about in accordance with the ordinance commanded by his *ka*.

I was one beloved of his father, praised by his mother, (50/51) gracious to his brothers. The count, true governor of Upper Egypt, honored by Osiris, Weni.

NOTES

1. On this rather obscure title consult Junker, *Gîza*, VI, 15-19, Helck, *Beamtentitel*, pp. 107-109, 115 f., and the additional evidence of the *Abusir Papyri*, where *ḫnty-š* and *ḥm-ntr* are paired.

2. Three ceremonial functions; the second is literally "making the king's way." On this ceremony see B. Grdseloff, *ASAE*, 51 (1951), 131.

3. The term "Two-Sides-of-the-House" refers to the Delta; Sedjer and Khen-sedjru are unknown.

4. The title *imi-r 'w* has been much discussed and variously rendered: "caravan-leader," (Faulkner, *Dict.*, p. 39); "overseer of dragomans," (Gardiner, *Egypt*, pp. 96, 99); "overseer of mercenaries," (H. Goedicke, *JEA*, 46 (1960), 62, and *idem*, *JEA*, 52 (1966), 173; "chief interpreter" (Fischer, *Inscriptions*, p. 29).

5. Three unknown geographical terms; it is not clear whether Weni is leading "from" or "to" these places. It is also not clear just where these campaigns against the "Asiatic Sand-dwellers" took place. In *Rivista degli studi orientali*, 38 (1963), 187-197, Goedicke has proposed to locate the campaigns in the eastern Delta rather than in Sinai and Palestine.

6. For this passage I have adopted the rendering of Edel, *Altäg. Gr.*, § 992. An alternate interpretation is that of Wilson in *ANET*, p. 228; see also G. Kadish, *JEA*, 52 (1966), 24 ff.

7. The location of "Gazelle's-head" is unknown. Weni's successful strategy consisted in ferrying half his army by boat and landing it in the enemy's rear, while the other half, traveling overland, made a frontal attack.

8. The office of Governor of Upper Egypt had been introduced in the Fifth Dynasty. Apparently Weni means that the office had never been held by a commoner.

9. "Countable" means "taxable." It is not clear what is meant by having counted everything twice; in *JEA*, 31 (1945), 15, Gardiner surmised that Weni "squeezed out of the unfortunate inhabitants of Upper Egypt twice as much in the way of taxes and work as his predecessors." But other and more charitable interpretations are possible, for instance that he was in office long enough to be responsible for tax-collecting on two successive occasions.

10. Each royal pyramid had its own name and could be referred to in personal terms as a divinity.

11. To "do" a distant place is an Egyptian idiom comparable with our "doing" a foreign country.

12. *Ḥḳꜣw ḫꜣswt*, "rulers of foreign countries," the term from which the name *Hyksos*, used by Manetho to denote the Asiatic invaders of Egypt, was derived.

THE AUTOBIOGRAPHY OF HARKHUF

Assuan
Sixth Dynasty

This most famous of the autobiographies of Old Kingdom officials is carved in fifty-eight lines on the facade of the tomb. Cut in a soft, flaking stone, the inscription is now in very poor condition. Harkhuf served kings Mernere and Pepi II and, like Weni before him, he became governor of Upper Egypt. In this capacity he led four expeditions to Nubia. His account of these expeditions is the most important source for Egypt's relations with Nubia at this time. To the account of his expeditions Harkhuf added the text of a letter he received from the boy-king Neferkare Pepi II in which the latter vividly and touchingly expresses his eagerness to see the dancing pygmy whom Harkhuf was bringing back with him.

The narration of his career is preceded by the standardized elements of tomb-autobiography—the prayers for offerings and for a good burial, and the catalog of virtues.

Publication: E. Schiaparelli, *Una tomba egiziana inedita* (Memorie della Accademia dei Lincei, ser. 4, Vol. 10/1) (Rome, 1893).   Sethe, *Urkunden*, I, 120-131.

Translation: *BAR* I, §§ 325-336, 350-354.

Study and partial translation: E. Edel in *Ägyptologische Studien*, pp. 51-75.

Comments: J. Yoyotte, *BIFAO*, 52 (1953), 173-178; D. M. Dixon, *JEA*, 44 (1958), 40-55; E. Edel, *ZÄS*, 85 (1960), 18-23.

Above the Entrance
(eight lines)

(1) An offering which the king gives and Anubis, he who is upon his mountain, before the god's shrine, in the place of embalming, the lord of the necropolis: May he be buried in the necropolis in the western desert, in great old age as one honored by the great god. ——————. The Count, Governor of Upper Egypt, Royal Seal-bearer, Sole Companion, Lector-priest, Chief of scouts, honored by Ptah-Sokar, Harkhuf.

An offering which the king gives and Osiris, lord of Busiris: May he journey in peace on the holy ways of the West, journeying on them as one honored. May he ascend to the god, lord of heaven, as one honored by [the god, lord of heaven]. The Count, Chamberlain,

Warden of Nekhen, Mayor of Nekheb, Sole Companion, Lector-priest, honored by Osiris, Harkhuf.

An offering which the king gives, to provide for him in the necropolis; and may he be transfigured[1] by the lector-priest on every New Year's day, every Thoth feast, every First-of-the-Year feast, every *wag*-feast, every Sokar-feast, on every great feast, ――――. The Royal Seal-bearer, Sole Companion, Lector-priest, Chief of scouts, Harkhuf.

> I have come here from my city,
> I have descended from my nome;
> I have built a house, set up (its) doors,
> I have dug a pool, planted sycamores.
> The king praised me,
> My father made a will for me.
> I was one worthy ―――
> One beloved of his father,
> Praised by his mother,
> Whom all his brothers loved.
> (5) I gave bread to the hungry,
> Clothing to the naked,
> I brought the boatless to land.
> O you who live upon earth,
> Who shall pass by this tomb
> Going north or going south,
> Who shall say: "a thousand loaves and beer jugs
> For the owner of this tomb,"
> I shall watch over them in the necropolis.
> I am an excellent equipped spirit (*akh*),
> A lector-priest who knows his speech.
> As for any man who enters this tomb unclean,
> I shall seize him by the neck like a bird,
> He will be judged for it by the great god!
> I was one who spoke fairly, who repeated what was liked,
> I never spoke evilly against any man to his superior,
> For I wished to stand well with the great god.
> Never did I judge between two [contenders]
> In a manner which deprived a son of his father's legacy.

An offering which the king gives and Anubis, who is upon his mountain and before the god's shrine, as provision for him in the necropolis, for one honored by Anubis, he upon his mountain and before the god's shrine ——————. The Count, Lector-priest —————— Sole Companion, Lector-priest, Chief of scouts, the honored Harkhuf.

Right side of entrance
(Fourteen lines)

(1) The Count, Sole Companion, Lector-priest, Chamberlain, Warden of Nekhen, Mayor of Nekheb, Royal Seal-bearer, Chief of scouts, Privy-councillor of all affairs of Upper Egypt, favorite of his lord, Harkhuf.

The Royal Seal-bearer, Sole Companion, Lector-priest, Chief of scouts, who brings the produce of all foreign lands to his lord, who brings gifts to the Royal Ornament,[2] Governor of all mountain-lands belonging to the southern region, who casts the dread of Horus into the foreign lands, who does what his lord praises; the Royal Seal-bearer, Sole Companion, Lector-priest, Chief of scouts, honored by Sokar, Harkhuf, says:

The majesty of Mernere, my lord, sent me together with my father, the sole companion and lector-priest, Iri, to Yam, to open[3] the way to that country. (5) I did it in seven months; I brought from it all kinds of beautiful and rare gifts, and was praised for it very greatly.

His majesty sent me a second time alone. I went up on the Yebu road and came down via Mekher, Terers, and Irtjetj (which are in) Irtjet in the space of eight months. I came down bringing gifts from that country in great quantity, the likes of which had never before been brought back to this land. I came down through the region of the house of the chief of Setju and Irtjet, I explored those foreign lands. I have not found it done by any companion and chief of scouts who went to Yam (10) previously.

Then his majesty sent me a third time to Yam. I went up from the nome of This upon the Oasis road. I found that the ruler of Yam had gone off to Tjemeh-land, to smite the Tjemeh to the western corner of heaven. I went up after him to Tjemeh-land and satisfied him, so that he praised all the gods for the sovereign.

Left side of entrance
(Ten lines)

(1) [I dispatched the courtier X with a man from Yam][4] to the retinue of [Horus], to let the majesty of Mernere, my lord, know [that I had gone to Tjemeh-land] after the ruler of Yam. Now when I had satisfied this ruler of Yam, [I came down through] ——————

south of Irtjet and north of Setju. I found the ruler of [the confederacy of] Irtjet, Setju, and Wawat. I came down with three hundred donkeys laden with incense, ebony, *ḥknw*-oil, *s3t*, (5) panther skins, elephant's-tusks, throw sticks, and all sorts of good products. Now when the ruler of Irtjet, Setju, and Wawat saw how strong and numerous the troop from Yam was which came down with me to the residence together with the army that had been sent with me, this ruler escorted me, gave me cattle and goats, and led me on the mountain paths of Irtjet—because of the excellence of the vigilance I had employed beyond that of any companion and chief of scouts who had been sent to Yam before.

Now when this servant fared down to the residence, the sole companion and master of the cool-rooms, Khuni, was sent to meet me with ships laden with date wine, cake, bread, and beer. (10) The Count, Royal Seal-bearer, Sole Companion, Lector-priest, God's Seal-bearer, Privy-councillor of ordinances, the honored Harkhuf.

On the far right
(Twenty-six lines)

(1) The King's own seal: Year 2, third month of the first season, day 15. The King's decree to the Sole companion, Lector-priest, Chief of scouts, Harkhuf. Notice has been taken of this dispatch of yours which you made for the King at the Palace, to let one know that you have come down in safety from Yam with the army that was with you. You have said in this dispatch of yours that you have brought (5) all kinds of great and beautiful gifts, which Hathor mistress of Imaau has given to the *ka* of King Neferkare, who lives forever. You have said in this dispatch of yours that you have brought a pygmy of the god's dances from the land of the horizon-dwellers,[5] like the pygmy whom the god's seal-bearer Bawerded brought from Punt in the time of King Isesi. You have said to my majesty that his like has never been brought by anyone who did Yam previously.[6]

Truly you know (10) how to do what your lord loves and praises. Truly you spend day and night planning to do what your lord loves, praises, and commands. His majesty will provide your many worthy honors for the benefit of your son's son for all time, so that all people will say, when they hear what my majesty did for you: "Does anything equal what was done for the sole companion Harkhuf when he came down from Yam, on account of the vigilance he showed in doing what his lord loved, praised, and (15) commanded?"

Come north to the residence at once! Hurry and bring with you this pygmy whom you brought from the land of the horizon-dwellers live, hale, and healthy, for the dances of the god, to gladden the heart, to delight the heart of King Neferkare who lives forever! When he goes down with you into the ship, get worthy men to be around him on deck, lest he fall into the water! When he lies down at night, get worthy (20) men to lie around him in his tent. Inspect ten times at night! My majesty desires to see this pygmy more than the gifts of the mine-land[7] and of Punt![8]

When you arrive at the residence and this pygmy is with you live, hale, and healthy, my majesty will do great things for you, more than was done for the god's seal-bearer Bawerded in the time of King Isesi, in accordance with my majesty's wish to see this pygmy. (25) Orders have been brought to the chief of the new towns and the companion, overseer of priests to command that supplies be furnished from what is under the charge of each from every storage depot and every temple that has not been exempted.

NOTES

1. A reference to the ritual by which the deceased was made an *akh*, a term usually rendered "spirit," "transfigured spirit," or "effective spirit."

2. Apparently a reference to the queen, although the title is used more generally for honored ladies.

3. On the implications of Harkhuf's exploratory journeys and on the location of the land of Yam consult especially the studies by Edel cited above.

4. Restored in accordance with Edel in *Ägyptologische Studien*, pp. 54 ff.

5. The term "horizon-dwellers" was a loose and vague designation of foreign peoples to the east and southeast of Egypt. The term was studied by C. Kuentz in *BIFAO*, 17 (1920), 121-190.

6. I.e., a dancing dwarf had once been brought from Punt but none had ever been brought from Yam.

7. The "mine-land" was a name for Sinai.

8. The often discussed location of Punt has been studied anew by R. Herzog, *Punt*, Abhandlungen des deutschen archäologischen Instituts, Abteilung Kairo. Ägyptologische Reihe, 6 (Cairo, 1968). His conclusions require the modifications outlined by K. Kitchen in his review in *Orientalia*, 40 (1971), 184-207: Punt extended from the shore of the Red Sea inland into the eastern Sudan.

II. A Royal Decree

CHARTER OF KING PEPI I FOR THE CHAPEL OF HIS MOTHER

From the Temple of Min at Coptus
Cairo Museum No. 41.890

This is one of a number of charters by which kings of the Sixth Dynasty and after granted immunity from all taxation to a particular sanctuary, in this case the mortuary chapel of the king's mother, which was connected with the temple of Min. A considerable number of such charters, carved on slabs, were found in this temple.

In the upper part of this stela King Merire Pepi I presents an offering to Min. The king's mother stands behind him. Below the scene is the inscription in nine lines.

Publication: Weill, *Décrets royaux*, pp. 40-43 and pl. vii.   Sethe, *Urkunden*, I, 214.   Goedicke, *Königliche Dokumente*, pp. 42-54 and fig. 4.

(1) First jubilee of Merire, given life, duration, and dominion; may he live like Re. (3) District of the Two-Falcons: Coptus: chapel of Queen-mother Iput. My majesty has commanded the exemption of this chapel [and what belongs to it] (5) in serfs and large and small cattle. [There is no] claim [whatever against it]. As to any commissioner who shall travel south on any mission, my majesty does not permit (him) (7) to charge any travel expenses to the chapel. Nor does my majesty permit to supply the royal retinue. For my majesty has commanded the exemption of this chapel. (9) My majesty does not permit to place any impost levied for the residence upon this chapel.

III. From The Pyramid Texts

The Pyramid Texts are carved on the walls of the sarcophagus chambers and adjoining rooms and corridors that together form the royal burial suites inside the pyramids of Saqqara. They were discovered in 1881 in five of the Saqqara pyramids; those of Unas, the last king of the Fifth Dynasty, and of Kings Teti, Pepi I, Mernere, and Pepi II, the principal kings of the Sixth Dynasty.

Since the 1920s some additional texts were found in the pyramids of the three queens of Pepi II, and in the pyramid of King Ibi of the Eighth Dynasty.

Taken together they constitute a corpus of incantations, the purpose of which is to promote the resurrection and well-being of the deceased kings. As carved on the walls, the incantations are clearly separated from one another by means of an introductory term and by dividing lines. Thus they form distinct, self-contained "utterances."

The oldest group, that in the pyramid of Unas, consists of 228 utterances. This stock was reused, though not in its entirety, in the pyramids of the subsequent kings, with new utterances added. Kurt Sethe's standard edition of the Pyramid Texts comprises a total of 714 distinct utterances; and the additional texts, discovered after the completion of his edition, bring the total to 759.

In assigning fixed numbers to the individual utterances Sethe, and Maspero before him, began the numbering in the sarcophagus chambers and ended in the outermost corridors. Some scholars think that the reverse order of numbering, beginning with the corridors and ending in the sarcophagus chambers, is preferable, for it would reveal a logical order in the distribution of the utterances. The problem whether a logical order of some kind existed is a complex one which requires much additional study. For the time being Sethe's method of numbering the utterances is the standard one.

The utterances translated here are drawn from the pyramids of Unas, Teti, and Pepi I. In each case the translation presents the original version of the text without regard to the later parallel versions of the same spells, which may contain variations. That is to say, "Unas Texts" are drawn from the Unas pyramid, and their reuse in the later pyramids is ignored, and Teti and Pepi I texts are drawn from their respective pyramids in the forms in which they first appeared. This method is designed to pinpoint the first appearance of each text cited and thus, within the limits of the small selection, allow a sampling of the specific characteristics of the successive generations of Pyramid Texts. The sample is of course too small to permit an overview of all the themes, and of the evolution of thought which shaped the growth and change of certain themes and the disappearance of others.

The disappearance of some topics, or viewpoints, is as significant as the creation of new ones. For example, the famous "Cannibal Hymn" of the Unas pyramid (Utterance 273-274) was reused in the pyramid of Teti but not thereafter, a clear indication that this very primitive text was not suited to the thinking of later generations.

The central theme and purpose of the Pyramid Texts is the resurrection of the dead king and his ascent to the sky. The principal stages of his dramatic conquest of eternal life are: the awakening in the tomb from the sleep of death; the ascent to the sky; and the admission to the company of the immortal gods. These stages are envisioned with a variety of detail, and joined to them are ancillary themes. Thus numerous texts are concerned with purification and with the offering of food and drink, and the texts of this type were originally recited by the priests during the several stages of the king's burial and in the subsequent funerary cult performed at the pyramid. Other texts, such as the spells against snakes, come from the sphere of daily life. Yet others are primarily speculative and concerned with envisioning the realm of the gods.

The utterances vary greatly in length. By and large, the short ones are unified and consistent, while the long ones tend to be repetitious and diffuse. This also means that the compositions most successful as poetry will be found among the shorter texts. All Pyramid Texts are composed in the "orational style," a recitative that depends for its effects on a strong regular rhythm. Here and there, when suffused with feeling and imagination, the incantations attain the heightened intensity which is the universal hallmark of poetry.

Publication: Sethe, *Pyramidentexte*.   A. Piankoff, *The Pyramid of Unas*, Bollingen series, 40:5 (Princeton, 1968).

Translation and commentary: Sethe, *Übersetzung*.   Mercer, *Pyramid Texts*.   Faulkner, *Pyramid Texts*.

UNAS PYRAMID TEXTS

Utterance 217

Sarcophagus Chamber, South Wall

The king joins the sun-god[1]

Re-Atum, this Unas comes to you,
A spirit[2] indestructible
Who lays claim to the place of the four pillars!
Your son comes to you, this Unas comes to you,
May you cross the sky united in the dark,
May you rise in lightland, the place in which you shine!
Seth, Nephthys, go proclaim to Upper Egypt's gods
And their spirits:
"This Unas comes, a spirit indestructible,
If he wishes you to die, you will die,

If he wishes you to live, you will live!"
Re-Atum, this Unas comes to you,
A spirit indestructible
Who lays claim to the place of the four pillars!
Your son comes to you, this Unas comes to you,
May you cross the sky united in the dark,
May you rise in lightland, the place in which you shine!
Osiris, Isis, go proclaim to Lower Egypt's gods
And their spirits:
"This Unas comes, a spirit indestructible,
Like the morning star above Hapy,
Whom the water-spirits worship;
Whom he wishes to live will live,
Whom he wishes to die will die!"

Re-Atum, this Unas comes to you,
A spirit indestructible
Who lays claim to the place of the four pillars!
Your son comes to you, this Unas comes to you,
May you cross the sky united in the dark,
May you rise in lightland, the place in which you shine!
Thoth, go proclaim to the gods of the west
And their spirits:
"This Unas comes, a spirit indestructible,
Decked above the neck as Anubis,
Lord of the western height,
He will count hearts, he will claim hearts,
Whom he wishes to live will live,
Whom he wishes to die will die!"

Re-Atum, this Unas comes to you,
A spirit indestructible
Who lays claim to the place of the four pillars!
Your son comes to you, this Unas comes to you,
May you cross the sky united in the dark,
May you rise in lightland, the place in which you shine!
Horus, go proclaim to the powers of the east
And their spirits:
"This Unas comes, a spirit indestructible,
Whom he wishes to live will live,
Whom he wishes to die will die!"

Re-Atum, your son comes to you,
Unas comes to you,
Raise him to you, hold him in your arms,
He is your son, of your body, forever!

NOTES

1. The utterance consists of four parts in each of which the king announces his arrival in the sky to the sun-god and commands certain gods, associated with the four cardinal points, to broadcast his coming to the four sides of the universe. The symmetry of the composition is heightened by repetitions and relieved by variations.

2. The word rendered "spirit" and "spirits" is *akh* in the singular and plural forms.

Utterance 239

Sarcophagus Chamber, West Gable

The triumph of the White Crown

White-crown goes forth,
She has swallowed the Great;
White-crown's tongue swallowed the Great,
Tongue was not seen![1]

NOTES

1. The text recalls the cardinal event with which Egyptian dynastic history begins: the victory of the South over the North which preceded the unification of the land. The event is symbolically represented as the victory of the white crown of Upper Egypt over the red crown of Lower Egypt. Because Lower Egypt was also represented by the Cobra goddess Wadjet, the text could be used as a spell against snakes. The very brevity of the phrasing—in Egyptian the whole text consists of ten words—is characteristic of sorcerer's spells.

Utterance 245

Passage to the Sarcophagus Chamber, South Wall

The king joins the stars

This Unas comes to you, O Nut,
This Unas comes to you, O Nut,
He has consigned his father to the earth,
He has left Horus behind him.[1]

Grown are his falcon wings,
Plumes of the holy hawk;
His power[2] has brought him,
His magic has equipped him!

The sky-goddess replies

Make your seat in heaven,
Among the stars of heaven,
For you are the Lone Star,[3] the comrade of Hu!
You shall look down on Osiris,[4]
As he commands the spirits,
While you stand far from him;
You are not among them,
You shall not be among them!

NOTES

1. The meaning seems to be that the resurrected king has left his earthly affairs in good order: he has provided a proper burial for his father and has installed his son as king.

2. His *ba*.

3. In *JNES*, 25 (1966), 153-161, Faulkner discussed the identification of the king with certain stars, and he suggested that the "Lone Star" is Venus as seen just after sunset.

4. As a star, the king will be able to look down on Osiris who rules the dead in the netherworld, and he will not share their fate. This is one text in which Osiris is viewed as confined to the netherworld, while in many later Pyramid Texts Osiris has been given a place in the sky.

Utterance 253

Antechamber, West Gable

The king is cleansed in the Field of Rushes

Cleansed is he who is cleansed in the Field of Rushes:
Cleansed is Re in the Field of Rushes;
Cleansed is he who is cleansed in the Field of Rushes:
Cleansed is this Unas in the Field of Rushes.[1]
Hand of Unas in hand of Re!
O Nut, take his hand!
O Shu, lift him up!
O Shu, lift him up![2]

NOTES

1. Just as the sun-god Re takes a daily purifying morning bath in the Field of Rushes, located in the eastern sky, so will the king bathe there in the company of the sun-god. This litany of purification occurs in several versions.

2. The king's ascent to the sky is imagined in a variety of ways. Here it is Shu, the god of air, who is asked to lift him up, while the sky-goddess Nut bends down to take his hand.

Utterance 263

Antechamber, South Wall

The king crosses over to the eastern sky

The sky's reed-floats are launched for Re,
That he may cross on them to lightland;
The sky's reed-floats are launched for Harakhty,
That Harakhty may cross on them to Re;
The sky's reed-floats are launched for Unas,
That he may cross on them to lightland, to Re;
The sky's reed-floats are launched for Unas
That he may cross on them to Harakhty, to Re.[1]

It is well with Unas and his *ka*,
Unas shall live with his *ka*,
His panther skin is on him,
His staff in his arm, his scepter in his hand.
He subjects to himself those who have gone there,
They bring him those four elder spirits,
The chiefs of the sidelock wearers,
Who stand on the eastern side of the sky
Leaning on their staffs,
That they may tell this Unas's good name to Re,
Announce this Unas to Nehebkau,[2]
and greet the entry of this Unas.
Flooded are the Fields of Rushes
That Unas may cross on the Winding Water:[3]
Ferried is this Unas to the eastern side of lightland,
Ferried is this Unas to the eastern side of sky,
His sister is Sothis,[4] his offspring the dawn.

NOTES

1. This utterance is the oldest version of several texts concerned with the crossing of the sky by means of reed-floats (see Sethe, *Kommentar*, II, 24 ff.). The floats, made of two reedbundles tied together, represent a far more primitive form of transport than the boats in which the sun-god is said to travel in texts of later origin.

2. A divinity in serpent form who is in the retinue of Re and serves as a guardian.

3. The Winding Water is a frequently mentioned feature of the celestial topography.

4. The goddess who personified the dog-star, Sirius. She was frequently identified with Isis.

Utterance 270

Antechamber, South Wall

The king summons the ferryman

Awake in peace, you of back-turned face, in peace,
You who looks backward, in peace,
Sky's ferryman, in peace,
Nut's ferryman, in peace,
Ferryman of gods, in peace![1]
Unas has come to you
That you may ferry him in this boat in which you ferry the gods.
Unas has come to his side as a god comes to his side,
Unas has come to his shore as a god comes to his shore.
No one alive accuses Unas,
No dead accuses Unas;
No goose accuses Unas,
No ox accuses Unas.[2]
If you fail to ferry Unas,
He will leap and sit on the wing of Thoth,[3]
Then *he* will ferry Unas to that side!

NOTES

1. This is one of several "ferryman" texts in which the king asks the celestial ferryman to ferry him across the body of water that separated the sky from the earth. The ferryman is called "he who looks backward" apparently because being alone in operating the ferry he must look in both directions. The ferryman is hailed by means of the litany "awaken in peace" with which the gods were greeted each morning by the priests performing the daily cult in the temples.

36   ANCIENT EGYPTIAN LITERATURE

2. The king has done no wrong to man, bird, or beast. This affirmation of innocence shows that the king's admittance to the sky required not only power and persuasion but moral purity as well.

3. Thoth in his appearance as ibis will transport the king. The alternation between pleading and threatening is characteristic of the Pyramid Texts as it is of all magic and sorcery.

Utterances 273-274

Antechamber, East Wall

The king feeds on the gods

Sky rains, stars darken,
The vaults quiver, earth's bones tremble,
The ⌜planets⌝[1] stand still
At seeing Unas rise as power,
A god who lives on his fathers,
Who feeds on his mothers!

Unas is master of cunning
Whose mother knows not his name;
Unas's glory is in heaven,
His power is in lightland;
Like Atum, his father, his begetter,
Though his son, he is stronger than he!

The forces of Unas are behind him,
His helpers[2] are under his feet,
His gods on his head, his serpents on his brow,
Unas's lead-serpent is on his brow,
Soul-searcher whose flame consumes,
Unas's neck is in its place.

Unas is the bull of heaven
Who rages in his heart,
Who lives on the being of every god,
Who eats their entrails
When they come, their bodies full of magic
From the Isle of Flame.[3]

Unas is one equipped who has gathered his spirits,
Unas has risen as Great One, as master of servants,
He will sit with his back to Geb,
Unas will judge with Him-whose-name-is-hidden

On the day of slaying the eldest.[4]
Unas is lord of offerings who knots the cord,
Who himself prepares his meal.

Unas is he who eats men, feeds on gods,
Master of messengers who sends instructions:
It is Horn-grasper ⌐in Kehau⌐ who lassoes them for Unas,
It is Serpent Raised-head who guards, who holds them for him,
It is He-upon-the-willows who binds them for him.[5]
It is Khons, slayer of lords, who cuts their throats for Unas,
Who tears their entrails out for him,
He the envoy who is sent to punish.
It is Shesmu[6] who carves them up for Unas,
Cooks meals of them for him in his dinner-pots.

Unas eats their magic, swallows their spirits:
Their big ones are for his morning meal,
Their middle ones for his evening meal,
Their little ones for his night meal,
And the oldest males and females for his fuel.
The Great Ones in the northern sky light him fire
For the kettles' contents with the old ones' thighs,
For the sky-dwellers serve Unas,
And the pots are scraped for him with their women's legs.

He has encompassed the two skies,
He has circled the two shores;
Unas is the great power that overpowers the powers,
Unas is the divine hawk, the great hawk of hawks,
Whom he finds on his way he devours whole.
Unas's place is before all the nobles in lightland,
Unas is god, oldest of the old,
Thousands serve him, hundreds offer to him,
Great-Power rank was given him by Orion, father of gods.

Unas has risen again in heaven,
He is crowned as lord of lightland.
He has smashed bones and marrow,
He has seized the hearts of gods,
He has eaten the Red, swallowed the Green.[7]
Unas feeds on the lungs of the wise,
Likes to live on hearts and their magic;

Unas abhors licking the coils of the Red[8]
But delights to have their magic in his belly.

The dignities of Unas will not be taken from him,
For he has swallowed the knowledge of every god;
Unas's lifetime is forever, his limit is eternity
In his dignity of "If-he-likes-he-does if-he-hates-he-does-not,"
As he dwells in lightland for all eternity.
Lo, their power is in Unas's belly,
Their spirits are before Unas as broth of the gods,
Cooked for Unas from their bones.
Lo, their power is with Unas,
Their shadows (are taken) from their owners,
For Unas is of those who risen is risen, lasting lasts.
Not can evildoers harm Unas's chosen seat
Among the living in this land for all eternity!

NOTES

1. Faulkner, *Pyramid Texts*, p. 83 n. 3, has suggested the meaning "planets" for *gnmw*.

2. His *kзw* and *ḥmwst*, the male and female personifications of faculties.

3. The Isle of Flame is an often mentioned part of the celestial topography. It was studied by H. Kees in *ZÄS*, 78 (1943), 41-53.

4. An obscure passage which has been variously rendered; see Faulkner, *op. cit.*, pp. 81 and 83 nn. 10-11.

5. Three divinities will catch and bind the king's victims: a "grasper of horns," a serpent, and *ḥry ṭrwt*, whom Sethe rendered as "he who is over the reddening," i.e., the blood. This demon only binds the victims, however, the slaughter being subsequently done by Khons. Hence I take *ṭrwt* to be the word for "willows," and "he upon the willows" to be the demon who binds the victims with willow branches.

6. After Khons has slain the gods, Shesmu, the god of the oil and wine press, cooks them.

7. The "Red" is the red crown of Lower Egypt; the "Green" is Wadjet, the cobra goddess of Lower Egypt.

8. Sethe, *Kommentar*, II, 169, interpreted *šbsw* as the coil that protruded from the red crown.

Utterance 304

Antechamber, North Wall

The king climbs to the sky on a ladder

Hail, daughter of Anubis, above the hatches of heaven,
Comrade of Thoth, above the ladder's rails,

Open Unas's path, let Unas pass!
Hail, Ostrich on the Winding Water's shore,
Open Unas's path, let Unas pass!
Hail, four-horned Bull of Re,
Your horn in the west, your horn in the east,
Your southern horn, your northern horn:
Bend your western horn for Unas, let Unas pass!
"Are you a pure westerner?"[1]
"I come from Hawk City."[2]
Hail, Field of Offerings,
Hail to the herbs within you!
"Welcome is the pure to me!"[3]

NOTES

1. The bull questions the king.
2. Perhaps the royal residence is meant.
3. The Field's reply to the king's greeting.

Utterance 309

Antechamber, North Wall

The king serves the sun-god

Unas is gods' ⌈steward⌉,[1] behind the mansion of Re,
Born of Wish-of-the-gods, who is in the bow of Re's bark;[2]
Unas squats before him,
Unas opens his boxes,
Unas unseals his decrees,
Unas seals his dispatches,
Unas sends his messengers who tire not,
Unas does what Unas is told.[3]

NOTES

1. The meaning of *ḏḥ₃i* is unknown; the sense of "steward" or "secretary" seems indicated. "Behind the mansion" means "looking after the mansion."
2. Probably a reference to the goddess Maat, the daughter of Re (see Sethe, *Kommentar*, II, 327).
3. The modest role that the king assumes in this spell conflicts radically with the cannibalistic bluster of Utterance 273-274.

Utterance 317

Entrance to the Antechamber, West Wall

The king appears as the crocodile-god Sobk

Unas has come today from the overflowing flood,
Unas is Sobk, green-plumed, wakeful, alert,
The fierce who came forth from shank and tail of the Great
      Radiant one,[1]
Unas has come to his streams
In the land of the great flowing flood,
To the seat of contentment
Which lies, green-pastured, in lightland,
That Unas may bring greenness to the Great Eye in the field.
Unas takes his seat in lightland,
Unas arises as Sobk, son of Neith;
Unas eats with his mouth,
Unas spends water, spends seed with his phallus;
Unas is lord of seed who takes wives from their husbands,
Whenever Unas wishes, as his heart urges.

NOTES

1. The mother of Sobk is Neith, a warfaring goddess whose cult-center
was at Sais. Frequently associated with the primordial floodwaters, she
is here identified with the celestial cow who gave birth to the sun-god.

TETI PYRAMID TEXTS

Utterance 337

Sarcophagus Chamber, West Wall

The king ascends to the sky

Heaven shouts, earth trembles
In dread of you, Osiris, at your coming![1]
O you milch-cows here, O you nursing cows here,
Turn about him, lament him, mourn him, bewail him,[2]
As he comes forth and goes to heaven
Among his brothers, the gods!

NOTES

1. The king is identified with Osiris, an identification now generally
made, and Osiris as ruler of the dead is no longer confined to the netherworld but also has a seat in the sky.

2. The ritual of mourning which accompanies the king's ascent to the
sky is alluded to in terms recalling the mourning over the slain Osiris.

Utterance 350

Sarcophagus Chamber, East Wall

The king prays to the sky-goddess

O great strider
Who sows greenstone, malachite, turquoise—stars!
As you are green so may Teti be green,
Green as a living reed!¹

NOTES

1. When entrance into the sky had become the central goal of the royal
funerary cult, the sky-goddess Nut, mother of gods, became the protecting
mother of the dead. The prayers addressed to her are suffused with feeling
and are among the finest creations of Egyptian religious poetry. The
splendid image of the sky-goddess sowing stars—whose light was thought
of as green—joined to the image of the green plant as the symbol of life,
makes this brief prayer a poetic gem.

Utterance 373

Antechamber, West Wall

The king is raised from his tomb

Oho! Oho! Rise up, O Teti!
Take your head,
Collect your bones,
Gather your limbs,
Shake the earth from your flesh!
Take your bread that rots not,
Your beer that sours not,
Stand at the gates that bar the common people!
The gatekeeper comes out to you,
He grasps your hand,
Takes you into heaven, to your father Geb.
He rejoices at your coming,
Gives you his hands,
Kisses you, caresses you,

Sets you before the spirits, the imperishable stars.
The hidden ones worship you,
The great ones surround you,
The watchers wait on you.
Barley is threshed for you,
Emmer is reaped for you,
Your monthly feasts are made with it,
Your half-month feasts are made with it,
As ordered done for you by Geb, your father,
Rise up, O Teti, you shall not die!

Utterance 402

Antechamber, East Wall

The king roams the sky

Spacious is Teti's seat with Geb,
High is Teti's star with Re,
Teti roams the Fields of Offering,
Teti is that Eye of Re,
Conceived at night, born every day!

Utterance 403

Antechamber, East Wall

The king prays for abundance

O you whose '3b-tree greens on his field,
O Blossom-opener on his sycamore,
O you of gleaming shores upon his *im3*-tree,
O lord of verdant fields: rejoice today!
Henceforth Teti is among you,
Teti will go in your midst,
Teti will live on what you live!
O you bulls of Atum,
Make Teti green, make Teti fresh,
More than the crown on his head,
More than the flood on his lap,
More than the dates in his fist!

Utterance 406

Antechamber, East Wall

The king prays to the sun-god

Hail, O Re, in your beauty, your splendor,
On your thrones, in your radiance![1]
Do bring Teti milk of Isis,
Flowing water from Nephthys,
Flood of the lake, surge of the sea,
Life, prosperity, health, and joy,
Bread, beer, and clothing,
Things on which Teti may live!
May the brewers obey me throughout the day
And provide for me at night,
I shall eat when they are sated with their fare!
May Teti see you when you go forth as Thoth,[2]
When the waterway is made for the bark of Re,
To his fields that lie in Yasu,
And you surge at the head of your helpers![3]

NOTES

1. Whatever the precise meaning of *sзswy* (see Sethe, *Kommentar*, III, 297, and Faulkner, *Pyramid Texts*, p. 133 n. 2), a term denoting the sun's radiance is meant.
2. In his nightly journey, the sun-god becomes Thoth, the moon-god.
3. *Yasu* is a region of the night sky. The *hyw* (or *hhw*) were interpreted by Sethe as gods who carry the sky (*ibid.*, p. 304), and by Faulkner as "chaos-gods."

Utterance 407

Antechamber, East Wall

The king joins the sun-god

Teti has purified himself:
May he take his pure seat in the sky!
Teti endures:
May his beautiful seats endure!
Teti will take his pure seat in the bow of Re's bark:
The sailors who row Re, they shall row Teti!
The sailors who convey Re about lightland,
They shall convey Teti about lightland!

Teti's mouth has been parted,
Teti's nose has been opened,
Teti's ears are unstopped.[1]
Teti will decide matters,
Will judge between two,
Teti will command one greater than he!
Re will purify Teti,
Re will guard Teti from all evil!

NOTES

1. The ritual of the "opening of the mouth" has restored the king's physical and mental powers, so that he can function as judge and ruler in the beyond.

PEPI I PYRAMID TEXTS

Utterance 432

Sarcophagus Chamber, West Wall

The king prays to the sky-goddess

O Great One who became Sky,
You are strong, you are mighty,
You fill every place with your beauty,
The whole earth is beneath you, you possess it!
As you enfold earth and all things in your arms,
So have you taken this Pepi to you,
An indestructible star within you![1]

NOTES

1. By ornamenting the ceiling of the sarcophagus chamber with stars, the chamber was made to represent the night sky; and the prayers addressed to the sky-goddess Nut ask her, as mother of the dead king, to take him in her arms and transform him into a star.

Utterance 440

Sarcophagus Chamber, West Wall

The king asks for admittance to the sky

If you love life, O Horus, upon his life staff of truth,[1]
Do not lock the gates of heaven,
Do not bolt its bars,[2]

After you have taken Pepi's *ka* into heaven,[3]
To the god's nobles, the god's friends,
Who lean on their staffs,
Guardians of Upper Egypt,
Clad in red linen,
Living on figs,
Drinking wine,
Anointed with unguent,
That he may speak for Pepi to the great god
And let Pepi ascend to the great god!

NOTES

1. A wordplay on '*nḫ*, "life," and *m'nḫt*, a word for "staff."
2. Another wordplay, with *ḫsf*, "to repel, prevent, bar," and *ḫsfw*, "bars."
3. *Ḏr*, "after, since," not "before," in accordance with Anthes's study in *Wilson Festschrift*, pp. 1-13. The *ka* has made its way into the sky ahead of the king and will announce his coming.

Utterance 442

Sarcophagus Chamber, West Wall

The king becomes a star

Truly, this Great One has fallen on his side,
He who is in Nedyt was cast down.[1]
Your hand is grasped by Re,
Your head is raised by the Two Enneads.[2]
Lo, he has come as Orion,
Lo, Osiris has come as Orion,
Lord of wine at the *wag*-feast.
"Good one," said his mother,
"Heir," said his father,
Conceived of sky, born of dusk.[3]
Sky conceived you and Orion,
Dusk gave birth to you and Orion.
Who lives lives by the gods' command,
You shall live!
You shall rise with Orion in the eastern sky,
You shall set with Orion in the western sky,
Your third is Sothis, pure of thrones,

She is your guide on sky's good paths,
In the Field of Rushes.

NOTES

1. A reference to the slaying of Osiris at the place called Nedyt, and a wordplay on *ndi* "cast down," and *ndyt*, the place-name.
2. The term "two enneads" stands for "all the gods."
3. The complex term *dwȝt* (or *dȝt*) embraced the concepts of dawn, dusk, and netherworld. Both "dawn" and "dusk" seem suitable here.

Utterance 446

Sarcophagus Chamber, West Wall

The sky-goddess protects the king

O Osiris Pepi,
Nut, your mother, spreads herself above you,
She conceals you from all evil,
Nut protects you from all evil,
You, the greatest of her children!

Utterance 454

Sarcophagus Chamber, West Wall

The king's power embraces sky and earth

O Osiris Pepi,
You enfold every god in your arms,
Their lands and all their possessions!
O Osiris Pepi,
You are great and round
Like the ring that circles the islands![1]

NOTES

1. The *nbwt* were thought to be the islands of the Aegean Sea, an interpretation upheld by Gardiner in *AEO*, I, 206* ff. The exhaustive study by J. Vercoutter (*BIFAO*, 46 (1947), 125-158, and 48 (1949), 107-209), however, has shown the term to have been used more widely for foreign regions to the north and east. Yet in this context the narrower meaning "islands" appears suitable.

Utterance 486

Antechamber, West Wall

The king is a primordial god

Hail, O waters brought by Shu,
Which the twin springs raised,
In which Geb has bathed his limbs,
So that hearts lost fear, hearts lost dread.[1]
Pepi was born in Nun
Before there was sky,
Before there was earth,
Before there were mountains,[2]
Before there was strife,
Before fear came about through the Horus Eye.[3]

Pepi is one of that great group born aforetime in On,[4]
Who are not carried off for a king,
Who are not brought before magistrates,
Who are not made to suffer,
Who are not found guilty.
Such is Pepi: he will not suffer,
He will not be carried off for a king,
He will not be brought before magistrates,
The foes of Pepi will not triumph.
Pepi will not hunger,
His nails will not grow long,
No bone in him will be broken.

If Pepi goes down into water,
Osiris will lift him up,
The Enneads will support him,
Re will take Pepi by the hand,
To where a god may be.
If he goes down ⟨to earth⟩
Geb will lift him up,
The Enneads will support this Pepi,
He will be led by the hand to where a god may be.[5]

NOTES

1. It is not clear how the sentence *ibw m-ḫt snḏ ḥ3tyw m-ḫt š't* is to be construed. I have preferred Sethe's interpretation to Faulkner's.

2. *Smnty*, according to Sethe, meant the two mountain chains that border the Nile valley and were viewed as supports of the sky.

3. An allusion to the myth of the sun-god's left eye, the moon, which was robbed by Seth and restored by Horus. The struggles between Seth and Osiris, and Seth and Horus, were the prototypes of strife in the world.

4. This section gives a different view of the king's origin: he is a member of the Ennead of Heliopolis. As a god he is not subject to the misfortunes that befall ordinary mortals.

5. When the king dies, neither water nor earth will retain him, for the gods will raise him up to the sky.

Utterance 517

Passage to the Antechamber

The king addresses the ferryman

O Boatman of the boatless just,
Ferryman of the Field of Rushes!
Pepi is just before heaven and earth,
Pepi is just before this isle of earth,
To which he has swum, to which he has come,
Which is between the thighs of Nut!
He is that pygmy of the dances of god,[1]
Bringer of joy before his great throne!
This is what you heard in the houses,
What you overheard in the streets
On the day Pepi was called to life,[2]
To hear what had been ordained.
Lo, the two on the great god's throne
Who summon Pepi to life, eternal,
They are Well-being and Health![3]

Ferry this Pepi to the Field,
The great god's beautiful throne,
That he may do what is done with the revered:
He commends them to the *ka*'s,[4]
He assigns them to the bird-catch;
Pepi is such a one:
He will assign Pepi to the *ka*'s,
He will assign Pepi to the bird-catch.

NOTES

1. That the king compares himself to a dancing pygmy shows the awe and esteem with which the Egyptians viewed them. See also the *Autobiography of Harkhuf.*

2. "Life" here stands for the eternal life of the resurrected.

3. "Well-being" and "Health" are here personified as divinities who share the throne with the sun-god. Together with "Life" they form the trio of terms which came to be regularly appended to all royal names.

4. "He" is the sun-god. The plural of the term *ka* denotes the sum of a person's physical and mental faculties; cf. Utterance 273-274, n. 2. In addition, the term had the meaning "food-offerings." Either meaning could apply here.

Utterance 573

Antechamber, West Wall

The king prays for admittance to the sky

Awake in peace, O Pure One, in peace!
Awake in peace, Horus of-the-East, in peace!
Awake in peace, Soul-of-the-East, in peace!
Awake in peace, Horus-of-Lightland, in peace![1]
You lie down in the Night-bark,
You awake in the Day-bark,
For you are he who gazes on the gods,
There is no god who gazes on you!

O father of Pepi, take Pepi with you
Living, to you mother Nut!
Gates of sky, open for Pepi,
Gates of heaven, open for Pepi,
Pepi comes to you, make him live!
Command that this Pepi sit beside you,
Beside him who rises in lightland!
O father of Pepi, command to the goddess beside you[2]
To make wide Pepi's seat at the stairway of heaven!

Command the Living One, the son of Sothis,
To speak for this Pepi,
To establish for Pepi a seat in the sky!
Commend this Pepi to the Great Noble,
The beloved of Ptah, the son of Ptah,
To speak for this Pepi,
To make flourish his jar-stands on earth,
For Pepi is one with these four gods:
Imsety, Hapy, Duamutef, Kebhsenuf,[3]
Who live by *maat*,

Who lean on their staffs,
Who watch over Upper Egypt.

He flies, he flies from you men as do ducks,
He wrests his arms from you as a falcon,
He tears himself from you as a kite,
Pepi frees himself from the fetters of earth,
Pepi is released from bondage![4]

NOTES

1. The litany "awake in peace" is addressed to the rising sun, envisaged in its various manifestations as "eastern Horus," "eastern *ba*," and "Horus-of-the-horizon" (Harakhty).

2. An obscure goddess named *Msḥ3t*.

3. The four sons of Horus, who guard the four canopic jars in which the inner organs were buried and protect the dead from hunger and thirst.

4. Beginning as a quiet invocation of the sun-god, rising to an intense vision of the opening sky, and concluding with the soaring image of the shedding of earthly fetters in the flight to the sky, the text is a fine piece of poetry.

IV. A Theological Treatise

"THE MEMPHITE THEOLOGY"

British Museum No. 498 (Shabaka Stone)

The text is carved on a rectangular slab of black granite, which measures 92 × 137 cm. It consists of two horizontal lines, written at the top across the entire width of the stone, and sixty-two columns which begin on the left side. In addition to numerous lacunae, the middle portion of the text, columns twenty-four to forty-seven, has been almost completely obliterated owing to the slab's reuse as a nether millstone.

As shown by its introduction, the text was copied onto the stone by order of King Shabaka of the Twenty-fifth Dynasty (ca. 710 B.C.), because the original, written on papyrus or leather, was found to be worm-eaten. The text is a work of the Old Kingdom, but its precise date is not known. The language is archaic and resembles that of the Pyramid Texts.

The present translation is based on the studies of Sethe and Junker, which have achieved an overall understanding of this difficult work. In matters of detail many obscurities remain. According to Sethe, the text was a dramatic play accompanied by explanatory prose narrations, and comparable to medieval mystery plays. Junker, however, saw in it an expository treatise, written partly in explicatory and partly in narrative prose and interwoven with speeches of the gods in dialogue form. These speeches would have been derived from dramatic performances of the sacred myths with which the text is concerned.

If the text is viewed as essentially a treatise rather than a drama, it is implied that it has an inner unity and cohesion, and Junker has striven to demonstrate that this is the case, and has pointed out that it treats consecutively of three interrelated topics: (1) Ptah is the king of Egypt and the unifier of the land. (2) Memphis is the capital of Egypt and the hinge of Upper and Lower Egypt. (3) Ptah is also the supreme god and the creator of the world.

Publication: J. H. Breasted, *ZÄS*, 39 (1901), 39-54 and pls. I-II. K. Sethe, *Das "Denkmal memphitischer Theologie," der Schabakostein des Britischen Museums*, Unters. z. Gesch. u. Altertumskunde Ägyptens, Bd. X, 1 (Leipzig, 1928; reprinted, Hildesheim, 1964). H. Junker, *Die Götterlehre von Memphis*, APAW, 1939, Phil.-hist. Kl. no. 23 (Berlin, 1940). H. Junker, *Die politische Lehre von Memphis*, APAW, 1941, Phil.-hist. Kl. no. 6 (Berlin, 1941).

Discussion and excerpts: A. Erman, *Ein Denkmal memphitischer Theologie*, SPAW, 1911 (Berlin, 1911), pp. 916-950. J. H. Breasted, *The Dawn of Conscience* (New York, 1933), pp. 29-42. J. A. Wilson in *Intellectual Adventure*, pp. 55-60. S. Sauneron and J. Yoyotte in *Sources Orientales*, I (1959), 62-64.

Translation of excerpts: J. A. Wilson in *ANET*, pp. 4-6.

(1-2 horizontally) The living Horus: Who prospers the Two Lands; the Two Ladies: Who prospers the Two Lands; the Golden Horus: Who prospers the Two Lands; the King of Upper and Lower Egypt: Neferkare; the Son of Re: Sha[baka], beloved of Ptah-South-of-his-Wall, who lives like Re forever.[1]

This writing was copied out anew by his majesty in the House of his father Ptah-South-of-his-Wall, for his majesty found it to be a work of the ancestors which was worm-eaten, so that it could not be understood from beginning to end. His majesty copied it anew so that it became better than it had been before, in order that his name might endure and his monument last in the House of his father Ptah-South-of-his-Wall throughout eternity, as a work done by the Son of Re [Shabaka] for his father Ptah-Tatenen, so that he might live forever.

(3) ––– [King of Upper and Lower Egypt] is this Ptah, who is called by the great name: [Ta-te]nen [South-of-his-Wall, Lord of eternity] –––. (4) ––– [the joiner] of Upper and Lower Egypt is he, this uniter who arose as king of Upper Egypt and arose as king of Lower Egypt. (5) –––––– (6) ––– "self-begotten," so says Atum: "who created the Nine Gods."[2]

Horus and Ptah Are One

(7) [Geb, lord of the gods, commanded] that the Nine Gods gather to him. He judged between Horus and Seth; (8) he ended their quarrel. He made Seth king of Upper Egypt in the land of Upper Egypt, up to the place in which he was born, which is Su. And Geb made Horus king of Lower Egypt in the land of Lower Egypt, up to the place in which his father was drowned (9) which is "Division-of-the-Two-Lands." Thus Horus stood over one region, and Seth stood over one region. They made peace over the Two Lands at Ayan. That was the division of the Two Lands.

(10a) Geb's words to Seth: "Go to the place in which you were born." (10b) Seth: Upper Egypt. (11a) Geb's words to Horus: "Go to the place in which your father was drowned." (11b) Horus: Lower Egypt. (12a) Geb's words to Horus and Seth: "I have separated you." (12b) ––– Lower and Upper Egypt.

(10c) Then it seemed wrong to Geb that the portion of Horus was like the portion of Seth. So Geb gave to Horus his inheritance, for he is the son of his firstborn son.[3]

(13a) Geb's words to the Nine Gods: "I have appointed (13b)

Horus, the firstborn." (14a) Geb's words to the Nine Gods: "Him alone, (14b) Horus, the inheritance." (15a) Geb's words to the Nine Gods: "To this heir, (15b) Horus, my inheritance." (16a) Geb's words to the Nine Gods: "To the son of my son, (16b) Horus, the Jackal of Upper Egypt ---. (17a) Geb's words to the Nine Gods: "The firstborn, (17b) Horus, the Opener-of-the-ways."[4] (18a) Geb's words to the Nine Gods: "The son who was born --- (18b) Horus, on the Birthday of the Opener-of-the-ways."

(13c) Then Horus stood over the land. He is the uniter of this land, proclaimed in the great name: Ta-tenen, South-of-his-Wall, Lord of Eternity. Then sprouted (14c) the two Great Magicians upon his head.[5] He is Horus who arose as king of Upper and Lower Egypt, who united the Two Lands in the Nome of the Wall, the place in which the Two Lands were united.[6]

(15c) Reed and papyrus were placed on the double door of the House of Ptah. That means Horus and Seth, pacified and united. They fraternized so as to cease quarreling (16c) in whatever place they might be, being united in the House of Ptah, the "Balance of the Two Lands" in which Upper and Lower Egypt had been weighed.

This is the land (17c) ------ the burial of Osiris in the House of Sokar. (18c) ------ Isis and Nepthys without delay, (19) for Osiris had drowned in his water. Isis [and Nephthys] looked out, [beheld him and attended to him]. (20a) Horus speaks to Isis and Nephthys: "Hurry, grasp him ---." (21a) Isis and Nephthys speak to Osiris: "We come, we take you ---."

(20b) ------ [They heeded in time] and brought him to (21b) [land. He entered the hidden portals in the glory of the lords of eternity]. ------. [Thus Osiris came into] the earth (22) at the royal fortress, to the north of [the land to which he had come. And his son Horus arose as king of Upper Egypt, arose as king of Lower Egypt, in the embrace of his father Osiris and of the gods in front of him and behind him.][7]

(23) There was built the royal fortress [at the command of Geb ---]. (24a) Geb speaks to Thoth: ------. (25a-30a) Geb speaks to Thoth: ------. (31a-35a) ------. (25b-26b) [Geb] speaks to Isis: ------. (27b) Isis causes [Horus and Seth] to come. (28b) Isis speaks to Horus and Seth: "[Come] ------." (29b) Isis speaks to Horus and Seth: "Make peace ------." (30b) Isis speaks to Horus and Seth: "Life will be pleasant for you when ------." (31b) Isis

speaks to Horus and Seth: "It is he who dries your tears ———." (32*b*-35*b*) ———. (36-47) ———.

Ptah the Supreme God

(48) The gods who came into being in Ptah:

(49*a*) Ptah-on-the-great-throne ———.

(50*a*) Ptah-Nun, the father who [made] Atum.

(51*a*) Ptah-Naunet, the mother who bore Atum.

(52*a*) Ptah-the-Great is heart and tongue of the Nine [Gods].

(49*b*) [Ptah] ——— who bore the gods.

(50*b*) [Ptah] ——— who bore the gods.

(51*b*) [Ptah] ———.

(52*b*) [Ptah] ——— Nefertem at the nose of Re every day.

(53) There took shape in the heart, there took shape on the tongue the form of Atum. For the very great one is Ptah, who gave [life] to all the gods and their *ka*s through this heart and through this tongue, (54) in which Horus had taken shape as Ptah, in which Thoth had taken shape as Ptah.

[*Alternative rendering*: (53) Heart took shape in the form of Atum, Tongue took shape in the form of Atum. It is Ptah, the very great, who has given [life] to all the gods and their *ka*s through this heart and through this tongue, (54) from which Horus had come forth as Ptah, from which Thoth had come forth as Ptah.][8]

Thus heart and tongue rule over all the limbs in accordance with the teaching that it (the heart, *or*: he, Ptah) is in every body and it (the tongue, *or*: he, Ptah) is in every mouth of all gods, all men, all cattle, all creeping things, whatever lives, thinking whatever it (*or*: he) wishes and commanding whatever it (*or*: he) wishes.[9]

(55) His (Ptah's) Ennead is before him as teeth and lips. They are the semen and the hands of Atum. For the Ennead of Atum came into being through his semen and his fingers. But the Ennead is the teeth and lips in this mouth which pronounced the name of every thing, from which Shu and Tefnut came forth, (56) and which gave birth to the Ennead.[10]

Sight, hearing, breathing—they report to the heart, and it makes every understanding come forth. As to the tongue, it repeats what the heart has devised.[11] Thus all the gods were born and his Ennead was completed. For every word of the god came about through what the heart devised and the tongue commanded.

(57) Thus all the faculties were made and all the qualities deter-

mined, they that make all foods and all provisions, through this word. ⟨Thus justice is done⟩ to him who does what is loved, ⟨and punishment⟩[12] to him who does what is hated. Thus life is given to the peaceful, death is given to the criminal. Thus all labor, all crafts are made, the action of the hands, the motion of the legs, (58) the movements of all the limbs, according to this command which is devised by the heart and comes forth on the tongue and creates the performance of every thing.[13]

Thus it is said of Ptah: "He who made all and created the gods." And he is Ta-tenen, who gave birth to the gods, and from whom every thing came forth, foods, provisions, divine offerings, all good things. Thus it is recognized and understood that he is the mightiest of the gods. Thus Ptah was satisfied after he had made all things and all divine words.

(59) He gave birth to the gods,
He made the towns,
He established the nomes,
He placed the gods in their (60) shrines,
He settled their offerings,
He established their shrines,
He made their bodies according to their wishes.
Thus the gods entered into their bodies,
Of every wood, every stone, every clay,
Every thing that grows upon him
(61) In which they came to be.
Thus were gathered to him all the gods and their *ka*s,
Content, united with the Lord of the Two Lands.[14]

Memphis the Royal City

The Great Throne that gives joy to the heart of the gods in the House of Ptah is the granary of Ta-tenen, the mistress of all life, through which the sustenance of the Two Lands is provided, (62) owing to the fact that Osiris was drowned in his water. Isis and Nephthys looked out, beheld him, and attended to him. Horus quickly commanded Isis and Nephthys to grasp Osiris and prevent his drowning (i.e., his submerging). (63) They heeded in time and brought him to land. He entered the hidden portals in the glory of the lords of eternity, in the steps of him who rises in the horizon, on the ways of Re at the Great Throne. (64) He entered the palace and joined the gods of Ta-tenen Ptah, lord of years.

Thus Osiris came into the earth at the Royal Fortress, to the north of the land to which he had come. His son Horus arose as king of Upper Egypt, arose as king of Lower Egypt, in the embrace of his father Osiris and of the gods in front of him and behind him.[15]

NOTES

1. The titulary of the king is repeated with Sokar substituted for Ptah.

2. This much damaged section appears to be a summary of Ptah's claims to supremacy: He is identical with the old Memphite earth-god Ta-tenen. He is king of Egypt because Horus is a manifestation of Ptah. And he is the self-begotten creator of all the other gods.

3. This section narrates, and enacts, the division of the rule of Egypt between Horus and Seth, which had been decided by the earth-god Geb. The division is viewed as a temporary settlement, subsequently replaced by the union of the Two Lands under the sole rule of Horus who now appears as son of Osiris and grandson of Geb. By viewing the origin of kingship as a two-stage process, the narration blends two distinct traditions: that of Horus and Seth as the original rulers of Lower and Upper Egypt, respectively; and that of Osiris, son of Geb and sole ruler of Egypt until slain by Seth, after which event the kingship over all of Egypt was awarded by the gods to his son Horus.

4. The jackal-god Wep-waut ("Opener-of-the-ways") was often identified with Horus.

5. The crowns of Upper and Lower Egypt.

6. This section stresses the identity of Horus and Ptah, an equation essential to the claim of Ptah's kingship. The "Wall" is the "White Wall," i.e., Memphis.

7. The body of the slain Osiris had floated downstream and was brought ashore at Memphis, thereby making Memphis the most sacred spot, and rightly cast as the place in which the Two Lands were joined. The restorations of the lacunae are made from lines 62-64, where this narrative is repeated.

8. The first rendering of this difficult passage is based on Sethe's translation; the alternative rendering reflects that of Junker. The difficulty centers on the two parallel phrases: *ḫpr m ḥȝty m tit Tm, ḫpr m ns m tit Tm*, in which the use of *ḫpr m* is ambiguous. Sethe's interpretation seems to me less strained. In any case, the passage expounds the central doctrine of this Memphite theology: Path, the god of Memphis, outranks Atum of Heliopolis and all the other gods.

9. Junker's rendering of this passage, to which I have given preference, differs from that of other scholars in that he took *wnt·f* to refer to heart and tongue respectively rather than to Ptah. In his view, this section embodies a "Naturlehre" which was not originally a part of the theology of Ptah.

10. Though not phrased as an outright repudiation of the Heliopolitan doctrine, according to which Atum created the gods through onanism, the Memphite theology attempts to supersede it by teaching that Ptah created the gods through commanding speech.

11. These two sentences have perhaps been misplaced by the copying scribe, for they seem to belong more naturally at the end of line 54.

12. Some such restoration is usually inserted here, for it looks as if the scribe omitted something.

13. The correct reading of *irrt sm n ḫt nb* was given by Grdseloff in *Arch. Or.*, 20 (1952), 484-486.

14. To Sethe and Junker this section appeared incongruous because, with the account of creation just completed, the text reverts to certain details of creation. It seems to me that the incongruity disappears if one realizes that this section is not a continuation of the narrative but a celebration of creation by means of a poetic hymn. The poem of praise, by which the narration of an action is summed up, makes an early appearance in the *Autobiography of Weni*, and becomes a major feature of Egyptian literature.

15. Since "in front" and "behind" also mean "before" and "after," the sentence has been variously rendered. Reasons for preferring the temporal rendering were adduced by R. Anthes in *ZÄS*, 86 (1961), 83.

V. Didactic Literature

THE INSTRUCTION OF PRINCE HARDJEDEF

Fragment

This is the earliest known example of the genre *Instruction*. As yet only the beginning of the text has come to light, pieced together from nine ostraca of the New Kingdom and one wooden tablet of the Late Period.

The problem of establishing the date of this Instruction, and of the related works—*Kagemni* and *Ptahhotep*—has been discussed in my Introduction. Briefly restated, the tentative conclusions outlined above are: (1) All three Instructions are pseudepigraphical works. (2) The most plausible date for the *Instruction of Hardjedef* is the time of the Fifth Dynasty, and for *Kagemni* and *Ptahhotep* the latter part of the Sixth Dynasty.

Publication: E. Brunner-Traut, *ZÄS*, 76 (1940), 3-9 and pl. I (the Munich ostracon). G. Posener, *RdE*, 9 (1952), 109-117, and *idem*, *RdE*, 18 (1966), 62-65.

On the tomb of prince Hardjedef and the worship of his person: Brunner-Traut, *op. cit.* H. Junker in *Studi Rosellini*, pp. 133-140. Junker, *Gîza*, VII, 26-27 and 114. H. Goedicke, *ASAE*, 55 (1958), 35-55.

Beginning of the Instruction made by the Hereditary Prince, Count, King's Son, Hardjedef, for his son, his nursling, whose name is Au-ib-re. [He] says:

Cleanse yourself before your (own) eyes,
Lest another cleanse you.
When you prosper, found your household,
Take a hearty wife,[1] a son will be born you.
It is for the son you build a house,
When you make a place for yourself.[2]
Make good your dwelling in the graveyard,
Make worthy your station in the West.[3]
Given that[4] death humbles us,
Given that life exalts us,
The house of death is for life.
Seek for yourself well-watered fields,[5]
——————.
Choose for him[6] a plot among your fields,

58

Well-watered every year.
He profits you more than your own son,
Prefer him even to your [heir].

NOTES

1. *Ḥmt nbt ib*, a woman who is "mistress of (her) heart."
2. Posener made two emendations and rendered: "Tu bâtiras une maison pour ton fils, tandis que j'ai fait pour toi le lieu où tu habites(?)."
3. This advice recurs in *Merikare*, line 127, and elsewhere; see H. Brunner, *MDIK*, 14 (1956), 17-19 and *MDIK*, 19 (1963), 53.
4. The iterated *šsp* may of course have the literal meaning, "accept," and it is so taken by Posener who rendered: "Adopte (cette règle), car la mort pour nous est décourageante (?), adopte (cette règle), car la vie pour nous est exaltante (?): la maison de la mort sert à la vie." I suspect, however, that it has an idiomatic meaning comparable with our "granted that."
5. Fields that are inundated by the annual overflowing of the Nile.
6. The funerary priest is meant. He should be well endowed, so that he will perform the cultic services for the dead.

THE INSTRUCTION ADDRESSED TO KAGEMNI

Papyrus Prisse, pp. 1-2
Fragment

This is the final portion of an Instruction that is addressed to *Kagemni* by a sage whose name stood in the lost beginning. The text occupies the first two pages of the great Papyrus Prisse of the Bibliothèque Nationale. After a blank stretch, from which another text had been erased, it is followed by the *Instruction of Ptahhotep*.

Publication: G. Jéquier, *Le Papyrus Prisse et ses variantes* (Paris, 1911), Pl. I.   A. Scharff, *ZÄS*, 77 (1941), 13-21.   A. H. Gardiner, *JEA*, 32 (1946), 71-74.   K. Sethe, *Lesestücke*, pp. 42-43 (abridged).

Translation: Gunn, *Ptah-Hotep and Ke'gemni*, pp. 62-64.   Erman, *Literature*, pp. 66-67.   Bissing, *Lebensweisheit*, pp. 52-53.

Comments: W. Federn, *JEA*, 36 (1950), 48-50.   A. H. Gardiner, *JEA* 37 (1951), 109-110.

(I, 1) The respectful man prospers,
Praised is the modest one,
The tent is open to the silent,
The seat of the quiet is spacious.[1]
Do not chatter!
Knives are sharp against the blunderer,
Without hurry except when he faults.[2]

When you sit with company,
Shun the food you love;

Restraint is a brief moment,[3]
Gluttony is base (5) and is reproved.
A cup of water quenches thirst,
A mouthful of herbs strengthens the heart;
One good thing stands for goodness,
A little something stands for much.
Vile is he whose belly covets when (meal)-time has passed,
He forgets those in whose house his belly roams.[4]

When you sit with a glutton,
Eat when his greed has passed;
When you drink with a drunkard,
Take when his heart is content.[5]
Don't fall upon meat by the side of a glutton,[6]
(10) Take when he gives you, don't refuse it,
Then it will soothe.
He who is blameless in matters of food,
No word can prevail against him;
⌐He who is gentle, even timid,⌐[7]
The harsh is kinder to him than to his mother,[8]
All people are his servants.

Let your name go forth
(II, 1) While your mouth is silent.
When you are summoned, don't boast of strength
Among those your age, lest you be opposed.
One knows not what may happen,
What god does when he punishes.

The vizier had his children summoned, after he had understood the ways of men, their character having become clear to him.[9] Then he said to them: "All that is written in (5) this book, heed it as I said it. Do not go beyond what has been set down." Then they placed themselves on their bellies. They recited it as it was written. It seemed good to them beyond anything in the whole land. They stood and sat accordingly.[10]

Then the majesty of King Huni died; the majesty of King Snefru was raised up as beneficent king in this whole land. Then Kagemni was made mayor of the city and vizier.

Colophon: It is finished.

NOTES

1. The four sentences express one idea: the quiet, modest person is well liked and hence successful. Thus, "the tent is open to the silent," not: "the tent of the silent is open." To have a "spacious seat" is "to be well received," and "to be made comfortable." Cf. "Spacious is Teti's seat with Geb," PT, Utterance 402. See also *Ptahhotep*, line 225.

2. *Nn ḥn n is ḥr sp·f* is ambiguous and has been variously rendered. Gardiner: "There is no speedy advance except at its proper time." Scharff and Federn took *nn ḥn* to refer to the "knives" and *sp* in the sense of "fault."

3. I.e., to control one's desire requires only a moment's effort.

4. This is substantially Scharff's and Gardiner's rendering. But in *JEA*, 36 (1950), 112 Gunn proposed: "He is a wretch who is grasping for the sake of his belly, . . . (and) who is gluttonous at home," and Gardiner accepted this. By omitting the middle portion of the sentence, however, Gunn failed to supply a meaning for the whole.

5. This was Gardiner's rendering of *iw ib·f ḥtpw* in the first edition of his *Grammar*, p. 248, top. In the third edition of the *Grammar*, and in *JEA*, 32 (1946), 73, he changed it to "and his heart will be content."

6. For *m sdw r iwf* I hold with Scharff against Gardiner and Federn. In the presence of a glutton one should not grab the meat but wait until one is given.

7. *Ḥrr (or: ḥtr) n ḥr r dfꜣ-ib* is obscure and perhaps corrupt. Federn cited two examples of *ḥrr* and, deriving *dfꜣ-ib* from *wdf*, "to lag," proposed: "meek to the degree of slow-wittedness." Gardiner did not accept this and left it unresolved, as Scharff had done.

8. Or: " The harsh is kinder to him than his (own) mother."

9. Literally, "having come upon him."

10. In addition to its literal meaning, "stand and sit" is used in the metaphorical sense of "to conduct oneself." It recurs in that sense in *Ptahhotep*, line 221. Its counterpart in biblical Hebrew was noted by Williams in *Wilson Festschrift*, p. 94.

THE INSTRUCTION OF PTAHHOTEP

This long work has survived in four copies, three of which are written on papyrus rolls while the fourth, containing only the beginning, is on a wooden tablet. The only complete version is that of Papyrus Prisse of the Bibliothèque Nationale, which dates from the Middle Kingdom. The other two papyri, both in the British Museum, are from the Middle and New Kingdoms, respectively. The wooden tablet, Carnarvon Tablet I in the Cairo Museum, also dates from the New Kingdom. The version of P. Prisse differs considerably from that of the other three copies. The translation here given reproduces the text of P. Prisse only.

The work consists of thirty-seven maxims framed by a prologue and an epilogue. Each maxim is developed as a unit of at least four, and rarely more than twelve, sentences and clauses. In one case, maxims 2-4, a theme is developed over three consecutive maxims thus forming a larger whole. Some themes and topics recur several times, an indication of their importance in the scale of values.

Taken together, the thirty-seven maxims do not amount to a comprehensive moral code, nor are they strung together in any logical order. But they touch upon the most important aspects of human relations and they focus on the basic virtues. The cardinal virtues are self-control, moderation, kindness, generosity, justice, and truthfulness tempered by discretion These virtues are to be practiced alike toward all people. No martial virtues are mentioned. The ideal man is a man of peace.

As stated in the Introduction, in my opinion the most plausible date for the composition of this work is the latter part of the Sixth Dynasty, a time in which Old Egyptian had evolved considerably in the direction of Middle Egyptian, a time in which the autobiographies in private tombs show an intellectual and literary capability comparable with the Maxims of Ptahhotep, and a time in which the monarchy was still serene and society ordered and secure.

Publication: G. Jéquier, *Le Papyrus Prisse et ses variantes* (Paris, 1911). Budge, *Facsimiles*, pls. xxxiv-xxxviii.   E. Dévaud, *Les Maximes de Ptahhotep* (Fribourg, 1916).   Z. Žába, *Les Maximes de Ptahhotep* (Prague, 1956).   Sethe, *Lesestücke*, pp. 36-42 (excerpts).

Additional fragments: R. A. Caminos, *Literary Fragments in the Hieratic Script* (Oxford, 1956), pls. 28-30.

Translation: Gunn, *Ptah-Hotep and Ke'gemni*, pp. 41-61.   Erman, *Literature*, pp. 54-67.   F. Lexa, *Enseignement de Ptahhotep et fragment de l'enseignement de Kagemni* (Prague, 1928).   *Idem*, "Quelques corrections," *Griffith Studies*, pp. 111-118.   J. A. Wilson in *ANET*, pp. 412-414 (excerpts).   Spiegel, *Hochkultur*, pp. 455 ff. (excerpts). Bissing, *Lebensweisheit*, pp. 45-51 (excerpts).

Studies of individual passages: R. O. Faulkner in *Ägyptologische Studien*, pp. 81-84 (maxims 2-4).   G. Fecht, *Der Habgierige und die Maat in der Lehre des Ptahhotep*, Abhdl. d. deutschen archäol. Instituts, Kairo, Ägyptologische Reihe, 1 (Glückstadt, 1958), maxims 5 and 19.   H. Goedicke, *JARCE*, 5 (1966), 130-133 (maxims 5 and 19), and *idem*, *JARCE*, 6 (1967), 97-102 (maxim 32).   F. Lexa, *Arch. Or.*, 7 (1935), 200-207 (maxim 6).   A. Volten in *Miscellanea Gregoriana*, pp. 371-373 (maxim 6).   Seibert, *Charakteristik*, pp. 71-84 (maxim 19 and lines 575-587).   Fecht, *Literarische Zeugnisse*, pp. 125-130 (lines 534-563).

The text is exceedingly difficult, and the translations differ widely. The best translation is that of Žába in his new and standard edition of 1956. I have frequently departed from all translations without mentioning these departures in notes, so as not to create an excessively heavy apparatus of annotations.

The numbers in parentheses are the line numbers that were assigned by Dévaud and Žába, which are equated with the page and line numbers of Papyrus Prisse, where the text begins on page 4. The numbers in the margin identify the individual maxims.

(1 = 4, 1) Instruction of the Mayor of the city, the Vizier Ptahhotep, under the Majesty of King Isesi, who lives for all eternity. The mayor of the city, the vizier Ptahhotep, said:

O king, my lord!
Age is here, old age arrived,

Feebleness came, weakness grows,
(10) ⌜Childlike⌝[11] one sleeps all day.
Eyes are dim, ears deaf,
Strength is waning through weariness,
The mouth, silenced, speaks not,
The heart, void, recalls not the past,
The bones ache throughout.
Good has become evil, all taste is gone,
(20 = 5, 2) What age does to people is evil in everything.
The nose, clogged, breathes not,
⌜Painful⌝[12] are standing and sitting.

May this servant be ordered to make a staff of old age,[3]
(30) So as to tell him the words of those who heard,[4]
The ways of the ancestors,
Who have listened to the gods.
May such be done for you,
So that strife may be banned from the people,
And the Two Shores may serve you!
Said the majesty of this god:
Instruct him then in the sayings of the past,
May he become a model for the children of the great,
(40) May obedience[5] enter him,
And the devotion of him who speaks to him,
No one is born wise.

Beginning of the formulations of excellent discourse spoken by the Prince, Count, God's Father, God's beloved, Eldest Son of the King, of his body, Mayor of the city and Vizier, Ptahhotep, in instructing the ignorant in knowledge and in the standard of excellent discourse, as profit for him who will hear, (50) as woe to him who would neglect them. He spoke to his son:

1. Don't be proud[6] of your knowledge,
    Consult the ignorant and the wise;
    The limits of art are not reached,
    No artist's skills are perfect;
    Good speech is more hidden than greenstone,
    Yet may be found among maids at the grindstones.

2. If you meet a disputant in action,[7]
    (61 = 5, 11) A powerful man, superior to you,

Fold your arms, bend your back,
To flout him will not make him agree with you.
Make little of the evil speech
By not opposing him while he's in action;
He will be called an ignoramus,
Your self-control will match his pile (of words).

3. If you meet a disputant in action
Who is your equal, on your level,
(70) You will make your worth exceed his by silence,
While he is speaking evilly,
There will be much talk by the hearers,
Your name will be good in the mind[8] of the magistrates.

4. If you meet a disputant in action,
A poor man, not your equal,
Do not attack him because he is weak,
Let him alone, he will confute himself.
Do not answer him to relieve your heart,
Do not vent yourself[9] against your opponent,
(81 = 6, 3) Wretched is he who injures a poor man,[10]
One will wish to do what you desire,
You will beat him through the magistrates' reproof.

5. If you are a man who leads,
Who controls the affairs of the many,
Seek out every beneficent deed,
That your conduct may be blameless.
Great is justice, lasting in effect,
Unchallenged since the time of Osiris.
(90) One punishes the transgressor of laws,
Though the greedy overlooks this;
Baseness may seize riches,
Yet crime never lands its wares;
In the end it is justice that lasts,
Man says: "It is my father's ground."[11]

6. (99 = 6, 8) Do not scheme against people,
God punishes accordingly:
If a man says: "I shall live by it,"
He will lack bread for his mouth.

If a man says: "I shall be rich,"
He will have to say: "My cleverness has snared me."
If he says: "I will snare for myself,"
He will be unable to say: "I snared for my profit."[12]
(111) If a man says: "I will rob someone,"
He will end being given to a stranger.
People's schemes do not prevail,
God's command is what prevails;
Live then in the midst of peace,
What they give comes by itself.[13]

7.　(119 = 6, 11) If you are one among guests
At the table of one greater than you,
Take what he gives as it is set before you;
Look at what is before you,
Don't shoot many glances at him,
Molesting him offends the *ka*.
Don't speak to him until he summons,
One does not know what may displease;
Speak when he has addressed you,
(130) Then your words will please the heart.
The nobleman, when he is behind food,[14]
Behaves as his *ka* commands him;
He will give to him whom he favors,
It is the custom when night has come.
It is the *ka* that makes his hands reach out,
(140) The great man gives to the chosen man;[15]
Thus eating is under the counsel of god,
A fool is who complains of it.

8.　If you are a man of trust,
Sent by one great man to another,
Adhere to the nature of him who sent you,
Give his message as he said it.
Guard against reviling speech,
(150) Which embroils one great with another;
Keep to the truth, don't exceed it,
But an outburst[16] should not be repeated.
Do not malign anyone,
(160 = 7, 5) Great or small, the *ka* abhors it.

9. If you plow and there's growth in the field,
    And god lets it prosper in your hand,
    Do not boast at your neighbors' side,
    One has great respect for the silent man:
    Man of character is man of wealth.
    If he robs he is like a crocodile in court.[17]
    Don't impose on one who is childless,
    (170) Neither decry nor boast of it;[18]
    There is many a father who has grief,
    And a mother of children less content than another;
    It is the lonely whom god fosters,
    While the family man prays for a follower.[19]

10. If you are poor, serve a man of worth,
    That all your conduct may be well with the god.
    Do not recall if he once was poor,
    Don't be arrogant[20] toward him
    For knowing his former state;
    Respect him for what has accrued to him,
    For wealth does not come by itself.
    It is their law for him whom they love,[21]
    His gain, he gathered it himself;
    It is the god who makes him worthy
    And protects him while he sleeps.

11. Follow your heart as long as you live,[22]
    Do no more than is required,
    Do not shorten the time of "follow-the-heart,"
    Trimming its moment offends the *ka*.
    (190) Don't waste time on daily cares
    Beyond providing for your household;
    When wealth has come, follow your heart,
    Wealth does no good if one is glum!

12. If you are a man of worth
    And produce a son by the grace of god,
    (199) If he is straight, takes after you,
    Takes good care of your possessions,
    Do for him all that is good,
    He is your son, your *ka* begot him,
    Don't withdraw your heart from him.

But an offspring can make trouble:
If he strays, neglects your counsel,
(210) Disobeys all that is said,
His mouth spouting evil speech,
Punish him for all his talk!
They hate him who crosses you,
His guilt was fated in the womb;
He whom they guide can not go wrong,
Whom they make boatless can not cross.[23]

13. (220 = 8, 2) If you are in the antechamber,
Stand and sit as fits your rank,[24]
Which was assigned you the first day.
Do not trespass—you will be turned back,
Keen is the face to him who enters announced,
Spacious the seat of him who has been called.[25]
The antechamber has a rule,
All behavior is by measure;
It is the god who gives advancement,
(231) He who uses elbows is not helped.[26]

14. If you are among the people,
Gain supporters through being trusted;[27]
The trusted man who does not vent his belly's speech,
He will himself become a leader.
A man of means—what is he like?
(240) Your name is good, you are not maligned,
Your body is sleek, your face benign,[28]
One praises you without your knowing.
He whose heart obeys his belly
Puts contempt of himself in place of love,
His heart is bald, his body unanointed;
The great-hearted is god-given,
He who obeys his belly belongs to the enemy.[29]

15. Report your commission without faltering,
(250 = 8, 12) Give your advice in your master's council.
If he is fluent in his speech,
It will not be hard for the envoy to report,[30]
Nor will he be answered, "Who is he to know it?"
As to the master, his affairs will fail

If he plans to punish him for it,
He should be silent upon (hearing): "I have told."[31]

16. If you are a man who leads,
Whose authority reaches wide,
You should do outstanding things,
(260 = 9, 2) Remember the day that comes after.
No strife will occur in the midst of honors,
But where the crocodile enters hatred arises.

17. If you are a man who leads,
Listen calmly to the speech of one who pleads;
Don't stop him from purging his body
Of that which he planned to tell.
A man in distress wants to pour out his heart
More than that his case be won.
(273) About him who stops a plea
One says: "Why does he reject it?"
Not all one pleads for can be granted,
But a good hearing soothes the heart.

18. If you want friendship to endure
In the house you enter
As master, brother, or friend,
(280) In whatever place you enter,
Beware of approaching the women!
Unhappy is the place where it is done,
Unwelcome[32] is he who intrudes on them.
A thousand men are turned away from their good:
A short moment like a dream,
Then death comes for having known them.
Poor advice is "shoot the opponent,"
When one goes to do it the heart rejects it.
He who fails through lust of them,
No affair of his can prosper.

19. (298 = 10, 1) If you want a perfect conduct,
To be free from every evil,
Guard against the vice of greed:
A grievous sickness without cure,
There is no treatment for it.

It embroils fathers, mothers,
And the brothers of the mother,
It parts wife from husband;
It is a compound[33] of all evils,
A bundle of all hateful things.
That man endures whose rule is rightness,
Who walks a straight line;[34]
(314) He will make a will by it,
The greedy has no tomb.

20. Do not be greedy in the division,
    Do not covet more than your share;
    Do not be greedy toward your kin,
    The mild has a greater claim than the harsh.
    Poor is he who shuns[35] his kin,
    He is deprived of ⌈interchange⌉.[36]
    Even a little of what is craved
    Turns a quarreler into an amiable man.[37]

21. (325) When you prosper and found your house,
    And love your wife with ardor,
    Fill her belly, clothe her back,
    Ointment soothes her body.
    Gladden her heart as long as you live,
    She is a fertile field for her lord.
    Do not contend with her in court,
    Keep her from power, restrain her—
    Her eye is her storm when she gazes—
    Thus will you make her stay in your house.
    _____.[38]

22. (339 = 11, 1) Sustain your friends with what you have,
    You have it by the grace of god;
    Of him who fails to sustain his friends
    One says, "a selfish *ka*."
    One plans the morrow but knows not what will be,
    The (right) *ka* is the *ka* by which one is sustained.
    If praiseworthy deeds are done,[39]
    Friends will say, "welcome!"
    One does not bring supplies to town,
    One brings friends when there is need.

23. (350 = 11, 5) Do not repeat calumny,
    Nor should you listen to it,
    It is the spouting of the hot-bellied.
    Report a thing observed, not heard,
    If it is negligible, don't say anything,
    He who is before you recognizes worth.
    ⌈If a seizure is ordered and carried out,
    Hatred will arise against him who seizes;⌉[40]
    Calumny is like a dream against which one covers the face.[41]

24. (362) If you are a man of worth
    Who sits in his master's council,
    Concentrate on excellence,
    Your silence is better than chatter.[42]
    Speak when you know you have a solution,
    It is the skilled who should speak in council;
    Speaking is harder than all other work,
    He who understands it makes it serve.

25. If you are mighty, gain respect through knowledge
    (371) And through gentleness of speech.
    Don't command except as is fitting,
    He who provokes[43] gets into trouble.
    Don't be haughty, lest you be humbled,
    Don't be mute, lest you be chided.
    When you answer one who is fuming,
    Avert your face, control yourself.
    The flame of the hot-heart[44] sweeps across,
    He who steps gently, his path is paved.
    He who frets all day has no happy moment,
    He who's gay all day can't keep house.
    ------.[45]

26. (388) Don't oppose a great man's action,
    Don't vex the heart of one who is burdened;
    If he gets angry at him who foils him,
    The ka[16] will part from him who loves him.
    Yet he is the provider along with the god,
    What he wishes should be done for him.
    When he turns his face back to you after raging,
    There will be peace from his ka;

As ill will comes from opposition,
So goodwill increases love.

27. Teach the great what is useful to him,
(400 = 12, 10) Be his aid before the people;
If you let his knowledge impress his lord,
Your sustenance will come from his *ka*.
As the favorite's belly is filled,
So your back will be clothed by it,
And his help will be there to sustain you.
For your superior whom you love
And who lives by it,
He in turn will give you good support.
Thus will love of you endure
In the belly[47] of those who love you,
He is a *ka* who loves to listen.

28. (415 = 13, 1) If you are a magistrate of standing,
Commissioned to satisfy the many,
⌐Hew a straight line.¬[48]
When you speak don't lean to one side,
Beware lest one complain:
"Judges, he distorts the matter!"
And your deed turns into a judgment (of you).

29. If you are angered by a misdeed,
Lean toward a man on account of his rightness;
Pass it over, don't recall it,
Since he was silent to you the first day.[49]

30. (428) If you are great after having been humble,
Have gained wealth after having been poor
In the past, in a town which you know,
⌐Knowing¬[50] your former condition,
Do not put trust in your wealth,
Which came to you as gift of god;
So that you will not fall behind one like you,
To whom the same has happened.

31. (441) Bend your back to your superior,
Your overseer from the palace;
Then your house will endure in its wealth,

Your rewards in their right place.
Wretched is he who opposes a superior,
One lives as long as he is mild,
Baring the arm does not hurt it.[51]
Do not plunder a neighbor's house,
Do not steal the goods of one near you,
Lest he denounce you before you are heard.
A quarreler is a mindless person,[52]
If he is known as an aggressor
The hostile man will have trouble in the neighborhood.

32. *This maxim is an injunction against illicit sexual intercourse. It is very obscure and has been omitted here.*[53]

33. If you probe the character of a friend,
Don't inquire, but approach him,
Deal with him alone,
So as not to suffer from his manner.
Dispute with him after a time,
(470) Test his heart in conversation;
If what he has seen escapes him,[54]
If he does a thing that annoys you,
Be yet friendly with him, don't attack;[55]
Be restrained, don't let fly,
Don't answer with hostility,
Neither part from him nor attack him;
His time does not fail to come,
One does not escape what is fated.

34. (481) Be generous[56] as long as you live,
What leaves the storehouse does not return;
It is the food to be shared which is coveted,
One whose belly is empty is an accuser;
One deprived[57] becomes an opponent,
Don't have him for a neighbor.
Kindness is a man's memorial
For the years after the function.[58]

35. (489 = 15, 3) Know your helpers, then you prosper,
Don't be mean toward your friends,
They are one's watered field,
And greater then one's riches,

For what belongs to one belongs to another.
The character of a son-of-man is profit to him;[59]
Good nature is a memorial.

36. Punish firmly, chastise soundly,
Then repression of crime becomes an example;
Punishment except for crime
Turns the complainer into an enemy.[60]

37. (499) If you take to wife a *špnt*[61]
Who is joyful[62] and known by her town,
If she is ⌐fickle⌐[63] and likes the moment,
Do not reject her, let her eat,
The joyful brings ⌐happiness.⌐[64]

Epilogue

If you listen to my sayings,
All your affairs will go forward;
In their truth resides their value,
Their memory goes on in the speech of men,
Because of the worth of their precepts;
If every word is carried on,
They will not perish in this land.
If advice is given for the good,[65]
The great will speak accordingly;
It is teaching a man to speak to posterity,
He who hears it becomes a master-hearer;
It is good to speak to posterity,
It will listen to it.

(520 = 15, 12) If a good example is set by him who leads,
He will be beneficent for ever,
His wisdom being for all time.
The wise feeds his *ba* with what endures,[66]
So that it is happy with him on earth.
The wise is known by his wisdom,
The great by his good actions;
His heart ⌐matches⌐[67] his tongue,
His lips are straight when he speaks;
(530) He has eyes that see,
His ears are made to hear what will profit his son,
Acting with truth he is free of falsehood.

Useful is hearing to a son who hears;
If hearing enters the hearer,
The hearer becomes a listener,
Hearing well is speaking well.
(540 = 16, 5) Useful is hearing to one who hears,
Hearing is better than all else,
It creates good will.
How good for a son to grasp his father's words,
He will reach old age through them.

He who hears is beloved of god,
He whom god hates does not hear.
(550) The heart makes of its owner a hearer or non-hearer,[68]
Man's heart is his life-prosperity-health!
The hearer is one who hears what is said,
He who loves to hear is one who does what is said.
How good for a son to listen to his father,
How happy is he to whom it is said:
"The son, he pleases as a master of hearing."
The hearer of whom this is said,
He is well-endowed
And honored by his father;
His remembrance is in the mouth of the living,
Those on earth and those who will be.

(564) If a man's son accepts his father's words,
No plan of his will go wrong.
Teach your son to be a hearer,
One who will be valued by the nobles;
One who guides his speech by what he was told,
One regarded as a hearer.
This son excels, his deeds stand out,
While failure follows him who hears not.
The wise wakes early to his lasting gain,
While the fool is hard pressed.

(575) The fool who does not hear,
He can do nothing at all;
He sees knowledge in ignorance,
Usefulness in harmfulness.
He does all that one detests

And is blamed for it each day;
He lives on that by which one dies,
His food is distortion of speech.
His sort is known to the officials,
Who say: "A living death each day."
One passes over his doings,
Because of his many daily troubles.

(588 = 17, 10) A son who hears is a follower of Horus,
It goes well with him when he has heard.
When he is old, has reached veneration,
He will speak likewise to his children,
Renewing the teaching of his father.
Every man teaches as he acts,
He will speak to the children,
So that they will speak to their children:
Set an example, don't give offense,
If justice stands firm your children will live.

As to the first who gets into trouble,
(600) When they see (it) people will say:
"That is just like him."
And will say to what they hear:
"That's just like him too."[69]

To see everyone is to satisfy the many,
Riches are useless without them.[70]
Don't take a word and then bring it back,
Don't put one thing in place of another.
Beware of loosening the cords in you,[71]
Lest a wise man say:
"Listen, if you want to endure in the mouth of the hearers,
Speak after you have mastered the craft!"
If you speak to good purpose,
All your affairs will be in place.

(618) Conceal your heart, control your mouth,
Then you will be known among the officials;
Be quite exact before your lord,
Act so that one will say to him: "He's the son of that one."
And those who hear it will say:
"Blessed is he to whom he was born!"

Be deliberate when you speak,
So as to say things that count;
Then the officials who listen will say:
"How good is what comes from his mouth!"
Act so that your lord will say of you:
"How good is he whom his father taught;
When he came forth from his body,
He told him all that was in (his) mind,
And he does even more than he was told."

(633 = 19, 5) Lo, the good son, the gift of god,
Exceeds what is told him by his lord,
He will do right when his heart is straight.
As you succeed me, sound in your body,
The king content with all that was done,
May you obtain (many) years of life!
Not small is what I did on earth,
I had one hundred and ten years of life
As gift of the king,
Honors exceeding those of the ancestors,
By doing justice for the king,
Until the state of veneration!

(645 = 19, 9) *Colophon*: It is done from its beginning to its end as
it was found in writing.

NOTES

1. Assuming with Žába that *ḥdr* is for *ḥrd*, but it is quite uncertain;
a word *ḥdr*, with a different determinative occurs in *Peasant*, B 138 in an
obscure context.
2. Instead of the *ksn* of the other versions Prisse has an obscure *n tnw*.
3. "Staff of old age" is a metaphor for son or successor.
4. *Sḏmyw*, "those who heard," or "the listeners," often has the
specific meaning "judges."
5. Literally, "hearing."
6. Literally, "Do not let your heart be big." Ptahhotep distinguishes
between '*ȝ-ib*, "big-hearted," in the sense of "proud, arrogant," and
wr-ib, "great-hearted," in the sense of "high-minded, magnanimous."
Elsewhere this distinction is not made; for example the courtier Tjetji
calls himself '*ȝ n ib·f* (BM 614, 7) which is of course "great of heart" in
the positive sense. Yet the pejorative sense of '*ȝ* recurs; see G. Posener,
RdE, 16 (1964), 37-43.
7. Faulkner's study of maxims 2-4 provided the correct overall understanding. Some details concerning shades of meaning remain uncertain,
e.g., the precise meaning of *ḥrp-ib*.

8. The word is *rḫ*, "knowledge."

9. Literally, "Do not wash your heart." "To wash the heart" *(tʿ ib)* is to relieve the heart of feelings, be they of anger or of joy. In *Peasant*, B 205 the hunter "washes his heart" by indulging in the joy of killing animals. When the heart is "washed" it is "appeased," as in *Sinuhe*, B 149. The expression was studied by A. Moret, *RT*, 14 (1893), 120-123; Gardiner, *Sinuhe*, p. 57; and Faulkner, *loc. cit.*, p. 84.

10. As Faulkner, *loc. cit.*, pointed out, *ksn pw* here and also in 13, 11 = 446 is applied to a person. Contrary to Faulkner and Žába, I separate *ib* from *ḥwrw* and read *ib·tw* at the beginning of line 82.

11. On this much studied maxim consult the literature cited. I have omitted lines 95-96 which are generally thought to be out of place here, and have inserted them after line 107.

12. Lines 95-96; the meaning is doubtful.

13. "They" are the gods. The maxim is interesting as a working of the theme of divine retribution through the reversal of fortune. This aspect was studied by Volten, *loc. cit.* ("Nemesis-Gedanken").

14. Egyptian says "behind food" rather than "before food."

15. I take *pḥ n s* to be an idiom for "chosen man" or "lucky man." If one renders "the great man gives to the man whom he can reach" (Wilson, Žába), the giving becomes a merely passive matter and does not result from the will of the *ka*.

16. A "washing of the heart"; see n. 9.

17. This sentence appears to be out of place here.

18. I.e., neither decry childlessness nor boast of having children.

19. Deleting the *s* before *šms·f*.

20. *ʿ3-ib* as above, n. 6.

21. Taking "they" to be "the gods"; see Žába's remarks, *op. cit.*, p. 127.

22. The recent attempt by D. Lorton in *JARCE*, 7 (1968), 41-54, to see in *šms-ib*, "follow the heart," something other than an exhortation to enjoy life seems to me erroneous.

23. The idea that the gods determine a man's character and fate was not developed to the point where it would have overwhelmed the sense of free will and personal responsibility. On the notion of fate consult S. Morenz, *Untersuchungen zur Rolle des Schicksals in der ägyptischen Religion*, Abhandlungen der Sächsischen Akademie der Wissenschaften Phil.-hist. Kl. 52/1 (Berlin, 1960).

24. "Stand and sit" may be taken literally or metaphorically; cf. *Kagemni*, n. 10.

25. The meaning is that he who comes before the king in accordance with protocol will find a good welcome. Hence the "keen face" is that of the king, not of the audience-seeker; the latter receives a "spacious seat," i.e., he is made welcome; cf. *Kagemni*, n. 1.

26. The participle of *rdiw kʿḥ* could be either active or passive; and since *kʿḥ* is both "elbow" and "shoulder," the image could be "he who touches elbows," or "rubs shoulders," or "is steered by the elbow." See also the expression *ir kʿḥ*, "give support" in line 411.

27. The meaning of *kf3-ib* is unclear. Faulkner, *Dict.*, p. 285: "trustworthy," and for *kf3* without *ib*, "be discreet," based on *Merikare*, line 64. E. Hornung, *ZÄS*, 87 (1962), 115-116, proposed the meanings "openhearted, generous," and their extension to "profligate, extravagant." In

the *Ptahhotep* passage the *kf3-ib* is defined as one who does not *phr dd m ht·f.* That *phr* here means "distort," as Faulkner, *Dict.*, p. 93, suggested, is not likely, since the "speech" is that of the *kf3-ib's* own belly. More likely, and staying close to the basic meaning of *phr,* "circulate," would be the meaning "to broadcast," "to make public." If so, the *kf3-ib* is the discreet man who does not speak unguardedly. However, this is the opposite of what one expects if *kf3-ib* is derived from the verb *kf3,* "to reveal." I suggest tentatively that *kf3-ib* is derived not from *kf3,* "to reveal," but from the homonym that yielded the noun: "hinder-parts," "bottom of jar," etc.; and that it means "trustworthy" (by way of discretion), as well as "trusting." The latter meaning would apply to the second occurrence in *Ptahhotep,* line 433, and to *Piankhi stela,* line 66, cited by Hornung. Where *kf3-ib* appears as an epithet of treasury officials the meaning "trustee" appears appropriate.

28. Literally, "your face toward your people."

29. This maxim contrasts the "heart" as the seat of reason with the "belly" as the seat of unreasoning feelings, desires, and appetites. The same view of the "belly" is conveyed by the term hot-bellied in maxim 23. But elsewhere in the text "belly" and "heart" are used interchangeably, e.g., the "hot-heart" in line 378 is the unreasoning, uncontrolled person, while in "the belly of those who love you" in line 413, the belly is the seat of affection.

30. I read: *ir ttf ⟨·f⟩ rf hft dd.f/ nn ksn r wpwty smit.*

31. I.e., the master should be silent after hearing the report, assuming that *iw·f gr·f* means "he should be silent" rather than "he will be silent." The latter meaning would apply to the envoy.

32. *N spd·n hr,* "the face is not keen," i.e., the master of the house does not welcome the intruder.

33. *T33* is more likely to mean a "gathering," or the like, than the "sifting" which Seibert, *Charakteristik,* p. 77 has proposed. See also the *t3wt* which occurs in line 356 in connection with *iti,* "to take, seize."

34. Literally, "according to his stride."

35. *Pri hr,* "to come out under (or, with)" has been thought to have the meaning "to reveal, to betray," e.g., in Louvre Stela C 14, and *Urk. IV,* 1031. For the Louvre C 14 passage Barta, *Selbstzeugnis,* 126, has now substituted "to be knowledgeable" ("ein Kundiger"); but the passage in *Urk. IV,* 1031, can hardly mean anything other than "reveal." For the *Ptahhotep* passage I suggest "to come out from under" in the sense of "escape, shun."

36. *Šw m int mdt* looks like yet another idiom that we do not understand; the context suggests social intercourse, conversation.

37. So with Gunn, *Studies,* p. 62. Žába's rendering requires changing *šnty* to *šntt.* The "amiable" is the "cool-bellied."

38. The final three sentences are very obscure.

39. In *Ägyptologische Studien,* pp. 362-365, Volten has proposed the meaning "misfortune" for *hsswt* and has taken *ka* in the sense of "food." I have not accepted either suggestion. While the *spw nw hsswt* of line 346 could conceivably mean "misfortunes," either as a euphemism or on the strength of the negative connotations of *sp,* the *hssw ntr* in line 340 hardly lends itself to such an interpretation. Moreover, none of the three versions show the walking-legs determinative that *hsi,* "to attack," requires.

40. *Tȝwt*, "seizure" ?; see n. 33, above. The two lines are very obscure; see Žába's comments.

41. The text of Prisse appears to be corrupt; read *mski*, "calumny" with L 1, and *ḥbs·tw ḥr r·s* at the end of the line.

42. Spiegel, *Hochkultur*, p. 677 n. 99, proposed "sprudeln" as the meaning of *tftf*, and the plant determinative as a reading of *ts*, "old." I take *tftf* in the similar sense of "chatter," and the plant as no more than a misapplied determinative.

43. *Štm* = "provoke" received support from the fragment of an Instruction published by G. Posener in *RdE*, 7 (1950), 71-83.

44. On "hot of heart" see n. 29, above.

45. The final lines are obscure; see Žába's discussion of de Buck's rendering as reported in Frankfort, *Religion*, p. 68. I have not seen de Buck's original version; he may have understood the drift of the passage, but the details are obscure. Is *stw mḥ* (or, *šd*) a term for "reaching goal" ? And I would divide *stw mḥ mi ir/ ḥmw sp r tȝ*, rather than *stw mḥ mi ir ḥmw/ sp r tȝ*. Can *sp r tȝ* mean "it is released," rather than "it is left on the ground" ? And the rendering of the last line as: "He who listens to his heart [alone] will come to, 'had I but . . .!' " raises serious doubts. The insertion of "alone" is hardly warranted; and without the "alone" the sentence conflicts sharply with the usual praise of the heart as man's guide, e. g., line 552: "Man's heart is his life-prosperity-health!"

46. I.e., the *ka* of the master.

47. On "in the belly" see n. 29, above.

48. *Šd mȝdw mnw*; *mȝdw* is an unknown word. Žába rendered, "protège l'impartialité(?) de la justice(?)."

49. A rather obscure maxim which I take to mean: if a good man does something wrong, it should be passed over as if it had never happened.

50. *M sšȝw* here and in *Merikare*, line 143, has entered *Wb.*, IV, 281, as "im Gegensatz zu"(?), which is a guess that does not fit the context. I take it to be a writing of *šsȝ*, "to know, recognize." On *kfȝ ib*, "trust," see n. 27, above.

51. I.e., stretching the arm out of the sleeve in a gesture of greeting.

52. *Im(w) pw n ib bkbkw*. Žába: "C'est un défaut(?) de cœur (aussi) que la récalcitrance(?)." I take *im(w) n ib* to be a person "lacking in heart," and *bkbkw* to be an active participle denoting a person who is verbally aggressive. In Arabic, *baqbaq* is the "prattle of a chatterbox," as I learned from S. D. Goitein, *JAOS*, 90 (1970), 518.

53. A new translation of this maxim was offered by H. Goedicke in *JARCE*, 6 (1967), 97-102.

54. Does this mean "forgetful" or "indiscreet" ?

55. Žába rendered *m iṯ ḥr* as "ne détourne(?) pas la face," and this interpretation has entered Faulkner's *Dict.*, p. 34. But *šri ḥr* is "avert the face" (see line 377), and the context suggests an aggressive gesture, parallel to *m wbȝ n·f mdt*, which I render somewhat freely as "don't let fly."

56. Literally, "be bright-faced."

57. I take *sȝhhw* to be the passive participle of a causative of *ȝhw*, "lacking."

58. Žába explained *wȝs* as "scepter" in the sense of "official function"; but some doubt remains.

59. "Son-of-man" here and elsewhere in the sense of "wellborn," is well known. The parallel expressions in Hebrew and Aramaic had the same connotation.

60. A difficult sentence owing to the ambiguities of *sp*, *iyt*, and *ʿnʿyt*. Gunn, *Studies*, p. 188, rendered: "As for a (bad) deed—except because of misfortune—it is what turns a quiet(?) man (who suffers by it?) into a truculent one." Žába has: "Quant à un (mauvais) acte—excepté (celui) causé par accident—c'est ce qui fait que celui qui se plaint devient homme qui s'oppose." See also S. Morenz's discussion of the passage in his study of *iyt* in *Mélanges Michałowski*, pp. 139-150.

61. The meaning of *špnt* is unknown. Guesses have ranged from "fat woman" to "dancer."

62. *Wnft-ib*, "gay, joyful" as in line 382. Žába preferred "frivolous," following Gunn, *Studies*, p. 128. But other occurrences of the term do not bear out the pejorative sense.

63. What *iw·s m hpwy* means is anybody's guess; I am guessing it means a person who changes her mind.

64. The *ʿḳзз* in *síp·s ʿḳзз* is an unknown word.

65. I read *ir·t(w) sšsrt r nfr*; *sšsrt* occurs in *Urk. IV*, 1380.17 in parallelism with *nḏ-r*, "counsel."

66. I divide *ín rḫ sm bз·f m smnt/ nfr·f im·f tp tз*.

67. *Mʿn*, in *mʿn ib·f ns·f*, is obscure. Žába suggested the emendation *mʿḫз*, "match, equal."

68. Once again the note of determinism is sounded; and it is quickly countered by the assertion that it is a man's own heart that determines his behavior.

69. I do not understand this passage.

70. Two obscure lines; see Žába's suggestion for emendation.

71. It is not clear just what metaphor is intended. Žába thinks of "s'embarasser dans ses propres filets." I tend to think that the heart is envisaged as secured with string like a sealed papyrus roll; and loosening the string produces an undesirable torrent of words. This would agree with the exhortation to "conceal the heart" *(hrp ib)* which comes in the next lines. The metaphor of the "sealed" heart *(htm)* is well known, e.g., *Ankhtifi*, inscr. 4.

PART TWO

The Transition to the Middle Kingdom

I. Monumental Inscriptions from Private Tombs

The seven tomb inscriptions in this section illustrate the major themes that recur in the autobiographies of this brief period. Their owners are persons of various ranks who have in common an intense loyalty to their home districts, their nomes, which they rule or in which they serve a ruler.

The striving for local autonomy, and the power struggle between the Heracleopolitan and Theban dynasties, resulted in intermittent warfare, recurring famines, and shifting alliances. This is the picture we piece together from the tomb inscriptions; and along with these features there emerges a strong sense of independence and self-reliance on the part of the nomarchs who rule their districts in kingly fashion. And just as the nomarchs pride themselves on their achievements, so their subordinates wish to be remembered for their vigorous and beneficial activities in the service of their nomes and towns.

Royal power, if mentioned at all in these inscriptions, appears remote, until the long reign of Intef II, who forcefully enlarged the Theban realm and set the stage for the overthrow of the Heracleopolitan dynasty. In his reign royal power reappears in the fully autocratic style of the divine monarchy, as is vividly brought home by the king's inscriptions and even more by those of his followers.

At no time did this brief interlude of local autonomy produce a social upheaval, a revolution designed to overthrow the hierarchic order of the society. Claims that such a revolution took place, which haunt much of the older egyptological literature, have absolutely no basis in the inscriptions of the period. They are conclusions mistakenly drawn from a single Middle Kingdom literary work, the *Admonitions of Ipuwer*. What the inscriptions of the First Intermediate Period show is the very opposite of a social upheaval. In each nome the hierarchic fabric is intact and serves to promote the welfare of the region and its defense in times of trouble.

Count Indi of This prides himself on having been a good fighter. *Ankhtifi, Nomarch of Hieraconpolis and Edfu*, whose fine tomb has survived, speaks in some detail of his military exploits and draws a vivid self-portrait of the proudly independent nomarch. Ankhtifi may have been an ally of the Heracleopolitan dynasty, but he was no one's subject, and in his independence a determined enemy of the Thebans whose territory he invaded.

A person of much humbler status, the *Overseer of Slaughterers Merer* tells of his effective administrative work in the nome of Edfu. He may have been a contemporary of Ankhtifi, and if so was his subordinate. The *Treasurer Iti of Imyotru* prides himself on having supplied his town with food in times of famine. Similarly, the *Steward Seneni of Coptus* wishes to be remembered as the person who distributed the grain for his town during the years of famine. On the other hand, the citizen *Qedes of Gebelein* vaunts his prowess as a fighting man who stood out among his peers. Lastly, the *Treasurer Tjetji*, loyal servant of Kings Intef II and III, describes his devoted services in the ornate, courtly style which reflects the reemergence of the divine monarchy.

Six of the seven autobiographies come from tomb stelae. That is to say, they represent the capsuled autobiography which singles out the highlights of the career, so as to fit on the surface of the single slab of stone, though in the case of Tjetji a slab of considerable size was chosen. The significance of the stela as carrier of the autobiography is the result of an evolutionary process that culminates in the Middle Kingdom. Since the Eleventh Dynasty, such private biographical stelae are not only a feature of the tomb but appear as independent, self-contained monuments erected in the holy city of Abydos, in the vicinity of the great temple of Osiris, where they obtain for their owners the proximity to the god who has come to represent death and resurrection.

Stelae from tombs, and from Abydos, have survived in large numbers. But not many tombs from the First Intermediate Period, and from the Middle Kingdom, have been found. Among these, the tomb of the *Nomarch Ankhtifi*, with its remarkable inscriptions and scenes, has shed a vivid light on the character of nomarchic power. The first four sections of his lenghthy autobiography, which is carved on the seven pillars of his tomb, are included here.

STELA OF COUNT INDI OF THIS

Metropolitan Museum 25.2.3

Publication: D. Dunham, *Naga-ed-Dêr Stelae of the First Intermediate Period* (Boston, 1937), no. 78, pp. 92-94 and pl. xxviii, 2.   Hayes, *Scepter of Egypt*, I, 139 and 141, and fig. 83.

Translation: Schenkel, *Memphis*, no. 260, p. 183.

A rectangular, painted limestone stela, 67.3 × 47.5 cm, well carved in sunk relief. The inscription consists of four horizontal lines which fill the upper third of the surface, and three short columns in smaller hiero-glyphs on the lower right side. The remaining space is filled by the standing figure of Indi and his wife, facing right, two small servant figures, an offering stand, and three short lines above the pair's heads, containing a short offering formula and their names.

As Hayes has suggested, Indi who relates that he "ruled This" probably lived in the time of the Eighth Dynasty, that shadowy dynasty of Memphite kings who no longer exerted true control. Indi's titles are traditional court titles; and by neither naming a king nor yet specifying the extent of his autonomy he reflects the end of the Old Kingdom and the beginning of the nomarchical period.

(1) An offering which the king gives (and) Anubis, who is upon his mountain and in the place of embalming, the lord of the necropolis: an offering for the Count, Royal Seal-bearer, Sole Companion, Lector-priest, the revered Indi, (3) who says:

I was a citizen excellent in combat, a companion of. . . .[1]
I was one loved by his father, praised by his mother,
Loved by his brothers, (5) liked by his relations.

Raised from the back of his father's house by the might of Onuris; ruler of This with a will to excel, with a will to act for the best. One who spoke with his mouth, one who acted with his arm. (7) No man will be found who would speak against the revered Indi.

Above the heads of Indi and his wife: A thousand of bread, a thousand of beer, a thousand of oxen, a thousand of fowl, a thousand of ointment jars, a thousand of clothing, a thousand of everything good, for the revered Indi. His beloved wife, Sole Royal Ornament, Priestess of Hathor, honored by the gods of This, Mut-muti.

NOTES

1. The word *ḥꜣdw*, as spelled here, is not known. Schenkel proposed to read *dḥꜣw*, from *dḥi*, "humble": "ein Kamerad seiner Untergebenen(?)." Perhaps so; but one expects a term parallel to "combat." *Ḥꜣd* with basket determinative is of course "fishing with the plunge-basket"; and *Wb.*, III, 36, also lists a noun *ḥꜣdt*, meaning "excitement" or the like.

THE FIRST PART OF THE AUTOBIOGRAPHY OF ANKHTIFI

From his Tomb at Moʿalla

Publication: J. Vandier, *Moʿalla: La tombe d'Ankhtifi et la tombe de Sebekhotep*, Bibliothèque d'étude, 18 (Cairo, 1950).

Translation: Schenkel, *Memphis*, no. 37, pp. 45-57.

Comments: H. Kees, *Orientalia*, 21 (1954), 86-97.   H. G. Fischer, *WZKM*, 57 (1961), 59-77.   G. Fecht in *Schott Festschrift*, pp. 50-60.

The part of Ankhtifi's autobiography which is translated here consists of the sections numbered 1-4 in Vandier's publication (pp. 161-185 and pl. xv) and corresponds to section 37A in Schenkel's translation (pp. 45-47).

In this part, Ankhtifi, the nomarch of Hieraconpolis, the third nome of Upper Egypt, relates his conquest and pacification of the nome of Edfu, the second nome of Upper Egypt, and vaunts his power and accomplishments.

Ankhtifi's hometown, where his tomb was located, was Hefat, the present Moʿalla.

(1) The Prince, Count, Royal Seal-bearer, Sole Companion, Lector-priest, General, Chief of scouts, Chief of foreign regions, Great Chief of the nomes of Edfu and Hieraconpolis, Ankhtifi, says:

(2) Horus brought me to the nome of Edfu for life, prosperity, health, to reestablish it, and I did (it). For Horus wished it to be reestablished, because he brought me to it to reestablish it.

I found the House of Khuu inundated like a marsh, abandoned by him who belonged to it, in the grip of a rebel, under the control of a wretch.[1] I made a man embrace the slayer of his father, the slayer of his brother, so as to reestablish the nome of Edfu. How happy was the day on which I found well-being in this nome! No power in whom there is the heat of strife will be accepted,[2] now that all forms of evil which people hate have been suppressed.

(3) I am the vanguard of men and the rearguard of men. One who finds the solution where it is lacking. A leader of the land through active conduct. Strong in speech, collected in thought, on the day of joining the three nomes.[3] For I am a champion without peer, who spoke out when the people were silent, on the day of fear when Upper Egypt was silent.

(4) As to everyone on whom I placed my hand, no misfortune ever befell him, because my heart was sealed and my counsel excellent.[4] But as to any fool, any wretch, who stands up in ⌜opposition⌝[5]—I shall give according as he gives.[6] "O woe," will be said of one who is accused by me.[7] His *wʿr* will take water like a boat.[8] For I am a champion without peer!

NOTES

1. "House of Khuu" is a name for the nome of Edfu (see Vandier, *Moʿalla*, p. 166, and H. G. Fischer, *Kush*, 10 [1962], 333). The precise meaning of *grgt*, here rendered "marsh," is unknown. In any case it is a waterlogged piece of land, here used metaphorically: the nome is inundated not with water but with troubles.

2. Reading *nn šsp šḥm*, rather than *nn di(·i)*, in accordance with Fecht's interpretation in *Schott Festschrift*, p. 53.

3. In addition to ruling the nomes of Hieraconpolis and Edfu, Ankhtifi made an alliance with the nome of Elephantine, thus creating a union of the three southernmost nomes which was directed against the nome of Thebes.

4. "On whom I placed my hand" means "whom I protected." On the "sealed heart" see *Ptahhotep*, n. 71.

5. *Ḫft-ir* is difficult; see Vandier's discussion, *op. cit.*, p. 182.

6. Reading *di(·i)* rather than *šsp*, in accordance with Fecht's discussion, *op. cit.*, p. 57.

7. *Sʿḥ* = "accuse" is well attested (see Faulkner, *Dict.*, p. 215).

8. The word *wʿr*, with wood determinative, is unknown. Vandier: "sa coque(?)"; Schenkel: "sein Hausstand(??)"; Fecht: "sein Brett(?)." Fecht's gruesome conjecture that the "board" floats downstream carrying the corpse of the executed opponent, is unwarranted, as Ankhtifi has merely said that he will give as he is given. Nor has it been established that *šsp mw* can mean "take to water," i.e., "swim," rather than "take on water." The shallow boats and barges must have taken on a good deal of water and required much bailing. In *Siut*, IV, 12, "bailing water" is used metaphorically for struggling against troubles.

STELA OF THE BUTLER MERER OF EDFU

Cracow National Museum

Publication: J. Černý, *JEA*, 47 (1961), 5-9 and pl. 1.
Translation: Schenkel, *Memphis*, no. 42, pp. 62-64.
Comments: H. G. Fischer, *Kush*, 10 (1962), 333-334.
A rectangular limestone slab stela, 52.5 × 87 cm. The inscription
consists of one line on top across the width of the stone, ten vertical
columns on the right side, and three columns on the left, before and behind
the standing figures of Merer and his wife.

(1) An offering which the king gives (and) Anubis, who is upon his
mountain and in the place of embalming, the lord of the necropolis,
in all his good and pure places: an offering for the revered one, the
Sole Companion, Butler and Overseer of the slaughterers of the House
of Khuu in its entirety, who says:

I was the priest for slaughtering and offering (3) in two temples
on behalf of the ruler. I offered for thirteen rulers without a mishap
ever befalling me.[1] I was not robbed, I was not spat in the eyes, owing
to the worth of my speech, the competence of my counsel, and the
bending of my arm.[2] I did what the great ones liked, what my (5)
household praised; a person beloved of his companions. I have stood
out in front; I have attained reveredness, I have bowed brow and
feather.

Never did I hand a person over to a potentate, so that my name
might be good with all men. (7) I never lied against any person—an
abomination to Anubis. And when fear had arisen in another town, this
town was praised. I acquired cattle, acquired people, acquired fields,
acquired copper. I nourished my brothers and sisters.

(9) I buried the dead and nourished the living, wherever I went in
this drought which had occurred. I closed off all their fields and
mounds in town and countryside, not letting (11) their water inundate
for someone else, as does a worthy citizen so that his family may swim.
When it happened that Upper Egyptian barley was given to the town,
I transported it many times. I gave a heap[3] of white Upper Egyptian
barley and a heap of *ḥmi*-barley, (13) and measured out for every man
according to his wish.

His beloved wife, who shares (his) estate,[4] the Sole Royal Ornament,
Priestess of Hathor, Demyosnai, good of speech; who makes (15)
the offering of white bread, who pleases in all that one wishes, who
serves the heart in all that one wishes, the sister-of-the-estate, praised
of Hathor lady of Dendera, Demyosnai.

NOTES

1. As Schenkel observed, the reference to thirteen rulers cannot mean that thirteen nomarchs ruled the area in rapid succession. The point Merer makes is that he served his superiors without ever making a mistake. These superiors may have been dead rulers for whom he performed funerary sacrifices. Compare the similar statement on the stela of Tjebu (*TPPI*, no. 3, line 7): "I was steward for six rulers without having a mishap."

2. A difficult passage variously rendered; see Černý and Schenkel. It has meanwhile become clear that *n nfr n ḏd(·i)* is "owing to the excellence of my speech." See the stela of *Djemi* and E. Edel, *ZÄS*, 85 (1960), 83. I therefore propose: *n nfr n ḏd(·i), n rḫ n nk(ʒ·i), n ḥʒm n ʿ(·i)*. Furthermore, a much better sense is obtained if the verbs *twʒ* and *psg*, which had been rendered in the active sense ("I did not rob, I did not spit in the eyes"), are understood as passives: " I was not robbed," etc. For an official to declare that he did not rob is rather pointless; whereas the statement that he was not robbed and abused elaborates on his earlier assertion that he never suffered a mishap and is in turn explained by the threefold excellence of his behavior.

3. The sign that Černý had read *ʿḥʿ*, "heap," was read as *mḫr*, "granary," by Fischer. In any case the content of the granary is meant.

4. I take *ḏt* in the sense of "mortuary endowment." Family members participating in the offerings destined for the tomb-owner were called *sn-ḏt, snt-ḏt*, etc. (see Junker, *Giza*, II, 194, and III, 6 f.).

STELA OF THE TREASURER ITI OF IMYOTRU

Cairo Museum 20001

Publication: Lange-Schäfer, *Grabsteine*, I, 1-2, and IV, pl. i.   J. Vandier, "La stèle 20.001 du Musée du Caire," *Mélanges Maspero I*, pp. 137-145.

Translation: B*AR*, I, 457-59.   Schenkel, *Memphis*, no. 39, pp. 57-58.

Comments: Vandier, *Famine*, p. 106; *idem*, *Moʿalla*, pp. 38-40. Schenkel, *Fmäs*, pp. 150-154.   H. G. Fischer, *Kush*, 9 (1961), 44 n. 2

A limestone slab-stela, 47 × 75 cm. The inscription consists of one line across the top and ten vertical columns that fill the right side. On the left are the seated figures of Iti and his wife. The similarities in style and content make it virtually certain that Iti was a contemporary of Ankhtifi and of Merer. His town, Imyotru near Gebelein, belonged to the Theban nome; but at this time it strained away from Theban dominion and looked south for support. Iti relates that he supplied his town during the famine and also helped Hefat (Ankhtifi's town), and Iuni, while not attempting to help the hungry citizens of Thebes.

(1) An offering which the king gives (and) Anubis, who is upon his mountain and in the place of embalming, the lord of the necropolis: an offering for the revered one, the Royal Seal-bearer, Sole Companion, Seal-bearer of the God, Iti, who says:

I was a worthy citizen who acted with his arm. I was a great pillar (3) in the Theban nome, a man of standing[1] in the Southland. I nourished Imyotru in years of misery. Though four hundred men were in straits through it,[2] I did not (5) seize a man's daughter, nor did I seize his field.

I acquired ten herds of goats, with herdsmen for each herd. I acquired two herds of cattle, one herd of asses. I acquired all kinds of small cattle. I made a 50-cubit boat, another (7) of 30 cubits. I gave Upper Egyptian barley to Iuni, to Hefat, after Imyotru had been supplied. While the Theban nome traveled [downstream] and upstream,[3] I never allowed Imyotru to travel downstream and upstream to another nome.

I served (9) a great lord, I served a small lord, without there being a fault of mine.[4] I built a house and an [estate][5] filled with all kinds of riches. People said: "He is free of robbing others." (11) This is what his eldest son made for him, his beloved, —––.

NOTES

1. *Nḥb-kȝw·f*, "one whose *kas* are harnessed."
2. K. Baer pointed out to me that *ssȝ iry* means something like "in desperation as a result," by quoting *ssȝ mr* from *Hatnub*, Graffito 15.4 (p. 34).
3. In search of food.
4. The sentence has been variously interpreted. In addition to Vandier's discussion in *Mélanges Maspero I*, pp. 141 ff., see Gardiner, *Grammar*, § 217; H. G. Fischer, *WZKM*, 57 (1961), 69-72; Schenkel, *FmäS*, p. 151, and *idem*, *Memphis*, p. 58 n. c.
5. If *ḥȝt = ȝḥt*, followed by *smȝ*, is to be read, as Vandier suggested, a compound term, rather than two words for "fields," seems preferable.

STELA OF THE STEWARD SENENI OF COPTUS

Cairo Museum 20500

Publication: Lange-Schäfer, *Grabsteine* II, 91-92, and IV, pl. xxxiv. *TPPI*, no. 9, p. 6.   Fischer, *Inscriptions*, no. 19, pp. 67-68 and pl. xviii.   Vandier, *Famine*, pp. 111-112 (excerpt).
Translation: Schenkel, *Memphis*, no. 20, p. 31.
A painted limestone stela, 50 × 55 cm. The inscription is written in two long lines across the top and five shorter lines that fill the right side. On the left, facing right, are the standing figures of Seneni and his wife.

Like Merer and Iti, Seneni refers to a prolonged famine. He does not mention his town by name; but his chief, Djefi, is known from other inscriptions to have been the ruler of Coptus. The stela came from the necropolis of Naqada, which lay within the Coptite nome.

(1) An offering which the king gives (and) Anubis, who is upon his

mountain and in the place of embalming, the lord of the necropolis: an offering for the Eldest of the House Seneni, who says: I measured out Upper Egyptian barley as sustenance for this whole town (3) in the gateway of the Count and Chief Priest Djefi, in the painful years (5) of distress. Having acted in the proper manner, I was praised for it by the whole town. (7) Never did I do what everybody hates. The royal chamberlain Senen(i).

STELA OF THE SOLDIER QEDES FROM GEBELEIN
Berlin 24032

Publication: H. G. Fischer, *Kush*, 9 (1961), 44-56 and pl. X.
Translation: Schenkel, *Memphis*, no. 41, pp. 61-62.
A limestone stela, 46 × 49.5 cm, carved in sunk relief. On the left are the standing figures of Qedes, his mother, and his son. The inscription is written in two horizontal lines across the top and four vertical columns on the right side. The unpretentious monument belonged to a commoner whose chief claim is that he was an excellent soldier. His mention of Nubian fighters casts an interesting sidelight on the presence of Nubian mercenaries in the area of Gebelein, the evidence for which was assembled by Fischer in the article referred to above.

(1) An offering which the king gives (and) Anubis, he who is upon his mountain and in the place of embalming: an offering for the honored Qedes, who says: I was a worthy citizen who acted with his arm, the foremost of his whole troop. I acquired oxen and goats. (3) I acquired granaries of Upper Egyptian barley. I acquired title to a [great] field. I made a boat of 30 (cubits) and a small boat that ferried the boatless in the inundation season. I acquired these in (5) the household of my father Iti; (but) it was my mother Ibeb who acquired them for me.[1]

I surpassed this whole town in swiftness—its Nubians and its Upper Egyptians.

NOTES

1. This statement illustrates the fact that women had the right to own property and to dispose of it as they wished, a situation that already existed in the Old Kingdom.

STELA OF THE TREASURER TJETJI
From his Theban Tomb
British Museum 614

Publication: *Hieroglyphic Texts from Egyptian Stelae, etc., in the British Museum*, Vol. I (London, 1911), pls. 49 f.   E. A. W. Budge, *Egyptian*

Sculptures in the British Museum (1914), pl. viii.   A. M. Blackman,
JEA, 17 (1931), 55-61 and pl. viii.   *TPPI*, no. 20, pp. 15-17.
Translation: Schenkel, *Memphis*, no. 75, pp. 103-107.

The stela of Tjetji, treasurer of kings Intef II and III, is one of the most
important biographical stelae in the collection of the British Museum. It is
a tall, rectangular, unpainted limestone stela, 150 cm high, of very good
workmanship. The inscription consists of fourteen horizontal lines which
fill the upper half of the surface, and five vertical columns on the lower
right side. The remaining space on the left is filled by the standing figure
of Tjetji, who faces right toward offerings arranged in several rows.
Behind him are two small servant figures.

Both the carving and the text illustrate the courtly style that emerged
under the new Theban kings, a style both elegant and ornate. It spells
the end of the First Intermediate Period and the beginning of a new
orientation, even before the reunification of the country under the next
king, Mentuhotep II, which inaugurates the age customarily called the
Middle Kingdom.

(1) Horus Wahankh, King of Upper and Lower Egypt, Son of
Re, Intef, born of Nefru, who lives like Re forever. His true servant
who has his affection, who ranks in front in his lord's house, a magistrate whose heart is great, who knows his lord's wish, who follows
him wherever he goes; sole in his majesty's heart in truth, foremost
of the great ones of the palace; keeper of the treasure in the secret
place, which his lord has concealed from the great ones; who gladdens
the heart of Horus with what he wishes, his lord's intimate, his
beloved; keeper of the treasure that is in (3) the secret place which his
lord loves; the Keeper of treasure, the Royal Chamberlain, the honored
Tjetji, who says:

I was one loved by his lord, praised by him every day. I spent a
long period of years under the majesty of my lord, Horus Wahankh,
King of Upper and Lower Egypt, Son of Re, Intef, while this land
was under his command from Yebu to This in the Thinite nome,[1]
I being his personal servant, his chamberlain in very truth.

He made me great, he advanced my rank, he put me in the place
of (5) his trust, in his private palace. The treasure was in my hand
under my seal, being the best of every good thing brought to the
majesty of my lord from Upper Egypt, from Lower Egypt, of everything that gladdens the heart, as tribute from this entire land, owing
to the fear of him throughout this land; and what was brought to
the majesty of my lord by the chiefs who rule the Red Land,[2] owing
to the fear of him throughout the hill-countries. He gave these things
to me, for he knew the worth of my energy. I accounted for them to

him without any punishable (7) fault ever happening, because my competence was great.

I was thus his majesty's true intimate, an official of great heart and cool temper in his master's house, who bent the arm among the great ones. I did not follow after evil for which men are hated. I am one who loves what is good, who hates what is evil, a person beloved in his lord's house, who did every task in accordance with his master's will. As for any task to which he ordered me to attend, (9) be it presenting the case of a petitioner, be it attending to the case of one in need, I did it rightly.

I did not overstep the instruction he had given me. I did not put one thing in the place of another. I was not high-handed[3] because of my power. I did not take anything wrongfully for the sake of accomplishing a task. As for every royal department that the majesty of my lord entrusted to me, and for which he made me carry out a mission in whatever his *ka* desired, I did it for him. I improved all their procedures, and there was never (11) a fault, because my competence was great.

I built a barge for the city, and a boat for all service: the accounting with the nobles,[4] and all occasions of escorting or sending.

I am wealthy, I am great; I furnished myself from my own property, given me by the majesty of my lord, because of his great love for me— Horus Wahankh, King of Upper and Lower Egypt, Son of Re, Intef, who lives like Re forever—until he went in peace to his horizon.

Now when his son had taken his place—(13) Horus Nekht-neb-tep-nefer, King of Upper and Lower Egypt, Son of Re, Intef, born of Nefru, who lives like Re forever—I followed him to all his good places of heart's content. Never did he find fault with me because my competence was great. He gave me every function that had been mine in the time of his father, to pursue it under his majesty, and no mishap ever occurred in it. I passed all my time on earth as personal chamberlain of the king. I was wealthy, I was great under his majesty. I am a man of character, praised by his lord every day.

Lines 15-19, vertical

(15) An offering which the king gives (and) Osiris, lord of Busiris, First-of-the-Westerners, lord of Abydos, in all his places: an offering of a thousand of bread and beer, a thousand of ointment jars and clothing, a thousand of everything good and pure; the offering-array, the provisions of the offering table; the foods of the lord of Abydos,

the pure bread of the House of Mont; libations and food-offerings of which the spirits love to eat, to the Keeper of the treasure, the Royal Chamberlain, the honored Tjetji.

(17) May he cross the firmament, traverse the sky,[5]
Ascend to the great god, land in peace in the good west.
May the Desert open her arms to him,
May the West hold out her hands to him;
May he reach the council of the gods,
May "come in peace" be said to him by the great of Abydos;
May hands be held out to him in the neshmet-bark,
On the ways of the west,
May he stride in good peace to lightland,[6]
(19) To the place where Osiris dwells;
May he open the paths he desires to the gates of the graveyard,
May they-who-have-abundance give him their hands
On the desert that furnishes offerings,
His ka being with him, his offerings before him,
The honored Tjetji.

NOTES

1. Tjetji informs us that the realm of King Intef II consisted of the territory between Elephantine and This, i.e., the eight southernmost nomes of Egypt. Though he thus ruled less than a quarter of Egypt, the king's claims to the divine kingship are grandly phrased.
2. The term for the desert lands bordering the Nile Valley.
3. Literally, "high-tempered."
4. I.e., the assessment of their taxes.
5. Tjetji's stylized and rhythmic prose here changes into the symmetrically formed sentences of the orational style.
6. Originally denoting the eastern horizon, the term $3ht$ came to include the region of the setting sun, as in this case.

II. The Prayers of a Theban King

A STELA OF KING WAHANKH INTEF II

From his Theban Tomb
Metropolitan Museum 13.182.3

Publication: H. E. Winlock, *JNES*, 2 (1943), 258-259 and pl. xxxvi.
TPPI, no. 15, pp. 9-10.   Hayes, *Scepter of Egypt* I, 152 and fig. 90.
Translation: S. Allam, *Beiträge zum Hathorkult, bis zum Ende des mittleren Reiches*, Münchner ägyptologische Studien, 4 (Berlin, 1963), pp. 140-141.   Schenkel, *Memphis*, no. 70, pp. 96-99.   J. A. Wilson, *JNES* 12 (1953), 221 (the second hymn).   Hermann, *Liebesdichtung*, pp. 25-26 (the second hymn).

A finely carved limestone stela, 42.5 cm square. The inscription consists of two hymns addressed by the king to Re and Hathor, respectively. The hymn to Re, preceded by the prayer for offerings, is written in six horizontal lines across the upper third of the stela. The hymn to Hathor is written in nine columns on the lower right side. In the lower left corner is the standing figure of the king, holding a bowl of beer and a jar of milk as offerings to the two gods. In the upper third of the stela the left edge of the stone is broken away, and on the right side the beginning of the first line is missing.

The first hymn is an evening song addressed to the setting sun, the second a song to Hathor, goddess of the sky and mistress of love. Both are very fine hymnic poetry.

I

[An offering which the king gives (and) Osiris: an offering of a thousand of bread and beer], a thousand of ointment jars and clothing, a thousand of everything good, to one honored by Re-Atum in his evenings, honored by Hathor [who nurses the dawn].[1] He says:

Will you depart, father Re, before you commend me?
Will sky conceal you before you commend me?
Commend ⟨me⟩ to night and those dwelling in it,
So as to find [me among your adorers],[2] O Re,
Who worship you at your risings,
Who lament at your settings.[3]
May night embrace me, midnight shelter me
By your command, O Re ------

94

I am your deputy, you made me lord of life, undying.
Commend ⟨me⟩ to night's early hours:[4]
May they place their guard upon me;
Commend ⟨me⟩ to [early dawn]:[5]
(5) May he put his guard about me;
I am the nursling of early dawn,
I am the nursling of night's early hours,
Born at night, whose life is made [in darkness],
Whose fear [besets] the herds with back-turned horns.[6]
With your eye's red glow as my protection
You find me [hailing] your approach!

II

O you lords of the western sky,
O you gods of the western sky,
O you who rule the shores of the western sky,
Who rejoice at Hathor's coming,
Who love to see her beauty rise!
I let her know,[7] I say at her side
That I rejoice in seeing her!
My hands do "come to me, come to me,"
My body says, my lips repeat:
Holy music (5) for Hathor, music a million times,
Because you love music, million times music
To your *ka* wherever you are!
I am he who makes the singer waken music for Hathor,
Every day at any hour she wishes.
May your heart be at peace with music,
May you proceed in goodly peace,
May you rejoice in life and gladness
With Horus who loves you,[8]
Who feasts with you on your foods,
Who eats with you of the offerings,
May you admit me to it every day!
Horus Wahankh, honored by Osiris, Son of Re, Intef, born of
   Nefru.

NOTES

1. An epithet of Hathor is required; restore *snkt bks*, or similarly.
2. Restore *ih gm·k wi m swsšyw tw*. The restoration of *swsšyw* is owed
to B. Grdseloff, *BiOr*, 5 (1948), 160.

3. *Nḫi*, "lament," not *nḫi*, "endure."

4. O. Neugebauer and R. Parker, *Egyptian Astronomical Texts*, Vol. I (London, 1960), p. 35, have shown that *bkȝt* is the early night, after *ḫȝwy* and before *wšȝw*. Here the plural *bkȝwt* is used.

5. Restore: *wḏ wi n bkȝ iḫ*, at the end of line 4.

6. The *iȝwt wḏbwt 'bw* are obscure.

7. As Grdseloff recognized *(loc. cit.)*, the sign after *rḫ* is not *ḳd* but the book-roll determinative of *rḫ*; hence read *di·i rḫ·s*.

8. The king is meant.

III. The Testament of a Heracleopolitan King

THE INSTRUCTION ADDRESSED TO KING MERIKARE

The text is preserved in three fragmentary papyri which only partly complement one another. They are Papyrus Leningrad 1116A, dating from the second half of the Eighteenth Dynasty; P. Moscow 4658, from the very end of the Eighteenth Dynasty; and P. Carlsberg 6, from the end of the Eighteenth Dynasty or later. Unfortunately, the most complete manuscript, P. Leningrad, is also the most corrupt. The numerous lacunae and the many scribal errors make this text one of the most difficult.

The work is cast in the form of an Instruction spoken by an old king to his son and successor. The fragmentary beginning has preserved the name of the son: Merikare. But that of the father is lost except for the still visible outline of the cartouche and traces of two vertical hieroglyphs forming the end of the king's name. This name is assumed to be that of one of the several kings of the Ninth/Tenth Dynasty who bore the nomen *Khety* (Akhtoi). However, since the order of the kings of this dynasty has not yet been fully clarified, it has not been determined which of the several Khetys preceded Merikare. In a new study of the dynasty (in *ZÄS*, 93 (1966), 13-20), J. von Beckerath has proposed as the most suitable candidate the Khety whose prenomen was Nebkaure.

As an Instruction, it continues the genre Instruction which originated in the Old Kingdom. But a new element has been added: it is a royal instruction, and specifically, a royal testament. It is the legacy of a departing king which embodies a treatise on kingship.

The treatise on kingship in the form of a royal testament is a literary genre that was to flourish many centuries later in the Hellenistic world and subsequently in the Islamic East as well as in medieval Europe: the *speculum regum*. It is, of course, not possible to draw a connecting line from the ancient Egyptian type to its Hellenistic and medieval counterparts—far too little is preserved from all ancient literatures to make it possible to reconstruct their interconnections—but it is interesting to see the emergence of the genre. Not that the *Instruction to Merikare* was the first work of this type (an Instruction of an earlier king Khety is referred to in the text), but it is the earliest preserved, and probably also an early work of the genre, for it shows compositional weaknesses that suggest experimentation.

As stated in the Introduction, I believe the work to be pseudepigraphic in the sense of not having been composed by King Khety himself, but genuine in the sense of being a work composed in the reign of King Merikare, designed to announce the direction of his policy and containing valid, rather than fictitious, historical information.

Set beside such literary antecedents as the *Maxims of Ptahhotep*, the work shows intellectual and literary progress. Its morality has grown in depth and subtlety; and there is a parallel growth in the ability to formulate concepts, and to develop themes and topics at greater length. A fully sustained compositional coherence as found in comparable works of the Twelfth Dynasty has not been achieved. There are several instances in which the same topic reappears in different places, and in which a buildup to a climax is deflected. Yet an overall plan and progression can be recognized.

The first major portion, of which almost nothing is preserved, deals with rebellion and how to overcome it. The second major section gives advice on dealing wisely and justly with nobles and commoners and is climaxed by a view of the judgment in the hereafter. Next comes advice on raising troops and on performing the religious duties. Then follows the "historical section" in which the old king describes his accomplishments and advises on how to continue them. At this point there is the beginning of a paean on the glory of kingship which is interrupted by a reference to the tragic destruction of monuments in the holy region of Abydos, a matter that had previously been alluded to. This leads to a reflection on divine retribution and rises to the recognition that the deity prefers right doing to rich offerings. Then comes the true climax: a hymn to the creator-god, the benefactor of mankind. The concluding section exhorts acceptance of the royal teachings.

The scribes of the New Kingdom divided the work into sections by means of rubrication. At an average such sections consist of twelve sentences and clauses. Where these rubrics were logical I have maintained them; but not all of the rubrics of the principal manuscript, P. Leningrad, are judicious, for the scribes often introduced rubrics mechanically without regard to content. The major topics encompass more than one rubricated section. The building blocks within each section are the small units of two, three, and four sentences, which are joined together by parallelism in its several forms, such as similarities, elaborations, and contrasts. And since all sentences and clauses are of approximately the same length, there results a clearly marked, regular, sentence rhythm.

All Instructions are composed in this rhythmic style marked by symmetrical sentences which I call the orational style. On occasion, when specific events are told, it turns into prose. At other moments it rises into poetry, as in the hymn to the creator-god which crowns the Instruction addressed to Merikare.

Publication: Golenischeff, *Papyrus hiératiques*, pls. ix-xiv.   Volten, *Politische Schriften*, pp. 3-82 and pls. 1-4.

Translation: A. H. Gardiner, *JEA* 1 (1914), 20-36.   Erman, *Literature*, pp. 75-84.   J. A. Wilson in *ANET*, pp. 414-418.   Scharff, *Der historische Abschnitt der Lehre für König Merikare*, SPAW (1936), Heft 8 (lines 69-110 and most of lines 111-144).

Comments and translations of individual passages: G. Posener, *Annuaire du Collège de France*, 62 (1962), 290-295; 63 (1963), 303-305; 64 (1964), 305-307; 65 (1965), 343-346; 66 (1966), 342-345.   *Idem, RdE*, 7 (1950), 176-180.   E. Drioton, *RdE*, 12 (1960), 90-91 (line 92).   R. Williams, in *Essays in Honour of T. J. Meek* (Toronto, 1964), pp. 16-19.   Seibert, *Charakteristik*, pp. 90-98 (lines 91-94 and 97-98).   D. Müller, *ZÄS*, 94 (1967), 117-123 (lines 53-54).   H. Kees, *MDIK*, 18 (1962), 6 (lines 88-89).

––––––

(25) The hothead[1] is an inciter of citizens,
He creates factions among the young;
If you find that citizens adhere to him,

––––––

Denounce him before the councillors,
Suppress [him], he is a rebel,
The talker is a troublemaker for the city.
Curb the multitude, suppress its heat,

––––––

(30) ––––––
May you be justified before the god,
That a man may say [even in] your [absence]
That you punish in accordance [with the crime].
Good nature is a man's heaven,
The cursing of the [furious] is painful.

If you are skilled in speech, you will win,
The tongue is [a king's] sword;
Speaking is stronger than all fighting,
The skillful is not overcome.
–––––– on the mat,
The wise is a [ꜥschoolꜥ][2] to the nobles.
Those who know that he knows will not attack him,
No [crime] occurs when he is near;
Justice comes to him distilled,
Shaped in the sayings of the ancestors.
(35) Copy your fathers, your ancestors,

––––––

See, their words endure in books,
Open, read them, copy their knowledge,
He who is taught becomes skilled.
Don't be evil, kindness is good,
Make your memorial last through love of you.
Increase the [people], befriend the town,
God will be praised for (your) donations,
One will ––––––
Praise your goodness,
Pray for your health –––.

Respect the nobles, sustain your people,

Strengthen your borders, your frontier patrols;
It is good to work for the future,
One respects the life of the foresighted,
While he who trusts fails.
Make people come [to you] (40) through your good nature,
A wretch is who desires the land [of his neighbor],
A fool is who covets what others possess.
Life on earth passes, it is not long,
Happy is he who is remembered,
A million men do not avail the Lord of the Two Lands.
Is there [a man] who lives forever?
He who comes with Osiris passes,
Just as he leaves who indulged himself.

Advance your officials, so that they act by your laws,
He who has wealth at home will not be partial,
He is a rich man who lacks nothing.
The poor man does not speak justly,
Not righteous is one who says, "I wish I had,"
He inclines to him who will pay him.
Great is the great man whose great men are great,
Strong is (45) the king who has councillors,
Wealthy is he who is rich in his nobles.
Speak truth in your house,
That the officials of the land may respect you;
Uprightness befits the lord,
The front of the house puts fear in the back.[3]

Do justice, then you endure on earth;
Calm the weeper, don't oppress the widow,
Don't expel a man from his father's property,
Don't reduce the nobles in their possessions.
Beware of punishing wrongfully,
Do not kill, it does not serve you.
Punish with beatings, with detention,
Thus will the land be well-ordered;
Except for the rebel whose plans are found out,
For god knows the treason plotters,
(50) God smites the rebels in blood.
He who is merciful --- lifetime;
Do not kill a man whose virtues you know,

With whom you once chanted the writings,
Who was brought up . . . ––– before god,
Who strode freely in the secret place.
The *ba* comes to the place it knows,
It does not miss its former path,
No kind of magic holds it back,
It comes to those who give it water.

The Court that judges the wretch,[4]
You know they are not lenient,
On the day of judging the miserable,
In the hour of doing their task.
It is painful when the accuser has knowledge,
Do not trust in length of years,
(55) They view a lifetime in an hour!
When a man remains over after death,
His deeds are set beside him as treasure,
And being yonder lasts forever.
A fool is who does what they reprove!
He who reaches them without having done wrong
Will exist there like a god,
Free-striding like the lords forever!

Raise your youths and the residence will love you,
Increase your subjects with ⌐recruits¬,[5]
See, your city is full of new growth.
Twenty years the youths indulge their wishes,
Then ⌐recruits¬ go forth . . .
Veterans[6] return to their children . . .
. . . . . .[7]
(60) I raised troops from them on my accession.
Advance your officials, promote your [soldiers],
Enrich the young men who follow you,
Provide with goods, endow with fields,
Reward them with herds.

Do not prefer the wellborn to the commoner,
Choose a man on account of his skills,
Then all crafts are done ––– . . .
Guard your borders, secure your forts,
Troops are useful to their lord.

Make your monuments [worthy] of the god,
This keeps alive their maker's name,
A man should do what profits his *ba*.
In the monthly service, wear the white sandals,
Visit the temple, ⌜observe⌝[18] the mysteries,
Enter (65) the shrine, eat bread in god's house;
Proffer libations, multiply the loaves,
Make ample the daily offerings,
It profits him who does it.
Endow your monuments according to your wealth,
Even one day gives to eternity,
An hour contributes to the future,
God recognizes him who works for him.
. . . . . . [9]

Troops will fight troops
As the ancestors foretold;
Egypt (70) fought in the graveyard,
Destroying tombs in vengeful destruction.
As I did it, so it happened,
As is done to one who strays from god's path.
Do not deal evilly with the Southland,
You know what the residence foretold about it;
As this happened so that may happen.
⌜Before they had trespassed⌝ . . . ---
I attacked This ⌜straight to⌝ its southern border ⌜at Taut⌝,
I engulfed it like a flood;
King Meriyebre, justified, had not done it;
Be merciful on account of it,
----- renew the treaties.
(75) No river lets itself be hidden,
It is good to work for the future.

You stand well with the Southland,
They come to you with tribute, with gifts;
I have acted like the forefathers:
If one has no grain to give,
Be kind, since they are humble before you.
Be sated with your bread, your beer,
Granite comes to you unhindered.
Do not despoil the monument of another,

But quarry stone in Tura.
Do not build your tomb out of ruins,
(Using) what had been made for what is to be made.
Behold, the king is lord of joy,
(80) You may rest, sleep in your strength,
Follow your heart, through what I have done,
There is no foe within your borders.

I arose as lord of the city,
Whose heart was sad because of the Northland;
From Hetshenu to ⌈Sembaqa⌉, and south to Two-Fish Channel[10]
I pacified the entire West as far as the coast of the sea.
It pays taxes, it gives cedar wood,[11]
One sees juniper wood which they give us.
The East abounds in bowmen,
⌈Their labor⌉ ------
The inner islands are turned back,
And every man within,
The temples say, "you are greater (85) than I."[12]

The land they had ravaged has been made into nomes,
All kinds of large towns [⌈are in it⌉];
What was ruled by one is in the hands of ten,
Officials are appointed, tax-[lists drawn up].
When free men are given land,
They work for you like a single team;
No rebel will arise among them,
And Hapy will not fail to come.
The dues of the Northland are in your hand,
For the mooring-post is staked in the district I made in the East
From Hebenu to Horusway;[13]
It is settled with towns, filled with people,
Of the best in the whole land,
To repel (90) attacks against them.
May I see a brave man who will copy it,
Who will add to what I have done,
A wretched heir would ⌈disgrace⌉ me.

But this should be said to the Bowman:[14]
Lo, the miserable Asiatic,
He is wretched because of the place he's in:

Short of water, bare of wood,
Its paths are many and painful because of mountains.
He does not dwell in one place,
Food propels his legs,
He fights since the time of Horus,
Not conquering nor being conquered,
He does not announce the day of combat,
Like a thief who darts about a group.[15]

But as I live (95) and shall be what I am,
When the Bowmen were a sealed wall,
I breached [⌈their strongholds⌉],
I made Lower Egypt attack them,
I captured their inhabitants,
I seized their cattle,
Until the Asiatics abhorred Egypt.
Do not concern yourself with him,
The Asiatic is a crocodile on its shore,
It snatches from a lonely road,
It cannot seize from a populous town.

Medenyt has been restored to its nome,
Its one side is irrigated as far as Kem-Wer,[16]
It is the ⌈defense⌉ against the Bowmen.[17]
(100) Its walls are warlike, its soldiers many,
Its serfs know how to bear arms,
Apart from the free men within.
The region of Memphis totals ten thousand men,
Free citizens[18] who are not taxed;
Officials are in it since the time it was residence,
The borders are firm, the garrisons valiant.
Many northerners irrigate it as far as the Northland,
Taxed with grain in the manner of free men;[19]
Lo, it is the gateway of the Northland,
They form a dyke as far as (105) Hnes.[20]
Abundant citizens are the heart's support,
Beware of being surrounded by the serfs of the foe,
Caution prolongs life.

If your southern border is attacked,
The Bowmen will put on the girdle,
Build buildings in the Northland!

As a man's name is not made small by his actions,
So a settled town is not harmed.
Build ------
The foe loves destruction and misery.
King Khety, the justified, laid down in teaching:
(110) He who is silent toward violence diminishes the offerings.
God will attack the rebel for the sake of the temple,
He will be overcome for what he has done,
He will be sated with what he planned to gain,
He will find no favor on the day of woe.[21]
Supply the offerings, revere the god,
Don't say, "it is trouble," don't slacken your hands.
He who opposes you attacks the sky,
A monument is sound for a hundred years;[22]
If the foe understood, he would not attack them,[23]
There is no one who has no (115) enemy.

The Lord of the Two Shores is one who knows,
A king who has courtiers is not ignorant;
As one wise did he come from the womb,
From a million men god singled him out.
A goodly office is kingship,
It has no son, no brother to maintain its memorial,
But one man provides for the other;
A man acts for him who was before him,
So that what he has done is preserved by his successor.
Lo, a shameful deed occurred in my time:
(120) The nome of This was ravaged;
Though it happened through my doing,
I learned it after it was done.[24]
There was retribution for what I had done,
For it is evil to destroy,
Useless to restore what one has damaged,
To rebuild what one has demolished.
Beware of it! A blow is repaid by its like,
To every action there is a response.

While generation succeeds generation,
God who knows characters is hidden;
One can not oppose the lord of the hand,[25]
He reaches all (125) that the eyes can see.

One should revere the god on his path,
Made of costly stone, fashioned of bronze.[26]
As watercourse is replaced by watercourse,
So no river allows itself to be concealed,
It breaks the channel in which it was hidden.
So also the *ba* goes to the place it knows,
And strays not from its former path.
Make worthy your house of the west,
Make firm your station in the graveyard,[27]
By being upright, by doing justice,
Upon which men's hearts rely.
The loaf[28] of the upright is preferred
To the ox of the evildoer.
Work for god, he will work for you also,
With offerings (130) that make the altar flourish,
With carvings that proclaim your name,
God thinks of him who works for him.

Well tended is mankind—god's cattle,
He made sky and earth for their sake,
He subdued the water monster,[29]
He made breath for their noses to live.
They are his images, who came from his body,
He shines in the sky for their sake;
He made for them plants and cattle,
Fowl and fish to feed them.
He slew his foes, reduced his children,
When they thought of making rebellion.[30]
He makes daylight for their sake,
He sails by to see them.
He has built (135) his shrine around them,
When they weep he hears.
He made for them rulers in the egg,
Leaders to raise the back of the weak.
He made for them magic as weapons
To ward off the blow of events,
Guarding[31] them by day and by night.
He has slain the traitors among them,
As a man beats his son for his brother's sake,
For god knows every name.

Do not neglect my speech,
Which lays down all the laws of kingship,
Which instructs you, that you may rule the land,
And may you reach me with none to accuse you!
Do not kill (140) one who is close to you,
Whom you have favored, god knows him;
He is one of the fortunate ones on earth,
Divine are they who follow the king!
Make yourself loved by everyone,
A good character is remembered
[⌜When his time⌝] has passed.
May you be called "he who ended the time of trouble,"
By those who come after in the House of Khety,
In thinking[32] of what has come today.
Lo, I have told you the best of my thoughts,
Act by what is set before you!

NOTES

1. The *ḥnn-ỉb*, the person whose heart is inflamed.

2. In place of Gardiner's restoration, "schoolhouse," Williams in *Essays*, p. 16, has proposed "storehouse."

3. The "back of the house" is the rear where women, children, and servants had their quarters.

4. K. Baer would render *sꜣry* as the "oppressed" and *wḏꜥ* as "providing justice" to the aggrieved, whence the judgment would be the vindication of those who were wronged on earth, rather than a general judgment of the dead. My feeling is that an overall judgment is envisaged in the passage as a whole; but the first part may well be the vindication of the innocent.

5. *Šwt* in *Ptahhotep*, line 489 means "neighbors, friends, helpers," or the like. Here it has been thought to mean "feathers" in the sense of "Nachwuchs" (Volten), "recruits" (Wilson), or "milice active" (Posener, *Annuaire*, 64 [1964], 305).

6. *Sꜥḳyw*, "veterans" (Volten, Posener), but it is uncertain.

7. One obscure sentence.

8. *Kfꜣ ḥr sštꜣ* has been translated "reveal the mysteries," except by Gardiner who rendered "be discreet concerning the mysteries." On *kfꜣ* in the compound *kfꜣ ỉb* see *Ptahhotep*, n. 27.

9. Four sentences which, though free of lacunae, are very obscure. The word written *tww·k* has been rendered as "your statues," but I cannot believe that the king is speaking of dispatching royal statues to foreign countries.

10. Literally, "its southern border at Two-Fish Channel." The "Two-Fish Channel," known from P. Westcar IX, 16 and elsewhere, appears to be the name for the Nile branch in the nome of Letopolis, i.e., the southernmost part of the Canopic branch. In this passage it designates the southern boundary of the western Delta.

11. *Mrw*-wood is rendered "Zedernholz" by Helck, *Materialien*, *passim*, see especially Pt. V, p. 906. The Merikare passage conveys the fact that imports of foreign timber again reach the Heracleopolitan realm.

12. I.e., the temples (or: "administrative districts"?) of the central Delta, called "the inner islands," acknowledge the king and pay homage to him.

13. In *MDIK*, 18 (1962), 6, Kees insisted that Hebenu is not an unknown locality in the eastern Delta, as Scharff and Volten had thought, but is the well-known metropolis of the sixteenth nome of Upper Egypt, hence that the king is speaking of an extensive system of border strongholds which stretched from the eastern side of the sixteenth nome all the way to the northeastern Delta, to the border fortress of Sile, where the "Horusway," the road to Palestine, began. "Horusway" and "Horusways" are synonymous with Sile.

14. This celebrated passage has been reexamined by Seibert, *Charakteristik*, I, 90-98. The principal difficulty lies in *štзw m ḫt ʿšзw*, which had been rendered "difficult from many trees," despite the fact that an arid landscape cannot have many trees. In *RdE*, 12 (1960), 90-91 Drioton proposed the meaning "debarred from having many trees." Seibert takes *m ḫt* to be the compound preposition "after," to which he assigns the meaning "despite," and proposes to read: *štзw m ḫt ʿšз ⟨ny⟩ wзwt ỉry/ ḳsn m-ʿ ḏww*, which he renders, "verborgen trotz der Menge der Wege dahin/ (Und) schlimm durch Berge." However, the meaning "despite" assigned to the alleged *m-ḫt* is impossible in this context. Only when *m-ḫt* serves as conjunction in a temporal clause can it acquire the overtone of "despite," as in the two references from *Urk. I*, pp. 49 and 283, cited in *Wb.*, III, 345.21, and in Edel, *Altäg. Gr.*, § 797: *m-ḫt nn ḏd·n(·ỉ)*, and *m-ḫt nn wḏ·n ḥm(·ỉ)*, where the literal meaning "after" has the overtone "despite," as is possible in any language. Said in a tone of rebuke, the sentence "after I told you to stay at home, you went out," means "despite my telling you to stay at home." But the spatial preposition "after" is not capable of such manipulation: "after many paths" does not yield "despite many paths."

I divide the sentences into: *зhw m mw/ štзw m ḫt/ ʿšзw wзwt ỉry/ ḳsn m-ʿ ḏww*; and following Drioton I take *štзw m ḫt* to mean "debarred from trees." For *зhw*, the meaning "short of," "lacking," is inescapable (Volten: "kümmerlich; Seibert, "dürftig"), and it agrees with the *sзhhw* of *Ptahhotep* line 485, which I have rendered "deprived." As to the initial *ḳsn pw n bw ntf ỉm*, Seibert rightly pointed out that the *n* cannot be ignored, hence "he (the Asiatic) is wretched." It may be recalled that the personal use of *ḳsn pw* occurs twice in *Ptahhotep*, lines 81 and 446.

15. *Šnʿ*, "dart about," as in *Peasant*, B 1, 61. The Moscow variant has *šn-ʿ*, an unknown compound for which Seibert proposed the meaning "to ban."

16. I.e., the east bank of the twenty-second nome was recovered by the Heracleopolitans and brought under cultivation up to the point where it joined the Fayum which they had held all along. This rendering was suggested to me by K. Baer. On *km-wr* of the Fayum see J. Yoyotte, *BIFAO*, 61 (1962), 116 f.

17. While P. Leningrad has *ḥpз*, "navel-cord," P. Carlsberg has *ḥpw* with fighting-man determinative. Scharff and Volten chose *ḥpw* and assigned it the meaning "Abwehr." Wilson and others preferred "navel-

cord." In any case "it" refers to Medenyt; hence the town and its nome are either "the defense against" the Asiatics or the "point of entry" that attracts the Asiatics.

18. Here, above in line 86 and below in line 103 I have, following Volten, rendered w'bw as "free men" rather than "priests." But it is uncertain; see Volten's discussion, op. cit., p. 54.

19. If b3kw is the passive, as I think it is, then the next sentence, sw3t pw ḥr·i n ir st, "it means surpassing me for him who does it," is out of place here.

20. "Dyke" here is surely metaphorical for "protection." A real dyke all the way from the Delta to Heracleopolis is hardly possible.

21. N in·tw ḥr mw·f, "one will not bring him on one's water." "To be on someone's water" is usually taken to mean "to be loyal to someone." This passage suggests a broader meaning, a mutual relationship of friendship and favor.

22. Posener, Annuaire, 65 (1965), 345, read the numeral "hundred" after rnpt.

23. The sentence m mrwt smnḫ ir·t·n·f etc. which follows here is out of place; it recurs in its proper context in line 118.

24. The destruction of tombs in the Thinite nome during warfare against the Thebans had already been mentioned in line 70. Here the king takes the blame for the action of his troops.

25. The sun-god in his aspect as creator.

26. Apparently a reference to the cult statues of the gods carried in procession during festivals.

27. Cf. the Instruction of Hardjedef, n. 3. Here in Merikare the advice on tomb-building is spiritualized: the funerary monument is to be built on rightdoing.

28. Bit, "loaf," rather than "character," as suggested by R. Williams in Essays, p. 19.

29. A reference to the concept of a primordial water monster, defeated at the time of creation.

30. An allusion to the myth of the "destruction of mankind," a text that forms part of the composition known as "the book of the cow of heaven," which is inscribed on the walls of three royal tombs of the Nineteenth Dynasty.

31. Rsi, "to watch," not rswt, "dream," as suggested by W. Federn, JNES, 19 (1960), 256-257.

32. Reading iw dd·tw·k, and taking ntyw m pḥwy m pr Ḥty in the temporal sense, in accordance with Posener, Annuaire, 66 (1966), 345. On m sšзw see Ptahhotep, n. 50; the rendering of m sšзw as "in contrast" negates the whole thrust of the king's speech—the description of his achievements which his son is asked to emulate and surpass.

PART THREE

The Middle Kingdom

I. Monumental Inscriptions

Assembled in this section are seven major inscriptions of the Middle Kingdom which range in date from the end of the Eleventh Dynasty to the end of the Thirteenth. Three of the inscriptions are from the royal sphere, the other four are autobiographies of officials.

Because of their precise dates, monumental inscriptions bring into focus the continual evolution of the literary forms and provide a frame of reference for the literary works on papyrus which, lacking dates, are dated by internal evidence only.

Though a very small sample, the seven inscriptions are representative of Middle Kingdom monumental texts. The royal inscriptions illustrate the chief topics of royal activity: the mining expeditions, the building of temples, and military action. The private inscriptions show the full flowering of the autobiography in the context of the funerary stela.

The bulk of Middle Kingdom private stelae that have survived have come from Abydos, where they had been erected in the vicinity of the temple of Osiris. Most worshipers contented themselves with a single round-topped stela. Some erected cenotaphs or small shrines. In all cases these are self-contained monuments, unrelated to whatever tombs their owners had constructed elsewhere. The majority of Abydene stelae are small and simple monuments, erected by average people representing many crafts and professions. Their very number reveals how widespread the custom of setting up a memorial at Abydos had become. The four here included are those of ranking officials, two of whom were associated with the annual mystery play that enacted the death and resurrection of Osiris.

ROCK STELA OF KING NEBTAWYRE MENTUHOTEP IV

In the Wadi Hammamat

The stela was executed on behalf of King Nebtawyre Mentuhotep IV, the last king of the Eleventh Dynasty, by the vizier Amenemhet, the future king and founder of the Twelfth Dynasty. As one of many quarry inscriptions, it commemorates the successful completion of a quarrying expedition in the desert region of the Wadi Hammamat, from which granite and other hard stones were brought back since the time of the First Dynasty. Min, the god of Coptus, was the lord of this eastern desert, and the expeditions placed themselves under his special care.

The stela is one of a group of four, all carved in the same month and referring to the same mission. The first inscription reports how the block of stone destined to become the lid of the royal sarcophagus was pointed out to the working party by a pregnant gazelle. The second inscription, the one here translated, is the official account of the purpose of the expedition. The third is the first-person account of the vizier Amenemhet, which commemorates his successful direction of the work, while the fourth reports the miraculous finding of a well of sweet water.

The text is written in two horizontal lines and nineteen columns.

Publication: Couyat-Montet, *Hammâmât*, no. 192, pp. 98-100 and pl. xxxvii.   C. Kuentz, *BIFAO*, 17 (1920), 121-125.

Translation: B*AR*, I, §§ 439-443 and 452-453.   Schenkel, *Memphis*, nos. 442 and 445, pp. 264-265 and 268-269.

(1) Year 2, second month of the inundation, day 15. Horus: Lord of the Two Lands; Two Ladies: Lord of the Two Lands; Gods of gold: King of Upper and Lower Egypt, *Nebtawyre*; the Son of Re: *Mentuhotep*, who lives forever.

(3) His majesty commanded to erect this stela for his father Min, lord of desert lands, at this august mountain,

> Primordial, first-ranking, in the land of horizon-dwellers,[1]
> God's palace endowed with life,
> Divine nest of Horus (5) in which this god flourishes,[2]
> His pure place of heart's content,
> Set above the deserts of god's land,[3]

in order to please his *ka* and to worship the god as he wishes, as does (7) a king who is on the great seat,

> First-ranking, of enduring monuments,
> Beneficent god, lord of joy,
> Great of fear, rich in love,
> Heir of Horus in his Two Lands,
> Nursling (9) of divine Isis,
> Mother of Min, great magician,[4]

for the kingship of Horus of the Two Shores. The king of Upper and Lower Egypt, *Nebtawyre*, who lives forever like Re, (11) says:

My majesty has sent the prince, mayor of the city, vizier, chief of royal works, royal favorite, Amenemhet, with a troop of ten-thousand men (13) from the southern nomes of Upper Egypt, and from the ⌜garrisons⌝[5] of Thebes, in order to bring me a precious block of the pure stone of this mountain, whose (15) excellence was made by Min, for the lord of life,[6] who recalls eternity even more than the monuments in the temples of Upper Egypt, as a mission of the king who rules the Two Lands, (17) so as to bring him his heart's desire from the desert lands of his father Min.

He made it as his monument to his father Min of Coptus, lord of desert lands, ruler of Bowmen,[7] that he may give very many [jubilees] and to live like Re forever.

(19) Day 27: descent of the lid of this sarcophagus, a slab of four by eight by two cubits, as it came from the works. Calves were slaughtered, goats sacrificed, incense was laid (21) on the flame. Now a troop of three thousand sailors from the nomes of Lower Egypt conduct it safely to Egypt.

NOTES

1. The terms "horizon" and horizon-dwellers" were studied by Kuentz in *BIFAO*, 17 (1920), 121-190, where he assembled evidence to show that *3ḫt*, "lightland," referred to the remote eastern regions of the *earth*, and that the *3ḫtyw* were the dwellers of those regions. The Egyptians, however, used the term so broadly as to include both earth and sky, and most scholars have retained the conventional rendering of *3ḫt* as "horizon."

2. Horus was often identified with Min.

3. Like the term "land of the horizon-dwellers," the expression "god's land" designated the foreign regions to the east and south of Egypt, including the land of Punt.

4. Here and above the foreward movement of the narration, rendered through finite verbs, is interrupted by an ornate heaping of epithets, the first group referring to the mountain, and the second to the king. Stylistically, these interruptions would be extremely awkward, were they not through their parallelistic structure endowed with a distinct rhythm which sets them apart from the prose narration.

5. The meaning of *prw wᶜbw* is uncertain. See Schenkel, *Memphis*, p. 256 n. a, for citation of discussions of the term.

6. "Lord of life" was a metaphor for sarcophagus.

7. *Iwntyw* = "Bowmen," designated the peoples of the southeastern deserts and of Nubia.

BUILDING INSCRIPTION OF SESOSTRIS I

Leather roll Berlin 3029

The original text was almost certainly carved on a stela or a wall of the temple of Atum at Heliopolis. The version that has survived is a hieratic copy on a leather roll, made by an Eighteenth Dynasty scribe. Apparently the text was considered a good literary composition worth copying. In making the copy, the New Kingdom scribe introduced verse-points, rubrics, and errors. Moreover, he omitted the final portion of the text.

The composition treats the founding of a temple as an action consisting of five steps: (1) The king appears before a full gathering of the courtiers. (2) The king makes a speech announcing his plan to build a temple. (3) The courtiers make an answering speech in which they applaud the royal plan. (4) The king turns to his chief architect and charges him with the execution of the plan. (5) The king presides over the founding ceremony in which a cord is stretched and released at the spot marked for the building. It is probable that these five stages correspond wholly or in part to the actual procedure followed on such an occasion.

The first part of the king's first speech is composed as a poem, while the remainder of the speeches and the description of the founding ceremony are rendered in prose. The king's poetic speech consists almost entirely of distichs.

Publication: L. Stern, ZÄS, 12 (1874), 85-96 and pls. i-ii.   A. de Buck in *Studia Aegyptiaca*, Vol. I, Analecta Orientalia, 17 (Rome, 1938), pp. 48-57.

Translation: BAR I, §§ 498-506.   Erman, *Literature*, pp. 49-52.

(I, 1) Year 3, third month of the inundation, day 8, under the Majesty of the King of Upper and Lower Egypt, *Kheperkare*, the Son of Re, *Sesostris*, the justified, who lives forever and ever. The king appeared in the double-crown; a sitting took place in the audience hall; a consultation with his followers, the companions of the palace, the officials of the private apartment. Command was uttered for them to hear; counsel was given for them to learn:

Behold, my majesty plans a work,
   thinks of a deed of value.
For (5) the future[1] will I make a monument,
   I will settle firm decrees for Harakhty.
He begat me to do what should be done for him,
   to accomplish what he commands to do.
He appointed me shepherd of this land,
   knowing him who would herd it for him.
He gave to me what he protects,
   what the eye in him illuminates.
He who does all as he desires
   conveys[2] to me what he wants known.
I am king by nature,
   ruler to whom one does not give.
I conquered as a fledgling,
   I lorded in the egg,
    I ruled as a youth.
He advanced me to Lord of the Two Parts,
   a child (10) yet wearing swaddling clothes.
He destined me to rule the people,
   made me to be before mankind.
He fashioned me as palace-dweller,
   an offspring not yet issued from the thighs.

[Mine is the land], its length and breadth,
   I was nursed to be a conqueror.
Mine is the land, I am its lord,
   my power reaches heaven's height.
I excel by acting for my maker,
   pleasing the god with what he gave.
[I am] his son and his protector,
   he gave me to conquer what he conquered.

Having come as Horus, I have taken thought. Having established[3] the offerings of (15) the gods, I will construct a great house for my father Atum. He will enrich himself inasmuch as he made me conquer. I will supply his altars on earth. I will build my house in his neighborhood. My excellence will be remembered in his house: the shrine[4] is my name, the lake my memorial. To do what profits is eternity. A king who is evoked by his works is not doomed. He who plans for himself does not know ⌜oblivion⌝,[5] for his name is still pronounced ⌜for it⌝. What pertains to eternity does not perish. What exists is what was made. It means seeking (20) what profits. A name is good sustenance. It means being alert to the concerns of eternity.

(II, 1) Then spoke the royal companions in answer to their god: *Hu* is ⟨in⟩ your mouth, *Sia* is behind you, O King! What you plan comes about: the King's appearance at the Uniting-of-the-Two-Lands, to stretch [the cord] in your temple. It is worthy to look to the morrow as something of value for a lifetime. The people cannot succeed without you. Your Majesty is everyone's eyes. It is very good that you will make your monument (5) in On, the sanctuary of the gods, near your father, the lord of the palace, Atum, the Bull of the Ennead. When your temple is built, it will provide for the altar. It will give service to your image. It will befriend your statues in all eternity.

The king spoke to the royal seal-bearer, sole companion, overseer of the two gold-houses and the two silver-houses, and privy-councillor of the two diadems: It is your counsel that carries out all the works that my majesty desires to bring about. You are the one who is in charge of them, who will act according to my wish. Skill (10) and alertness belong to him who is free of slackness. All works belong to the instructed. He who applies himself[6] is effective. The time of action is your hour. [Its means] accord with your needs in planning.[7] . . . . . . Order the workmen to do according to your design.

The king appeared in the plumed crown, with all the people following him. The chief lector-priest and scribe of the divine books stretched (15) the cord. The rope was released, laid in the ground, made to be this temple. His majesty ordered to proceed; the king turned round before the people. Joined together were Upper and Lower Egypt. . . . . . .

NOTES

1. De Buck connected "for the future" (*n m-ḫt*) with the preceding sentence; but the verse-point is before, not after, *n m-ḫt*; and with *n m-ḫt* at the beginning, the sentences have the right length and balance as well as a chiastic order, with *n m-ḫt* balanced by *n Ḥr-sḥty*. Admittedly, verse-points are often misplaced, and the word order here suggested is unusual.

2. Reading *sʿr*, "present," "announce."

3. I do not emend *smn·n·i* to *smn·i*, as de Buck has done. The point is not that the king will establish offerings—these he will have established as a matter of course at the beginning of his reign—but that he will build a new temple.

4. The word has been read as *bnbnt*, "pyramidion." But the house determinative is not suitable. I read *mrt*, a word for "temple" (see *Wb.*, II, 108.9). This has the added advantage of rendering a wordplay: *rn·i pw mrt, mnw·i pw mr*. The text has several such alliterating wordplays.

5. An illegible sign followed by *rw* and walking legs.

6. Literally, "he who has two arms."

7. I restore *ws[ḫ·s r] ḫft ḥrw·k* and take *wsḫ* to be "latitude" in the sense of "means." But it is uncertain; and the next sentence is rendered obscure by the lacuna after *ir*.

BOUNDARY STELA OF SESOSTRIS III

Berlin Museum 1157

The stela is one of a pair of boundary stelae that Sesostris III erected in the sixteenth year of his reign. It was found at Semna, while the duplicate copy was found on the island of Uronarti. Sesostris III conducted several vigorous Nubian campaigns and increased the fortresses which his predecessors had strung along the river between Elephantine and the second cataract. Already in his eighth year he had designated Semna, called Heh, as the boundary by setting up a stela with a brief text which enjoined all Nubians to halt there (Berlin Museum 14753).[1]

The fortress of Heh (Semna) marked the southern end of the second cataract region. Opposite Semna, on the east bank, stood the fortress of Kumma, and just north of Semna the newly erected fortress of Uronarti, the trio controlling all river and land traffic and making an effective boundary.

The stela is of red granite and has a rounded top which is filled by the representation of the winged sun disk. Below it is the text in twenty-one lines.

Publication: *Ägyptische Inschriften*, I, 257-258.   Sethe, *Lesestücke*,

pp. 83-84.   J. Janssen, *JNES*, 12 (1953), 51-55 (the duplicate Uronarti stela).
Translation: BAR I, §§ 653-660.

(1) The living Horus: Divine of Form; the Two Ladies: Divine of Birth; the King of Upper and Lower Egypt: *Khakaure*, given life; the living Gold-Horus: Being; the Son of Re's body, his beloved, the Lord of the Two Lands: *Sesostris*, given life-stability-health forever. (3) Year 16, third month of winter: the king made his southern boundary at Heh:

I have made my boundary further south than my fathers,
I have added (5) to what was bequeathed me.
I am a king who speaks and acts,
What my heart plans is done by my arm.
One who attacks to conquer, who is swift to (7) succeed,
In whose heart a plan does not slumber.
Considerate to clients, steady in mercy,
Merciless to the foe who attacks him.
One who attacks him who would attack,
Who stops when one stops,
(9) Who replies to a matter as befits it.
To stop when attacked is to make bold the foe's heart,
Attack is valor, retreat is cowardice,
A coward is he who is driven (11) from his border.
Since the Nubian listens to the word of mouth,[2]
To answer him is to make him retreat.
Attack him, he will turn his back,
Retreat, he will start attacking.
(13) They are not people one respects,
They are wretches, craven-hearted.
My majesty has seen it, it is not an untruth.
I have captured their women,
I have carried off (15) their dependents,
Gone to their wells, killed their cattle,
Cut down their grain, set fire to it.
As my father lives for me, I speak the truth!
It is no boast (17) that comes from my mouth.

As for any son of mine who shall maintain this border which my majesty has made, he is my son, born to my majesty. The true son is he who champions his father, (19) who guards the border of his begetter. But he who abandons it, who fails to fight for it, he is not my son, he was not born to me.

Now my majesty has had an image made (21) of my majesty, at this border which my majesty has made, in order that you maintain it, in order that you fight for it.

NOTES

1. The identification of ancient Heh with modern Semna rests first on the fact that two of the three boundary stelae (all of which name Heh as the boundary), were found at Semna, and the third just north of Semna, at Uronarti. In *RdE*, 16 (1963), 179-191, J. Vercoutter has proposed to identify Iken, the trading post to which, according to the stela of year 8, Nubians were admitted, with the great fortress of Mirgissa, some thirty miles north of Semna, a suggestion that appears very plausible. But Vercoutter's proposal to dissociate Heh from Semna and to see in it a place *north* of Iken, is not convincing. He reasoned that if the Nubians were allowed to trade at Iken and yet forbidden to pass Heh, then Heh must have been to the north of Iken. This argument misses the point made by the Heh stela of year 8. Its text says that all Nubian traffic from the south must halt at Heh; that Nubians wishing to trade at Iken will be permitted to proceed by an overland route; but no river traffic north of Heh will be allowed. In fact, this general prohibition of movement beyond Heh, with the specific exception of overland trading travel to Iken, proves that Heh was south of Iken. Hence the text of the stela of year 8 reinforces the identification of Heh with Semna, as had previously been understood; see for example T. Säve-Söderbergh, *Ägypten und Nubien* (Lund, 1941), pp. 75 ff. It goes without saying that overland trading traffic was easy to control and presented no threat.

2. I follow Sethe, *Erl.*, 84, 5, in taking *ḥr n r* as "word of mouth." Janssen's alternate rendering, "since the Nubian hears to fall at a word" (*JNES*, 12 (1953), 54) agrees with Gardiner, *Grammar*, p. 361.

STELA OF INTEF SON OF SENT

From Abydos
British Museum 581

This is one of three stelae in the British Museum belonging to the same person. It is dated to the reign of Sesostris I by the fact that the other two stelae contain this king's name. Coming from Abydos, it exemplifies the trend prevailing among private persons since the Eleventh Dynasty of erecting a small chapel, cenotaph, or single stela in the vicinity of the most hallowed sanctuary of Osiris.

The stela begins with an invocation of Osiris in his form as Foremost-of-the-Westerners (*Khentamentiu*). It also invokes his colleague the god Wep-waut ("Opener of the ways"), who played a prominent part in the annual procession and performance which enacted the life, death, and resurrection of Osiris. In addition, the text spells out the worshiper's association with Abydos through a short hymn which Intef addresses to the holy city, while Intef himself stands beside the seven horizontal lines of the text, his left arm raised in a gesture of greeting. This inscription and the figure of Intef on the left fill the upper third of the tall rectangular stela.

The upper portion is set off from the lower by means of a horizontal line drawn across the surface. The lower portion is subdivided by another horizontal line into two equal halves, each containing ten short vertical columns of text. Together these twenty text columns make up the biographical part of the stela.

Each column consists of a single period beginning with "I am" (*ink*) and including several dependent clauses. Each complete period has from two to four dependent clauses. Through the variations in length and sentence structure, the regularity of the pattern is sufficiently alleviated to escape extreme monotony. The style, then, is that of symmetrically structured speech at its most formal.

The twenty statements form a catalog of virtues that paint the portrait of the ideal courtier. Just as the poetic speech of Sesostris I in his building inscription drew the ideal portrait of the divine king, so the self-portrait of the courtier Intef is designed to perpetuate the image of the ideal servant. The virtues which Intef catalogs are essentially those that were taught in the maxims of Ptahhotep: the true gentleman is calm, self-controlled, friendly, helpful, generous, loyal, truthful and impartial.

Publication: *Hieroglyphic Texts from Egyptian Stelae, etc., in the British Museum*, Vol. II (London, 1912) pl. 23.   Sethe, *Lesestücke*, pp. 80-81.

Partial translation: J. Spiegel, *Die Idee vom Totengericht in der ägyptischen Religion*, Leipziger ägyptologische Studien, 2 (Glückstadt, 1935), pp. 38-40.

Lines 1-7, horizontal

(1) Kissing the ground of Khentamentiu, seeing the beauty of Wep-waut, by the Chamberlain Intef; he says:

As to this shrine,[1] I made (it)[2] (3) in the desert of Abydos,
This island to which one clings,
Walls designed by the All-Lord,
Seat hallowed since the time of Osiris,
Settled by Horus (5) for the forefathers,
Served by the stars in heaven,
Mistress of mankind,
To whom the great of Busiris come,
Equal of On in (7) holiness,
Upon which the All-Lord reposes!
An offering for the honored Chamberlain Intef, son of Sent.

Columns 8-17

(8) I am silent with the angry,
Patient with the ignorant,
So as to quell strife.

I am cool, free of haste,[3]
Knowing the outcome, expecting what comes.
(10) I am a speaker in situations of strife,
One who knows which phrase causes anger.
I am friendly when I hear my name
To him who would tell me (his) concern.[4]
(12) I am controlled, kind, friendly,
One who calms the weeper with good words.
I am one bright-faced[5] to his client,
Beneficent to his equal.
(14) I am a straight one in his lord's house,
Who knows flattery when it is spoken.
I am bright-faced, open-handed,
An owner of food who does not cover his face.[6]
(16) I am a friend of the poor,
One well-disposed to the have-not.
I am one who feeds the hungry in need,
Who is open-handed to the pauper.

Columns 18–27

(18) I am knowing to him who lacks knowledge,
One who teaches a man what is useful to him.
I am a straight one in the king's house,
Who knows what to say in every office.
(20) I am a listener who listens to the truth,
Who ponders it in the heart.[7]
I am one pleasant to his lord's house,
Who is remembered for his good qualities.
(22) I am kindly in the offices,
One who is calm and does not ⌜roar⌝.[8]
I am kindly, not short-tempered,[9]
One who does not attack a man for a remark.
(24) I am accurate like the scales,
Straight and true like Thoth.
I am firm-footed, well-disposed,
Loyal to him who advanced him.
(26) I am a knower who taught himself knowledge,[10]
An advisor whose advice is sought.
I am a speaker in the hall of justice,
Skilled in speech in anxious situations.

NOTES

1. As was pointed out by C. Boreux in *BIFAO*, 30 (1931), 45-48, many of the stelae erected at Abydos were not single stelae but were parts of small shrines consisting of three rectangular stelae. These small shrines, or cenotaphs, were called *ḥꜥt* or *mꜥḥꜥt*.

2. Sethe, *Erl.*, 80, 11 (p. 126), took *ir·n·i* to stand for the relative form *ir·t·n·i* and explained the whole long sentence as an anacoluthon, since the apodosis to "as to this shrine which I made in the desert," is lacking. It is however much simpler to see in *ir·n·i* the *sḏm·n·f* form, in which case the sentence is complete. The absence of "it" in "I made (it)," is analogous to the common formula *ir·n·f m mnw·f* which also lacks an "it." As it is, Intef's introductory statement that he set up his memorial at Abydos is complete and is followed by a short hymn.

3. *Ḥꜣẖ-ḥr*, see Faulkner, *Dict.*, p. 185.

4. The first-person suffix is a scribal error.

5. I.e., "generous."

6. The person who "covers his face" is the opposite of the "bright-faced"; he is the one who turns away from people in need.

7. *Swꜣwꜣ is st ḥr ib*. Sethe and Spiegel took *isst* for an unknown word. I take it to be the enclitic particle *is* followed by the dependent pronoun *st* which refers back to "truth."

8. For *rrit* Sethe guessed "Überheblichkeit," while Faulkner, *Dict.*, p. 151, connected it with *rri*, "pig," and suggested "piggishness"(?). Along these lines I have ventured "roaring."

9. *Sin-ḥr* recalls the *ḥꜣẖ-ḥr* of line 9 and is perhaps slightly stronger.

10. So with Brunner, *Erziehung*, p. 162, rather than Spiegel's "ich war einer, der wusste, wer ihn Wissen lehren konnte."

STELA OF IKHERNOFRET

From Abydos
Berlin Museum 1204

A round-topped limestone stela, 100 × 65 × 20 cm. Under the winged sun disk the standing figure of Osiris faces the titulary of Sesostris III. Below is the main text in twenty-four horizontal lines. At the bottom Ikhernofret sits facing an offering-table and members of his family. Subsidiary texts, consisting of the titulary of Sesostris III and the titles of Ikhernofret, run in vertical columns along the outer edges of the stela.

The text is of unusual interest because it provides an account, albeit a veiled one, of the annually performed "mysteries of Osiris." Holding high office under Sesostris III, Ikhernofret was charged with the organization of the annual festival of the god in which the statue of Osiris journeyed between his temple and his tomb amid scenes of combat which reenacted the god's kingship, death, and resurrection.

Publication: *Ägyptische Inschriften*, I, 169-175.   H. Schäfer, "Die Mysterien des Osiris in Abydos unter König Sesostris III," *Untersuchungen*, IV/2 (1904).   Sethe, *Lesestücke*, pp. 70-71.   *Idem*, *Erl.*, pp. 104-107.

Translation: *BAR*, I, 661-669.   J. A. Wilson in *ANET*, pp. 329-330.

(1) The living Horus: Divine of Form; the Two Ladies: Divine of Birth; the Gold-Horus: Being; the King of Upper and Lower

Egypt: *Khakaure*; the Son of Re: *Sesostris*, given life like Re forever. King's command to the Prince, Count, Royal Seal-bearer, Sole Companion, Overseer of the two gold-houses, Overseer of the two silver-houses, Chief Seal-bearer, Ikhernofret, the revered:

(3) My majesty deigns to have you journey upstream to Abydos in the nome of This, to make (my) monument for my father Osiris, Foremost-of-the-Westerners: to adorn his secret image with the fine gold which he has let my majesty bring back from Nubia in triumphant victory.

You will surely do this in (5) the best manner of acting for the benefit of my father Osiris. For my majesty sends you with my heart relying on your doing everything to the heart's content of my majesty. For you were brought up as a pupil of my majesty. You have grown up as foster child of my majesty, (7) the sole pupil of my palace. My majesty made you a Companion when you were a youth of twenty-six years. My majesty did this because I saw you as one of excellent conduct, keen of tongue, who had come from the womb as one wise. Now my majesty (9) sends you to do this, because my majesty knows that no one could do it but you. Go then and return when you have done all that my majesty has commanded.

I did all that his majesty commanded in executing my lord's command for his father Osiris, Foremost-of-the-Westerners, lord of Abydos, great power in the nome of This. (11) I acted as "his beloved son"[1] for Osiris, Foremost-of-the-Westerners. I furnished his great bark, the eternal everlasting one. I made for him the portable shrine that carries the beauty of the Foremost-of-the-Westerners, of gold, silver, lapis lazuli, bronze, *ssndm*-wood, and cedar wood. The gods (13) who attend him were fashioned, their shrines were made anew. I made the hour-priests [diligent] at their tasks; I made them know the ritual of every day and of the feasts of the beginnings of the seasons.

I directed the work on the *neshmet*-bark,[2] I fashioned the cabin. (15) I decked the breast of the lord of Abydos with lapis lazuli and turquoise, fine gold, and all costly stones which are the ornaments of a god's body. I clothed the god with his regalia in my rank of master of secrets, in my function of stolist.[3] (17) I was pure of hand in decking the god, a priest whose fingers are clean.

I conducted the Procession of Wep-waut, when he goes forth to champion his father.[4] I repulsed the attackers of the *neshmet*-bark, I felled the foes of Osiris.

I conducted the Great Procession, following the god in his steps.[5] (19) I made the god's boat sail, Thoth steering the sailing. I equipped with a cabin the bark "Truly-risen-is-the-Lord-of-Abydos." Decked in his beautiful regalia he proceeded to the domain of Peqer. I cleared the god's path to his tomb in Peqer. I protected Wen-nofer on that day of great combat. I felled all his foes on the shore of Nedyt.

I made him enter into the Great Bark. It bore his beauty. I gave joy to the eastern deserts; I caused rejoicing in the western deserts: (23) They saw the beauty of the *neshmet*-bark as it landed at Abydos. It brought [Osiris, Foremost-of-the-Westerners, Lord of] Abydos, to his palace. I followed the god to his house. His purification was done; his seat was made spacious. I loosened the knot in ---; [he came to rest among] his [followers], his retinue.

NOTES

1. A priestly office concerned with servicing the statue of the god.

2. Apparently three barks were used in the processions: the *neshmet*-bark which is always associated with Osiris; a "great bark" mentioned in lines 11 and 22; and a bark called "truly-risen-is-the-lord-of-Abydos." The last named is associated with the funeral of the god. The "great bark" may have been the actual river boat on which the small portable barks were carried.

3. The reading of this priestly title is uncertain; see P. Montet, *JNES*, 9 (1950), 18-27.

4. This was the first procession, in which Osiris appeared as living ruler with Wep-waut acting as his herald.

5. The central part of the performance included the god's death and the funeral procession to his tomb in Peqer, situated about a mile and a half to the southwest of the temple. It was followed by the final procession in which the resurrected god returned to his temple.

STELA OF SEHETEP-IB-RE

From Abydos
Cairo Museum 20538

Sehetep-ib-re served successively under Sesostris III and Amenemhet III. During the reign of the latter he erected for himself a funerary monument at Abydos in the shape of a tall, freestanding limestone stela which is inscribed on both faces and on the thickness of the sides. The stone measures 123 × 48 × 24 cm. On the recto, under the rounded top, the standing figure of Osiris faces the titulary of Amenemhet III, and on the verso that of Sesostris III.

The long text combines several distinct genres. The recto has a stylized autobiography limited to self-laudatory epithets. It is followed by an elaborate "appeal to the living," addressed to the priests of the several gods and to all other inhabitants of the town. The verso consists of three distinct topics: an autobiography in which the official recalls his participation in the cult of Osiris; an Instruction in which right conduct is defined in terms of loyalty to the king; and another "appeal to the living." The long middle portion, the Instruction, is of considerable interest, and the studies that have been devoted to it have clarified its origin and purpose.

Kuentz was able to show that the Instruction recurs in a somewhat different form in a Ramesside papyrus, and that both versions must have had a common ancestor. Subsequently Posener found portions of the same text in a Louvre papyrus, on a tablet, and on several ostraca; and he placed this newly won Instruction in its political and literary context (*Littérature*, pp. 117-128).

The author of the stela-text copied the first part of the Instruction and adapted it as a teaching addressed by Sehetep-ib-re to his children. In this form, the Instruction begins and ends with exhortations to worship and serve the king, and its middle portion is an encomium of the king in the form of a hymn.

The hymn to the king came from yet another literary tradition. It could be inserted into a narrative, as is the case in the *Story of Sinuhe*. It also existed as a literary category in its own right, as we see in the *Cycle of Hymns to Sesostris III*, preserved in a papyrus from Illahun.

This Instruction, then, combines the form of the "teaching" with that of the "hymn" into a vigorous exhortation to loyalty. This point of view was of course already central to the morality of the Old Kingdom; but only now, in the Twelfth Dynasty, did it attain its full literary elaboration.

Publication: Mariette, *Abydos*, II, 34 and pls. 24-26.   Lange-Schäfer, *Grabsteine*, II, 145-150, and IV, pl. 40.   Sethe, *Lesestücke*, pp. 68-69. *Idem, Erl.*, pp. 99-104.   A. Kamal, *ASAE*, 38 (1938), 265-283, and 40 (1940), 209-229 (the verso).

Translation: *BAR* I, §§ 745-748.

Translation and study of the Instruction: Erman, *Literature*, pp. 84-85. C. Kuentz in *Griffith Studies*, pp. 97-110.   J. A. Wilson in *ANET*, p. 431.   H. Grapow, *ZÄS*, 79 (1954), 21-27.

Study: Posener, *Littérature*, pp. 117-128.

Recto

The first portion of the text is written in twelve horizontal lines across the middle of the stone, the second in nine vertical columns on the lower right side. In the lower left is the standing figure of Sehetep-ib-re.

(1) The Prince, Count, Royal Seal-bearer, beloved Sole Companion, Great one of the King of Upper Egypt, Grandee of the King of Lower Egypt; Magistrate at the head of the people, Overseer of horn, hoof, feather, scale, and pleasure ponds; whose coming is awaited by the courtiers; (3) to whom people tell their affairs; whose worth the Lord of the Two Lands perceived; whom he set before the Two Shores. Keeper of silver and gold; herdsman of cattle of all kinds; man of justice before the Two Lands; straight and true (5) like Thoth. Master of secrets in the temples; overseer of all works of the king's

house. More accurate than the plummet; the equal of the scales. Patient, effective in counsel; who says what is good, repeats what pleases; (7) whose patience is unequaled; good at listening, excellent in speaking. An official who unravels what is knotty; whom his lord distinguished before millions. Truly exemplary and beloved; free of wrongdoing. Single-minded for the lord who has tried him; pillar of the South (9) in the king's house; who follows his lord in his strides; his intimate before the courtiers. Who attends his lord alone; companion of Horus in the palace; true favorite of his lord; to whom secret matters are told. Who solves[1] the knotty (11), eases pains, acts for the best. The Royal Seal-bearer, Temple-overseer, Deputy Chief Seal-bearer, Sehetep-ib-re, says:

O you counts, chief priests, high priests, lector-priests, god's seal-bearers, Anubis priests; you many priests and chiefs of priestly phyles; and all who live in this town, who shall be in this temple, who shall pass by this monument,[2] who shall read this stela: as you love Osiris, Foremost-of-the-Westerners, and repeat performing his feasts; as you love Wep-waut, your kindly god, and rejoice in the king forever; as you love life and ignore death, and as your children thrive for you, so shall you say as your utterance:

An offering which the king gives of a thousand of bread and beer, oxen and fowl, ointment and clothing, and every pleasant thing on which a god lives, for the revered prince, count, royal seal-bearer, temple-overseer, deputy chief seal-bearer, Sehetep-ib-re, son of Dedet-Nekhbet, the justified.

Verso
Twenty-six horizontal lines

(1) The Prince, Count, Royal Seal-bearer, Temple-overseer, Deputy Chief Seal-bearer, Sehetep-ib-re, the justified, says:

I have had this monument consecrated. Its place has been established. I have made contracts for payments to the priests (3) of Abydos. I have officiated as "his beloved son" in the service of the gold-house, in the mystery of the lord of Abydos.[3]

I have directed the work on the sacred bark; I fashioned its cordage. I conducted (5) the *hȝkr*-ceremony for its lord,[4] and the Procession of Wep-waut. All the offerings were done for him, recited by the priests. I clothed the god in his regalia in my rank of master of secrets, my function of stolist. (7) I was openhanded in decking the god, a priest whose fingers are clean, so that I may be a follower of the god, so as to be a mighty spirit (*akh*) at the shrine of the lord of Abydos.

Beginning of the Instruction which he made for his children:

(9) I say a great thing, I let you hear,
I let you know counsel everlasting,
Right conduct of life, passing the lifetime in peace:
Worship King Nimaatre, ever-living, in (11) your bodies,
Cleave to His Majesty in your hearts!
He is Sia in the hearts,
His eyes seek out every body.
He is Re who sees with his rays,
Who lights the Two Lands more than the sun-disk,
Who makes verdant (13) more than great Hapy,
He has filled the Two Lands with life force.
Noses turn cold when he starts to rage,
When he is at peace one breathes air.
He gives food to those who serve him,
He nourishes him who treads (15) his path.

The king is sustenance, his mouth is plenty,
He who will be is his creation.
He is the Khnum of everybody,
Begetter who makes mankind.
He is Bastet who guards the Two Lands,
He who worships (17) him is sheltered by his arm.
He is Sakhmet to him who defies his command,
He whom he hates will bear distress.

Fight for his name, respect his oath,
Then you stay free of ⌐betrayal⌐.[5]
The king's beloved will be (19) honored,
His majesty's foe has no tomb,
His corpse is cast into the water.
Do this, then you prosper,
It serves[6] you forever!

The Prince, Count, Royal Seal-bearer, Temple-overseer, Sehetep-ib-re, says:

O beloved of the king, favorite of his city-god, (21) priests of Osiris, Foremost-of-the-Westerners, in Abydos, hour-priests of this god, priests of King Nimaatre, who lives forever, and of Khakaure, the justified, and their hour-priests in your city; (23) all people of Abydos, who shall pass by this monument in going downstream or upstream: as you love your king, as you praise your city-gods, as your children remain in your place, as you love life and ignore (25) death, you shall say:

A thousand of bread and beer, oxen and fowl, ointment and clothing, incense, unguent and all kinds of herbs, all kinds of offerings on which a god lives, for the *ka* of the revered prince, count, royal seal-bearer, beloved of his lord, favored sole companion, deputy chief seal-bearer, Sehetep-ib-re, the justified, son of Dedet-Nekhbet, the justified.

NOTES

1. *Gmi*, "find," in the sense of "find a solution," parallel to *wḥ'* in line 7.
2. As this passage shows, the basic sense of *m'ḥ't* is not "tomb," but rather "funerary monument," in this case a freestanding stela.
3. In the festivals of Abydos Sehetep-ib-re performed essentially the same functions as Ikhernofret.
4. A ceremony connected with the burial of Osiris.
5. The precise meaning of *sp n bgsw* is not known.
6. *Gmi*, "find," in the sense of "find useful."

STELA OF THE PRIEST HOREMKHAUF

From his Tomb at Hieraconpolis
Metropolitan Museum 35.7.55

A round-topped painted limestone stela, 58 × 35 × 15 cm. In the lunette is the pair of large magic eyes which, since the Twelfth Dynasty, commonly decorates the funerary stelae. Below is the text in eleven horizontal lines and five short vertical columns on the lower right side. On the lower left are the standing figures of Horemkhauf and his wife. The space between the figures and the text is filled by offerings and the names of the couple's children. The workmanship is crude.

The stela was found in 1935, when the Egyptian Expedition of the Metropolitan Museum of Art cleared the courtyard before the tomb entrance. The work of recording the tomb is currently being carried out by the American Research Center in Egypt.

Horemkhauf's trip to the capital, Itj-tawy—the main event of his biographical stela—took place in the last decade of the Thirteenth Dynasty. The decoration of his tomb was completed several decades later, at the beginning of the Seventeenth Dynasty, when the North and Itj-tawy had fallen into the hands of the Hyksos. Thus his life straddles the end of the Middle Kingdom and the beginning of the Hyksos period.

Publication: W. C. Hayes, *JEA*, 33 (1947), 3-11 and pl. II.

(1) An offering which the king gives (to) Horus of Nekhen, Osiris dwelling in Nekhen, Horus Avenger-of-his-Father, Thoth, and the Ennead of gods and goddesses in Nekhen, that they may give an

offering of bread and beer, oxen and fowl, ointment and clothing, incense and unguent, all things good and pure whereof one gives to (3) a god: foods and nourishments; transfiguration, power, and justification; smelling the sweet breath of the northwind; gifts of sky, produce of earth, bounty of Hapy. May hands give, may flood purify, may Thoth offer to the *ka* of (5) the Chief Inspector of priests of Horus of Nekhen, the Overseer of fields, Horemkhauf, the justified. He says:

Horus Avenger-of-his-Father ordered me to the Residence,[1] to bring back Horus of Nekhen and his mother Isis, the justified.[2] (7) He appointed me captain of a ship and crew, for he knew me to be a competent official of his temple, one alert in his duties. I traveled downstream in a good journey. I took (9) Horus of Nekhen upon my arms together with this goddess, his mother, in the Good Office of Itj-tawy in the presence of the king himself.

I, an excellent dignitary on earth, shall be an excellent spirit (*akh*) in the necropolis, since[3] I have given bread to the hungry, (11) clothes to the naked, and have nourished my brothers. I have not let one beg goods from another, and everyone opened[4] to his brothers. I looked after (13) the house of those who had raised me; they are buried and made to live.[5]

I gave labor to Horus, and Horus made that I was given a vacation from labor in the house,[6] inasmuch as (15) he loved me, the Chief Inspector of priests of Horus of Nekhen, the Overseer of fields, Horemkhauf, son of the Inspector of priests and Overseer of fields,[7] Thuty, justified, born of the Royal Ornament Tyetyeb, justified.

NOTES

1. The god Horus in his manifestation as the son of Osiris commissioned Horemkhauf to travel to the royal residence and bring back a new cult image of the Horus worshiped at Hieraconpolis, as well as a new image of Isis. This long journey apparently was the outstanding event of his career.
2. The epithet "justified," usually appended to the name of a deceased person, was sometimes added to the name of a deity.
3. Note that *m-ḥt*, "after," here has the meaning "since," or "because." Cf. *Merikare*, n. 14.
4. I.e., opened his door.
5. The eternal life of the resurrected dead.
6. The vacation was the journey to the capital.
7. An official of modest rank, Horemkhauf held the same positions as his father before him, possibly one step higher, since he calls himself "chief" inspector.

II. A Spell from the Coffin Texts

CT 1130 and 1031

Beginning in the First Intermediate Period, it became customary to inscribe the coffins of non-royal well-to-do persons with spells designed to protect the dead against the dangers of the netherworld and to bring about an afterlife modeled on that of the divine king. Like the king, the common man (and woman) now desired to rise up to the sky and to join the gods. Along with these grandiose wishes, the texts spell out more ordinary concerns and fears, such as the fear to suffer hunger and thirst, and the wish to be united with one's family.

In inspiration, the Coffin Texts descend directly from the Pyramid Texts, and some of their spells are direct borrowings. But the bulk of the material is new and reflects its non-royal origin. As a corpus, the Coffin Texts are far less coherent than the Pyramid Texts, for they lack a unifying point of view. Inspired by a reliance on magic, they lack the humility of prayer and the restraints of reason. Oscillating between grandiose claims and petty fears, they show the human imagination at its most abstruse. Fear of death and longing for eternal life have been brewed in a sorcerer's cauldron from which they emerge as magic incantations of the most phrenetic sort. The attempt to overcome the fear of death by usurping the royal claims to immortality resulted in delusions of grandeur which accorded so little with the observed facts of life as to appear paranoid.

Now and then a more reasonable attitude prevails, as in the first part of the spell here translated. It consists of a speech of the sun-god Re, in which the god takes credit for four good deeds which he did at the time of creation. In listing the four deeds, the god makes two assertions of prime importance: that he created all men as equals; and that it was not he who taught mankind to do wrong; rather, people do wrong of their own volition. This portion of the text is much above the usual level. The remainder is a typical Coffin Text spell, a grandiose claim that the dead will win entry into heaven and will be the equal of the sun-god.

The spell was used on a number of coffins, and the translation draws on the several versions as found side by side in de Buck's masterly edition.

Publication: de Buck, *Coffin Texts*, VII, 461-471 and 262.

Translation of the first part: J. A. Wilson in *ANET*, pp. 7-8.

Words spoken by Him-whose-names-are-hidden, the All-Lord, as he speaks before those who silence the storm, in the sailing of the court:[1]

Hail in peace! I repeat to you the good deeds which my own heart did for me from within the serpent-coil,[2] in order to silence strife. I did four good deeds within the portal of lightland:

I made the four winds, that every man might breathe in his time. This is one of the deeds.

I made the great inundation, that the humble might benefit by it like the great. This is one of the deeds.

I made every man like his fellow; and I did not command that they do wrong. It is their hearts that disobey what I have said. This is one of the deeds.

I made that their hearts are not disposed to forget the West, in order that sacred offerings be made to the gods of the nomes. This is one of the deeds.

I have created the gods from my sweat, and the people from the tears of my eye.[3]

The dead speaks

I shall shine[4] and be seen every day as a dignitary of the All-Lord, having given satisfaction to the Weary-hearted.[5]

I shall sail rightly in my bark, I am lord of eternity in the crossing of the sky.

I am not afraid in my limbs, for Hu and Hike[6] overthrow for me that evil being.

I shall see lightland, I shall dwell in it. I shall judge the poor and the wealthy.

I shall do the same for the evil-doers; for mine is life, I am its lord, and the scepter will not be taken from me.

I have spent a million years with the Weary-hearted, the son of Geb, dwelling with him in one place; while hills became towns and towns hills, for dwelling destroys dwelling.[7]

I am lord of the flame who lives on truth; lord of eternity maker of joy, against whom that worm shall not rebel.

I am he who is in his shrine, master of action[8] who destroys the storm; who drives off the serpents of many names when he goes from his shrine.

Lord of the winds who announces the northwind, rich in names in the mouth of the Ennead.

Lord of lightland, maker of light, who lights the sky with his beauty.

I am he in his name! Make way for me, that I may see Nun and Amun! For I am that equipped spirit (*akh*) who passes by the ⌜guards⌝.[9] They do not speak for fear of Him-whose-name-is-hidden, who is in my body. I know him, I do not ignore him! I am equipped and effective in opening his portal!

As for any person who knows this spell, he will be like Re in the eastern sky, like Osiris in the netherworld. He will go down to the circle of fire, without the flame touching him ever!

NOTES

1. *Sgrw nšn* might be either the active or the passive participle; Wilson construed it as the passive participle: "those stilled from tumult." In the active sense it would refer to the gods who accompany the sun-god. *Šnwt* are the courtiers, or entourage, of Re.

2. The serpent-dragon Apophis who symbolized the lurking dangers of the world.

3. A wordplay on *rmṭ*, "people," and *rmyt*, "tears," which occurs a number of times as an allusion to the creation of mankind.

4. Here begins the spell that is put in the mouth of the dead. In four of the versions it is cast in the first person, and in two version in the third person.

5. An epithet of Osiris. The meaning seems to be that the dead must first satisfy Osiris, the ruler of the dead, before he can join the sun-god.

6. The personifications of effective speech and of magic.

7. The claims get successively grander until the dead speaks as if he were the sun-god himself. That this identification is intended is shown by the explanatory remark with which the spell ends.

8. Does *spw* with knife determinative mean "slaughter"?

9. One version has *nhw*, another *hnw*, a third *msw*.

III. Didactic Literature

The first and the last of the seven works in this section belong to the genre *Instruction* in the specific sense in which the Egyptians used the term: a teaching of a father to his son. But all seven works are instructional in the wider sense. They formulate and ponder problems of life and death and seek solutions. Egypt and Mesopotamia were the earliest practitioners of this class of writings, to which the name *"Wisdom Literature"* has been given. Their example contributed significantly to the subsequent flowering of the genre among the Hebrews.

The compositional forms in which the evolved Wisdom Literature of the Middle Kingdom is cast are three: the didactic speech of a father to his son; the admonishing or prophetic speech, or speeches, whose speakers may be sages or other people in the role of defenders of the public good; and the dialogue in which two speakers defend contrasting points of view.

The *Instruction of King Amenemhet I* is, like the *Instruction for Merikare*, a royal testament that distills the experience of the old king for the benefit of his son and successor. In content it differs dramatically from the earlier work. For whereas Merikare had been advised to surround himself with competent officials, King Amenemhet warns his son against all his subjects, for all are potential traitors—a pessimism that resulted from the attempt on the king's life.

Though Amenemhet's thirty-year rule ended with his assassination, it had been a vigorous and successful reign. And near its beginning it had been glorified in the work known as the *Prophecies of Neferti*. These are prophecies after the event, and the fictional disguise is of the most transparent kind: the sage Neferti is transposed into the Old Kingdom, to the court of King Snefru, having been summoned in order to entertain the king with fine speeches. Asked to speak of the future rather than the past, he launches into a depiction of civil war and general distress, which eventually turns into happiness through the accession of king Amenemhet I.

The transition from the Eleventh to the Twelfth Dynasty, however, had not been particularly troublesome. There had been no general distress. It follows that the theme "national distress" was a literary *topos* that required no basis in reality, or almost none. A change of dynasty, or merely a succession within the same dynasty, sufficed as a point of departure for developing the topic: *order versus disorder*. In short, works such as the *Prophecies of Neferti* formulated a general social problem and treated it from an entirely loyalist point of view: the king was the guarantor of order and of justice. This point of view was of course inherited from the Old Kingdom. What is new is that it is now formulated through a depiction of chaos, the chaos that overtakes the nation when kingship is weak.

A pendant to the *Prophecies of Neferti* are the *Complaints of Khakheperre-sonb*. Here the depiction of national chaos is so vague and metaphorical that no scholar has tried to claim a historical reality for it. Clearly, what interested these authors was the topic as such. Moreover, as the freshness of invention wore off, it became a matter of literary ingenuity, of inventing ever more images by which to describe the alleged distress. In *Khakhperre-sonb* the literary intention seems especially pronounced.

The most ambitious work of the genre, the *Admonitions of Ipuwer*, is also the most obscure. Long, fragmentary, and difficult, it has ever since Gardiner's first edition been interpreted as a reflection of the disorders of the First Intermediate Period, despite the fact that the composition is certainly no older than the Twelfth Dynasty. The dissenting view of S. Luria, who through examples drawn from other literatures gave a telling demonstration of the purely literary nature of the theme "national calamity," did not receive the attention it deserved. I am convinced that the *Admonitions of Ipuwer* is nothing other than the latest and fullest working out of the topos "national distress," that is to say, a work of the late Middle Kingdom which did not draw on any particular historical situation, least of all on the long-past First Intermediate Period.

In the *Dispute between a Man and His Ba*, the problems are personal, not social. Specifically the focus is on the role of that mysterious life-force called the *ba*, the indwelling demonic power that controlled man's life, escaped from his body at the moment of death, and played a vital but ill-defined part in his afterlife. What would happen to a man if he were deserted by his *ba*? This and related problems are not so much resolved as dissolved in a series of four poems of transcending beauty.

In the *Eloquent Peasant*, two unrelated themes—the need for justice and the utility of eloquence—are intertwined in a dramatic and ironic manner which gives the work its special interest.

Lastly, in the *Satire of the Trades*, the vein of literary satire is worked for the first time.

THE INSTRUCTION OF KING AMENEMHET I
FOR HIS SON SESOSTRIS I

When first studied, the text was regarded as the genuine work of King Amenemhet I, composed by him after he had escaped an attempt on his life. The currently prevailing view is that the king was in fact assassinated in the thirtieth year of his reign, and that the text was composed by a royal scribe at the behest of the new king, Sesostris I.

The attack on the king's life is told in a deliberately veiled manner; yet there are sufficient hints in the account and elsewhere in the text to convey to the Middle Kingdom audience that the speaker is the deceased king who speaks to his son in a revelation, and to later audiences, including the sophisticated one of the New Kingdom, that the work was composed by a court writer.

It is a powerful and imaginative composition, distinguished by its personal tone and by the bitterness born of experience with which the old king castigates the treachery of his subjects, and warns his son not to place trust in any man. The theme, then, is regicide. In contrast with the theme "national distress," regicide was not a topic that could be treated fully and openly, for it conflicted too strongly with the dogma of the divine king. Hence the work is the only one of its kind.

The orational style is used throughout, except in the description of the assassination which is rendered in prose.

The text was preserved in Papyrus Millingen of the Eighteenth Dynasty, a copy of which was made by A. Peyron in 1843. Subsequently the original papyrus was lost. Portions of the work are preserved on three wooden tablets of the Eighteenth Dynasty, some papyrus fragments, and numerous ostraca of the New Kingdom.

The line numbers are those of Papyrus Millingen, which is a good manuscript but fragmentary in the final portion.

Publication: F. Ll. Griffith, "The Millingen Papyrus," ZÄS, 34 (1896), 35-51.   G. Maspero, Les enseignements d'Amenemhat Ier à son fils Sanouasrit Ier (Cairo, 1914).   Volten, Politische Schriften, pp. 104-128. J. Lopez, "Le Papyrus Millingen," RdE, 15 (1963), 29-33 and pls. 4-8. W. Helck, Der Text der Lehre Amenemhets I. für seinen Sohn (Wiesbaden, 1969).

Translation: BAR, I, §§474-483.   Erman, Literature, pp. 72-74.   J. A. Wilson in ANET, pp. 418-419.

Study: Posener, Littérature, chap. 2.

Comments: A. H. Gardiner in Mélanges Maspero I, pp. 479-496. M. Malinine, BIFAO, 34 (1934), 63-74.   A. de Buck in Mélanges Maspero I, pp. 847-52.   A. de Buck, Le Muséon, 59 (1946), 183-200. R. O. Faulkner in Griffith Studies, pp. 69-73.   R. Anthes, JNES, 16 (1957), 176-190, and JNES, 17 (1958), 208-209.   H. Goedicke, JARCE, 7 (1968), 15-21.

(I, 1) Beginning of the Instruction made by the majesty of King Sehetepibre, son of Re, Amenemhet, the justified,[1] as he spoke in a revelation of truth, to his son the All-Lord. He said:

Risen as god,[2] hear what I tell you,
That you may rule the land, govern the shores,
Increase well-being!
Beware of subjects who are nobodies,
Of whose plotting one is not aware.[3]
Trust not a brother, know not a friend,
Make no (5) intimates, it is worthless.
When you lie down, guard your heart yourself,
For no man has adherents on the day of woe.
I gave to the beggar, I raised the orphan,
I gave success to the poor as to the wealthy;
But he who ate my food raised opposition,
He whom I gave my trust used it to plot.[4]
Wearers of my fine linen looked at me as if they were needy,[5]
Those perfumed with my myrrh ⌈poured water while wearing it⌉.[6]
You my living peers, my partners among men,
Make for me mourning such as has not (10) been heard,
For so great a combat had not yet been seen!

If one fights in the arena forgetful of the past,
Success will elude him who ignores what he should know.

It was after supper, night had come. I was taking an hour of rest, lying on my bed, for I was weary. As my heart (II, 1) began to follow sleep, weapons for my protection were turned against me,[7] while I was like a snake of the desert. I awoke at the fighting, ⌐alert⌐,[8] and found it was a combat of the guard. Had I quickly seized weapons in my hand, I would have made the cowards retreat ⌐in haste⌐. But no one is strong at night; no one can fight alone; no success is achieved without a helper.

(5) Thus bloodshed occurred while I was without you; before the courtiers had heard I would hand over to you; before I had sat with you so as to advise you.[9] For I had not prepared for it, had not expected it, had not foreseen the failing of the servants.

Had women ever marshaled troops?
Are rebels nurtured in the palace?
Does one release water that destroys the soil
And deprives people of their crops?[10]
No harm had come to me since my birth,
No one equaled me as a doer of deeds.

(10) I journeyed to Yebu, I returned to the Delta,
Having stood on the land's borders I observed its interior.
I reached the borders of ⌐the strongholds⌐[11]
By my strength and my feats.
I was grain-maker, beloved of Nepri,
Hapy honored me on every field.
None hungered in my years,
None (III, 1) thirsted in them,
One sat because I acted and spoke of me,
I had assigned everything to its place.
I subdued lions, I captured crocodiles,
I repressed those of Wawat,
I captured the Medjai,
I made the Asiatics do the dog walk.

I built myself a house decked with gold,
Its ceiling of lapis lazuli,
Walls of silver, floors of [acacia wood],
(5) Doors of copper, bolts of bronze,

Made for eternity, prepared for all time,
I know because I am its lord.
Behold, much hatred is in the streets,
The wise says "yes," the fool says "no,"
For no one knows it ⌐without your presence⌐,[12]
Sesostris my son!
As my feet depart, you are in my heart,
My eyes behold you, child of a happy hour
⌐Before the people as they hail you⌐.
I have made the past and arranged the future,
I gave you the contents of my heart.
You (10) wear the white crown of a god's son,
The seal is in its place, assigned you by me,
Jubilation is in the bark of Re,
Kingship is again what it was in the past!
......[13]
Raise your monuments, establish your strongholds,
Fight......[14]

NOTES

1. In Papyrus Chester Beatty IV, a New Kingdom scribe drew up a list of famous authors of the past and assigned the composition of the *Instruction of Amenemhet* to a scribe by the name of Khety. Whether or not his attribution was correct, it reveals that the New Kingdom scribe understood the pseudepigraphic nature of the work (see Posener, *Littérature*, p. 67). But as regards the audience of the Middle Kingdom, it seems to me probable that it took the work to be the genuine testament of King Amenemhet; for pseudepigrapha would lose much of their effectiveness if they were not, at least initially, believed to be the works of the men whose name they bore.

2. The much debated introductory passage was reexamined by Goedicke, *loc. cit.*, who made a case for taking *ḏd·f ḥꜥ m nṯr* as a single sentence, in accordance with the verse-points, and having it refer to the dead king who is "risen as god," rather than to the accession of Sesostris I. If so taken, however, the address to Sesostris becomes very abrupt, consisting only of "listen to me," and the sentence lacks balance. Helck has summarized the previous renderings and has preferred to take *ḥꜥ* as imperative, "rise," rather than the participle, "risen."

3. As Helck and Goedicke observed, the two *tmmt* refer back to *smdt*. I take the passage to mean that subjects who are unknown are dangerous because they can plot in secrecy. *Ḥrw* in the sense of "plot" is well attested (see Volten, *op. cit.*, p. 108).

4. Literally, "he whom I gave my hands."

5. Following Gardiner, *op. cit.*, p. 483, I read *šwyw*, rather than *šw*, "grass."

6. *Stí mw* has generally been interpreted as an act of disrespect or defiance, e.g., Helck: "spuckten vor mir aus." The inner logic of the

composition requires, however, that the king, looking back on the treacherous behavior of the plotters, should describe it in terms of *covert* acts, since any open defiance would have drawn immediate punishment. The "pouring water" in *Admonitions*, 7, 5, suggests a menial task.

7. I take *sphr* in the literal sense of "turn around."

8. The meaning of *iw·i n h'w·i*, "I being to my body" is uncertain. Gardiner's "by myself" was disputed by Anthes and Helck; the latter suggested "kam zu mir," i.e., "became alert."

9. I.e., the old king was prevented from "sitting together" with his son in a formal ceremony of abdication.

10. The context here, and in *Neferti*, line 46, suggests that *iryt* means "produce" and "crops."

11. For *hpswt* Gardiner, *op. cit.*, p. 493, proposed "frontier-strongholds," while Helck assumes a corrupted writing of *hps*, the constellation "great bear."

12. The three sentences recur in *Admonitions*, 6, 13. Helck has pointed out that *msyt* is a corruption of *msd*, "hatred." The third sentence is obscure.

13. A garbled sentence, not preserved in P. Millingen.

14. The two concluding sentences are corrupt.

THE PROPHECIES OF NEFERTI

The sage Neferti is summoned to the court of King Snefru of the Fourth Dynasty, in order to entertain the king with fine speeches. Asked to speak of the future rather than the past, he prophesies the destruction of the nation by civil war and its eventual redemption through the rise of a great king. He calls the redeemer "Ameny"—the short form of Amenemhet—and thereby provides the clue to the understanding of the work. The readers, ancient and modern, are to understand that the "prophecy" is a literary disguise, veiling the contemporary character of a work composed in the reign of Amenemhet I, and designed as a glorification of that king. The work is a historical romance in pseudo-prophetic form.

Reflecting the successful early years of the reign, it is free of the gloom that pervades the *Instruction of Amenemhet I*, written about two decades later. Except, of course, for the artificial gloom of the prophecies of disasters that would precede the redemption. We have already said that the theme "national distress" was an intellectual problem that became a literary topos. It required no specific factual basis but merely the general phenomenon of civil disorders that could, and did, break out periodically. But no major calamities had preceded the accession of Amenemhet I.

The work is preserved in a single manuscript, P. Leningrad 1116B, which dates from the Eighteenth Dynasty. Small portions are preserved on two writing boards of the Eighteenth Dynasty and on numerous Ramesside ostraca.

Publication: Golenischeff, *Papyrus hiératiques*, pls. 23-25. W. Helck, *Die Prophezeiung des Nfr·tj* (Wiesbaden, 1970).

Translation: A. H. Gardiner, *JEA*, I (1914), 100-106. Erman, *Literature*, pp. 110-115. J. A. Wilson in *ANET*, pp. 444-446. Lefebvre, *Romans*, pp. 95-105.

Study: Posener, *Littérature*, pp. 21-60 and 145-157.

(1) There was a time when the majesty of King Snefru, the justified, was beneficent king in this whole land. On one of those days the magistrates of the residence entered the palace to offer greetings. And they went out having offered greetings in accordance with their daily custom. Then his majesty said to the seal-bearer at his side: "Go, bring me the magistrates of the residence who have gone from here after today's greetings."

They were ushered in to him (5) straightway and were on their bellies before his majesty a second time. His majesty said to them: "Comrades, I have had you summoned in order that you seek out for me a son of yours who is wise, or a brother of yours who excels, or a friend of yours who has done a noble deed, so that he may speak to me some fine words, choice phrases at the hearing of which my majesty may be entertained."

They were on their bellies before his majesty once more. Then they spoke before his majesty: "There is a great lector-priest of Bastet, O king, our lord, Neferti (10) by name. He is a citizen with valiant arm, a scribe excellent with his fingers, a gentleman of greater wealth than any peer of his. May he be brought for your majesty to see!" Said his majesty: "Go, bring him to me!" He was ushered in to him straightway, and he was on his belly before his majesty.

His majesty said: "Come, Neferti, my friend, speak to me some fine words, choice phrases at the hearing of which my majesty may be entertained!" Said the lector-priest Neferti: "Of what has happened or of what will happen, O king, my lord?" (15) Said his majesty: "Of what will happen. As soon as today is here, it is passed over." He stretched out his hand to a box of writing equipment, took scroll and palette and began to put into writing the words of the lector-priest Neferti, that wise man of the East, servant of Bastet in her East, and native of the nome of On.

As he deplored what had happened[1] in the land, evoked the state of the East, with Asiatics roaming in their strength, frightening those about to harvest and seizing cattle from the plough, (20) he said:

Stir, my heart,
Bewail this land, from which you have sprung!
When there is silence before evil,
And when what should be chided is feared,
Then the great man is overthrown in the land of your birth.[2]
Tire not while this is before you,

Rise against what is before you!
Lo, the great no longer rule the land,
What was made has been unmade,
Re should begin to recreate!
The land is quite perished, no remnant is left,
Not the black of a nail is spared from its fate.
(Yet) while the land suffers, none care for it,
None speak, none shed tears: "How fares this land!"
The sundisk, covered, (25) shines not for people to see,
One cannot live when clouds conceal,
All are numb[3] from lack of it.

I shall describe what is before me,
I do not foretell what does not come:
Dry is the river of Egypt,
One crosses the water on foot;
One seeks water for ships to sail on,
Its course having turned into shoreland.
Shoreland will turn into water,
Watercourse back into shoreland.
Southwind will combat northwind,
Sky will lack the single wind.

A strange bird will breed in the Delta marsh,[4]
Having made its nest beside (30) the people,
The people having let it approach by default.
Then perish those delightful things,
The fishponds full of fish-eaters,[5]
Teeming with fish and fowl.
All happiness has vanished,
The land is bowed down in distress,
Owing to those feeders,[6]
Asiatics who roam the land.
Foes have risen in the East,
Asiatics have come down to Egypt.
If the fortress is ⌈crowded⌉ ...
...... (35) ......[7]
Desert flocks will drink at the river of Egypt,
Take their ease on the shores for lack of one to fear;
For this land is to-and-fro, knowing not what comes,

What-will-be being hidden according as one says:[8]
"When sight and hearing fail the mute leads."
I show you the land in turmoil,
What should not be has come to pass.
Men will seize weapons of warfare,
The land will live in (40) uproar.
Men will make arrows of copper,
Will crave blood for bread,
Will laugh aloud at distress.
None will weep over death,
None will wake fasting for death,
Each man's heart is for himself.
Mourning is not done today,
Hearts have quite abandoned it.
A man sits with his back turned,
While one slays another.
I show you the son as enemy, the brother as foe,
A man (45) slaying his father.[9]

Every mouth is full of "how I wish"[10]
All happiness has vanished;
The land is ruined, its fate decreed,
Deprived of produce, lacking in crops,[11]
What was made has been unmade.
One seizes a man's goods, gives them to an outsider,
I show you the master in need, the outsider sated,
The lazy stuffs himself, the active is needy.[12]
One gives only with hatred,
To silence the mouth that speaks;
To answer a speech the arm thrusts a stick,
One speaks by killing him.
Speech falls on the heart like fire,
(50) One cannot endure the word of mouth.

The land is shrunk—its rulers are many,
It is bare—its taxes are great;
The grain is low—the measure is large,
It is measured to overflowing.
Re will withdraw from mankind:
Though he will rise at his hour,
One will not know when noon has come;

No one will discern his shadow,
No face will be dazzled by seeing [him],
No eyes will moisten with water.
He will be in the sky like the moon,
His nightly course unchanged,
His rays on the face as before.[13]

I show you the land in turmoil:
The weak-armed is strong-armed,
(55) One salutes him who saluted.
I show you the undermost uppermost,
What was turned on the back turns the belly.[14]
Men will live in the graveyard,
The beggar will gain riches,
The great [will rob] to live.
The poor will eat bread,
The slaves will be exalted.
Gone from the earth is the nome of On,
The birthplace of every god.

Then a king will come from the South,
Ameny, the justified, by name,[15]
Son of a woman of Ta-Seti, child of Upper Egypt.
He will take the white crown,
He will wear the red crown;
(60) He will join the Two Mighty Ones,[16]
He will please the Two Lords with what they wish,
With field-circler in his fist, oar in his grasp.[17]
Rejoice, O people of his time,
The son of man will make his name for all eternity!
The evil-minded, the treason-plotters,
They suppress their speech in fear of him;
Asiatics will fall to his sword,
Libyans will fall to his flame,
Rebels to his wrath, traitors to (65) his might,
As the serpent on his brow subdues the rebels for him.
One will build the Walls-of-the-Ruler,[18]
To bar Asiatics from entering Egypt;
They shall beg water as supplicants,
So as to let their cattle drink.
Then Order will return to its seat,

While Chaos is driven away.[19]
Rejoice he who may behold, he who may attend the king!
And he who is wise will libate for me,
When he sees fulfilled what I have spoken!

Colophon: It has come to its end succesfully by the scribe ———.

NOTES

1. The text has *ḫprt*, not *ḫpr·ty·sy*. Throughout the work, the tenses vary from past to present and future, as a result of the underlying double standpoint: the actual time of the writer who is hailing the present beneficent reign of Amenemhet I, and the fictitious time of the speaker who addresses King Snefru and foretells the distant future.

2. In *JNES*, 30 (1971), 69-72, I drew attention to the connective use of iterated *mk* which helps to explain this passage.

3. Here and in line 38, *idw* denotes the numbness of sight and hearing, rather than only deafness.

4. The "strange bird" means the Asiatics who have been able to settle in the eastern Delta because they were not resisted.

5. *Wnyw ḥr wgsw* is parallel to *wbnw ḥr rmw*, and the human determinative of *wnyw* is an error. *Wgsw* has been interpreted as fish-slitting people, but the context points to fish-eating birds. The *wgs*-bird appears in *Peasant*, R 29; see also *Wb.*, I, 377: *wgs*, "Art Vögel."

6. "Feeders," not "food." This meaning of *dfꜣw* is attested by *Wb.*, V, 571.8-10.

7. Several very obscure sentences. Posener, *op. cit.*, p. 151, suggested as the general meaning that the Egyptians fleeing from the Asiatics have crowded into the fortresses and the latecomers are kept waiting outside. Helck, *op. cit.*, p. 30, thinks of Asiatics breaking through the Egyptian border fortifications.

8. In agreement with Helck, I take *m dd* to denote that a proverb is being quoted; but his rendering of *ptr sdm ḥr idw iw gr ḫft ḥr* as "Siehe, der hören sollte, ist taub, und so ist der Schweigende vorn," does not seem to me to hit the mark. The essence of a proverbial phrase is the compact terseness of its formulation, which makes every word carry maximum weight. Hence *ptr* can hardly be the near-meaningless "behold," and is more likely to be the infinitive of "to see." Hence: "when sight and hearing are numb the mute is out in front," a proverb similar to our "among the blind the one-eyed is king." On *idw* = "numb" see n. 3, above.

9. Two major topics make up the theme of "national distress." The first is the infiltration of the Delta by Asiatics; the second is civil war among Egyptians. This second topic is described by means of three *topoi*, all of which recur in the *Admonitions of Ipuwer*, and all of which are loaded with hyperbole: indiscriminate bloodshed, indifference to suffering, and the reversal of the social order, by which the rich become poor and the have-nots become the masters.

10. In this context, *mr·wi* cannot mean "love me"; it is probably an idiom of the type "I wish I had."

11. If *iryt* means "produce, crops" (see *Amenemhet*, n. 10), *gmyt* might

be "things of use," in accordance with the pregnant sense of *gmi* = "find useful."

12. *Tm ir mḥ n·f ir šw*. Since Gardiner, all translators have construed *tm ir mḥ n·f* as the subject, "he who never was one who filled for himself," and explained it as meaning the rich man who has servants who fill his granaries (Lefebvre), or is so rich he does not insist on full measure (Wilson). The predicate *ir šw* then means either "he is empty (i.e., poor)", so Gardiner and Lefebvre, or "he empties" (Wilson, Helck). It seems to me that a more satisfactory sense is obtained if the passage is treated as two sentences: *tm ir mḥ n·f/ ir šw*, "he who did not make (i.e., acquire) fills for himself; he who made is needy." Or *tm ir* and *ir* might be taken to mean "lazy" and "active."

13. The description of the sun's withdrawal contains some difficulties; see Posener's discussion, *op. cit.*, pp. 154-156. I take the passage to mean that the sun-god in anger over men's evil deeds will veil his light so as to be as pale as the moon, without however altering his regular course. Thus the sage is not foretelling the total cosmic catastrophe which would result from the sun's failure to rise, but only a limited punitive action.

14. This seems to me to be the meaning of *phr·ti m sз phr ḥt*. He who was easily overthrown now overthrows others. The sentence is one of several that treat of the theme "the undermost will be uppermost." To be flung to the ground on one's back meant being vanquished, as when "falsehood is flung on its back" in *Peasant*, B 182/3 and 197/8.

15. That "Ameny" is Amenemhet I was incisively demonstrated by Posener, *op. cit.*, pp. 47 ff.

16. The "Two Mighty Ones" are the vulture goddess Nekhbet and the cobra goddess Wadjet whose union, like that of the "Two Lords" (Horus and Seth), represented the unified kingdom.

17. Objects carried by the king in the ritual dances he performed before the gods.

18. The great border fortress built by Amenemhet I in the eastern Delta.

19. The contrasted pair is *maat* and *isfet*, which is of course basically "right" and "wrong," but sometimes conveys the enlarged sense of "order" and "chaos."

THE COMPLAINTS OF KHAKHEPERRE-SONB

British Museum 5645, a Writing Board

In content and style this work is closely related to the *Prophecies of Neferti* and to the *Admonitions of Ipuwer*. The single preserved copy was dated by Gardiner to the middle of the Eighteenth Dynasty, while the work itself clearly belongs to the Middle Kingdom. In fact, it can be dated with some assurance to the reign of Sesostris II or shortly after, for, as Gardiner pointed out, the name of the sage is compounded with the prenomen of that king.

Unlike *Neferti*, the *Complaints of Khakheperre-sonb* reveal no political purpose. They appear to be a purely literary working of the theme "national distress." If a political criticism was intended, it is concealed behind the

generalized metaphors on the theme of anarchy and distress. The time
was one of peace and prosperity. Hence the laments on the "distress of the
land" are metaphors. They are either purely literary, designed to enlarge
the literary possibilities of the theme, or they may have conveyed a covert
political criticism, of a kind that could not be made openly and hence was
wrapped in metaphor. Dispensing with the fiction of a real audience, the
author addresses his plaints to his heart, a device that further enhances the
rhetorical character of the work.

The text consists of fourteen lines on the recto and six lines on the verso;
and the lines are grouped into four sections by means of short dividers. As
written on the board, the text is complete, for after the fourth section there
are two lines in a larger handwriting which are not connected with it.
The text, however, may be the first part of a lost longer work.

Publication: Gardiner, *Admonitions*, pp. 95-110 and pls. 17-18.

Translation: Erman, *Literature*, pp. 108-110.

(I, 1) The gathering of words, the heaping of sayings, the seeking
of phrases by a searching heart, made by a priest of On, Seni's [son],
Khakheperre-sonb, called Ankhu. He says:

Had I unknown phrases,
Sayings that are strange,
Novel, untried words,
Free of repetition;
Not transmitted sayings,
Spoken by the ancestors!
I wring out my body of what it holds,
In releasing all my words;
For what was said is repetition,
When what was said is said.
Ancestor's words are nothing to boast of,
They are found[1] by those who come after.

(5) Not speaks one who spoke,
There speaks one who will speak,
May another find what he will speak!
Not a teller of tales after they happen,
This has been done before;
Nor a teller of what might be said,
This is vain endeavor, it is lies,
And none will recall his name to others.
I say this in accord with what I have seen:
From the first generation to those who come after,
They imitate that which is past.[2]

Would that I knew what others ignore,
Such as has not been repeated,
To say it and have my heart answer me,
To inform[3] it of my distress,
Shift to it the load on my back,
The matters that afflict me,
Relate to it of what I suffer
And sigh "Ah" with relief!

(10) I meditate on what has happened,
The events that occur throughout the land:
Changes take place, it is not like last year,
One year is more irksome than the other.
The land breaks up, is destroyed,
Becomes [a wasteland].
Order is cast out,
Chaos is in the council hall;[4]
The ways of the gods are violated,
Their provisions neglected.
The land is in turmoil,
There is mourning everywhere;
Towns, districts are grieving,
All alike are burdened by wrongs.
One turns one's back on dignity,
The lords of silence are disturbed;
As dawn comes every day,
The face recoils from events.
I cry out about it,
My limbs are weighed down,
I grieve in my heart.
It is hard[5] to keep silent about it,
Another heart would bend;
But a heart strong in distress:
It is a comrade to its lord.
Had I a heart skilled in hardship,
I would take my rest upon it,
Weigh it down with words of grief,
Lay on it my malady!

(II, 1) He said to his heart:
Come, my heart, I speak to you,

Answer me my sayings!
Unravel for me what goes on in the land,
Why those who shone are overthrown.[6]
I meditate on what has happened:
While trouble entered in today,
And turmoil will not cease tomorrow,[7]
Everyone is mute about it.
The whole land is in great distress,
Nobody is free from crime;
Hearts are greedy.[8]
He who gave orders takes orders,
And the hearts of both submit.
One wakes to it every day,
And the hearts do not reject it.
Yesterday's condition is like today's
. . . . . .[9]
None is wise enough to know it,
None angry enough to cry out,
One wakes to suffer each day.

My malady is long and heavy,
The sufferer lacks strength to save himself
From that which overwhelms him.
It is pain to be silent to what one hears,
It is futile[10] to answer (5) the ignorant,
To reject a speech makes enmity;
The heart does not accept the truth,
One cannot bear a statement of fact,
A man loves only his own words.
Everyone builds on crookedness,
Right-speaking is abandoned.
I spoke to you, my heart, answer you me,
A heart addressed must not be silent,
Lo, servant and master fare alike,
There is much that weighs upon you!

NOTES

1. *Gmi*, "find," here and below in line 5, in the pregnant sense of "find useful," "make use of."

2. It is interesting that imitation of the past, which is usually recommended in the Instructions, is here rejected.

3. *Shd* is quite literally "to enlighten."

4. The pair is *maat* and *isfet*, as in *Neferti*, lines 68/9; see there, n. 19.

5. Or, "painful"; *whd* occurs four times, varying from "painful" to "suffer," and "endure," (I, 13-4, and II, 4-5).

6. *Ntiw ḥd ptḥ* recalls *sr m ptḥ*, "the great man is overthrown," in *Neferti*, line 21.

7. Note the chiastic order of *ihw bs m-min/ nhpw n sw3 drdrw*, where *nhpw* is surely the word for "morning" in the sense of tomorrow, as suggested by Sethe *apud* Gardiner, *op. cit.*, 106. For the word *drdrw*, which elsewhere means "stranger," a meaning parallel to *ihw* is required, e.g., "strange doings," "hostilities."

8. *Snm* here and in *Admonitions*, 2, 5, is probably "greedy" rather than "sad."

9. *Ḥr sn rs n ʿšsw/ ḥr dri* is obscure.

10. *Ihw* (= *3hw*) above in II, 1, was the noun; here it is the adjective and recalls the *3hw m mw* of *Merikare*, lines 91/2, where the sense is "lacking, deficient"; hence "futile" seems appropriate here.

THE ADMONITIONS OF IPUWER

Papyrus Leiden 344, Recto

Ever since Gardiner's pioneering edition of this difficult text, his view of the *Admonitions* as the work of a Twelfth Dynasty author who laments the alleged calamities of the First Intermediate Period has held sway. It is, however, contradictory and untenable. Gardiner maintained on the one hand that "the pessimism of Ipuwer was intended to be understood as the direct and natural response to a real national calamity" (*Admonitions*, p. 111), and on the other that "historical romance was always popular in Ancient Egypt, and there is no inherent reason why the Admonitions, even if referring to the conditions of the Tenth Dynasty, should not have been written under the Twelfth" (*ibid.*). I submit that there is strong inherent reason why this cannot be so. If the *Admonitions* is the "direct response to a real calamity," then it cannot also be a "historical romance." The two are mutually exclusive.

We have seen that *Neferti* has a political-propagandistic aim which it expresses through the poetic elaboration of the topos "national distress." In *Khakheperre-sonb* we have encountered the same topos in a work that seems to be largely rhetorical. Both works were written in times of peace and prosperity. When the *Admonitions* is placed alongside these two works, it reveals itself as a composition of the same genre and character which differs only in being longer, more ambitious, more repetitious, and more extreme in its use of hyperbole. Its very verbosity and repetitiveness mark it as a latecomer in which the most comprehensive treatment of the theme "national distress" is attempted, in short, as a work of the late Middle Kingdom and of purely literary inspiration.

The unhistorical character of the whole genre was recognized by S. Luria in an article that did not receive the attention it deserved.* Adducing strikingly similar compositions from other cultures he pointed out the

* "Die Ersten werden die Letzten sein," *Klio*, 22 (1929), 405-431.

fictional, mythologic-messianic nature of these works and the fixed cliches through which the theme of "social chaos" was expressed. From an Annamite song he quoted phrases that sound as if they came from the *Admonitions*:

"Ceux qui n'avaient pas de culotte ont aujourd'hui des souliers . . .
Les filles publiques sont devenu de grandes dames,
Les vauriens sont tout puissant. . . ."

Luria also made the telling point that the description of chaos in the *Admonitions* is inherently contradictory, hence historically impossible: On the one hand the land is said to suffer from total want; on the other hand the poor are described as having become rich, of wearing fine clothes, and generally of disposing of all that once belonged to their masters.

In sum, the *Admonitions of Ipuwer* has not only no bearing whatever on the long past First Intermediate Period, it also does not derive from any other historical situation. It is the last, fullest, most exaggerated and hence least successful, composition on the theme "order versus chaos."

The text is preserved in a single, much damaged copy, Papyrus Leiden 344, which dates from the Nineteenth Dynasty. In its present condition the papyrus measures 347 cm in length and consists of seventeen pages. The text occupies the recto, while the verso has hymns to a deity, written in a different hand. Each page had fourteen lines, except pages 10 and 11, which have only thirteen each. On the first page, less than one-third of each line is preserved; and beginning with page 8, every page has large lacunae.

Publication: Gardiner, *Admonitions*.

Translation: Erman, *Literature*, pp. 92-108.   J. A. Wilson in *ANET*, pp. 441-444.   R. O. Faulkner, *JEA*, 51 (1965), 53-62, and "Notes," *JEA*, 50 (1964), 24-36.

(I, 1) —————— The door[-keepers] say: "Let us go plunder." The pastry-makers ——————. The washerman does not think of carrying his load. ——————. The bird[-catchers] are lined up for battle. ——————. The Delta[-dwellers] carry shields. The brewers (5) —————— sad. A man regards his son as his enemy. Hostility —————— another. Come and conquer. —————— what was ordained for you in the time of Horus, in the age of [the Ennead]. ——————. The man of character walks in mourning on account of the state of the land. The ——— walks ——————. Foreigners have become people everywhere.[1]

Lo, the face is pale (10) ——————
What the ancestors foretold has happened.

——————

Lo, ——————
(2, 1) The land is full of gangs,
A man goes to plow with his shield.
Lo, the meek say ——————
—————— is a man of substance.

Lo, the face is pale, the bowman ready,
Crime is everywhere, there is no man of yesterday.
Lo, the robber ――― everywhere,
The servant takes what he finds.
Lo, Hapy inundates and none plow for him,
All say, "We don't know what has happened in the land."
Lo, women are barren, none conceive,
Khnum does not fashion because of the state of the land.
Lo, poor men have become men of wealth,
He who could not afford (5) sandals owns riches.
Lo, men's slaves, their hearts are greedy,
The great do not mingle with their people [˹when they rejoice˺].
Lo, hearts are violent, storm sweeps the land,
There's blood everywhere, no shortage of dead,
The shroud calls out before one comes near it.
Lo, many dead are buried in the river,
The stream is the grave, the tomb became stream.
Lo, nobles lament, the poor rejoice,
Every town says, "Let us expel our rulers."
Lo, people are like ibises, there's dirt everywhere,
None have white garments in this time.
Lo, the land turns like a potter's wheel,
The robber owns riches, [the noble] is a thief.
Lo, the trusted are like ――――
The citizen [says], "Woe, what shall I do!"

(2, 10) Lo, the river is blood,
As one drinks of it one shrinks from people
And thirsts for water.
Lo, doors, columns, coffers[2] are burning,
While the hall of the palace stands firm.
Lo, the ship of the South founders,
Towns are ravaged, Upper Egypt became wasteland.
Lo, crocodiles gorge on their catch,
People go to them of their own will.
˹The land is injured˺,
One says, "Don't walk here, there's a net,"
People flap like fish,
The scared does not discern it in his fright.
Lo, people are diminished,

He who puts his brother in the ground is everywhere.
⌜The word of the wise has fled without delay⌝.
Lo, the son of man is denied recognition,
The child of his lady became the son of his maid.

(3, 1) Lo, the desert claims the land,
The nomes are destroyed,
Foreign bowmen have come into Egypt.
Lo, ──────
There are no people anywhere,
Lo, gold, lapis lazuli, silver, and turquoise,
Carnelian, amethyst, *ibht*-stone and ───
Are strung on the necks of female slaves.
Noblewomen[3] roam the land,
Ladies say, "We want to eat!"
Lo, ────── noblewomen,
Their bodies suffer in rags,
Their hearts ⌜shrink⌝ from greeting [⌜each other⌝].
Lo, (5) chests of ebony are smashed,
Precious *ssndm*-wood is chopped ───
Lo, [⌜tomb⌝]-builders have become field-laborers,
Those who were in the god's bark are yoked [to it].[4]

None indeed sail north to Byblos today. What shall we do for pine trees for our mummies? Free men are buried with their produce, nobles are embalmed with their oil as far as Crete.[5] They come no more. Gold is lacking; exhausted are ⌜materials⌝ for every kind of craft. What belongs to the palace has been stripped. What a great thing it is when the oasis-peasants come with their festival offerings, mats and [skins], fresh *rdmt*-plants, (10) the ⌜fat⌝ of birds . . .

Lo, Yebu, ⌜This⌝ ─── are not taxed because of strife. Lacking are ⌜grain⌝, charcoal, *irtyw*, *mꜣʿw*-wood, *nwt*-wood, brushwood. The output of craftsmen is lacking ─── . . . What good is a treasury without its revenues? Happy is the heart of the king when gifts[6] come to him. And when every foreign land [comes], that is our success,[7] that is our fortune. What shall we do about it? All is ruin!

Lo, merriment has ceased, is made no more,
Groaning is throughout the land, mingled with laments.
Lo, every have-not[8] is one who has,

Those who were (4, 1) people are strangers whom one shows the
   way.
Lo, everyone's hair [has fallen out],
One can't distinguish the son of man from the pauper.
Lo, [⌐one is numb ⌐] from noise,
No ⌐voice is straight ⌐ in years of shouting,
No ⌐end of shouting ⌐.
Lo, great and small ⟨say⟩, "I wish I were dead,"
Little children say, "He should not have made me live!"
Lo, children of nobles are dashed against walls,
Infants are put out on high ground.
Lo, those who were entombed are cast on high ground,
Embalmers' secrets are thrown away.
(5) Lo, gone is what yesterday was seen,
The land is left to its weakness like a cutting of flax.
Lo, the whole Delta cannot be seen,[9]
Lower Egypt puts trust in trodden roads.
What can one do? One says, "There are no ——— anywhere."
One says "Woe" to the place of secrets,
Those who ignore it own it as if they knew it,
Foreigners are skilled in the works of the Delta.

Lo, citizens are put to the grindstones,
Wearers of fine linen are beaten with [sticks].
Those who never saw daylight go out unhindered,
Those who were on their husbands' (10) beds,
"Let them lie on boards,"[10] [one repeats].
If one says, "Those boards with myrrh are too heavy for me,"
She is loaded down with jars filled with ———.
[No longer] does she know the palanquin,
And the butler is lacking.[11]
There is no remedy for it,
Ladies suffer like maidservants,
Singers are at the looms in the weaving-rooms,
What they sing to the goddess are dirges,
Those who told ——— are at the grindstones.
Lo, all maidservants are rude in their speech,
When the mistress speaks it irks the servants.
Lo, trees are felled, branches stripped,
And the servant abandons (5, 1) his household.

People say when they hear it:
Gone is the gain of abundance of children.
Food is lacking ------
What does it taste like today?

Lo, the great hunger and suffer,
Servants are served ---
------ lamentations.
Lo, the hot-tempered says:
"If I knew where god is I would serve him."
Lo, [right] is in the land in name,
Standing on it one does wrong.
Lo, one runs and fights for the goods [of a man]
(5) He is robbed, all his things are taken.
Lo, all beasts, their hearts weep,
Cattle bemoan the state of the land.
Lo, children of nobles are dashed against walls,
Infants are put out on high ground,
Khnum groans in weariness.
Lo, terror kills; the frightened says ......
Lo, (10) --- throughout the land,
The strong man sends to everyone,
A man strikes his maternal brother.
What has been done? ......

Lo, the ways are [blocked], the roads watched. One sits in the bushes till the night-traveler comes, in order to plunder his load. What is upon him is seized; he is assaulted with blows of the stick; he is criminally slain.

Lo, gone is what yesterday was seen,
The land is left to its weakness like a cutting of flax.
Citizens come and go in desolation,

If only this were the end of man,
No more conceiving, no (6, 1) births!
Then the land would cease to shout,
Tumult would be no more!
Lo, [one eats] herbs, washed down with water,
Birds find neither fruit nor herbs,
One takes --- from the mouth of pigs,

No face is bright . . . hunger.
Lo, grain is lacking on all sides,
One is stripped of clothes,
Unanointed with oil,[12]
Everyone says, "There's nothing."
The storehouse is bare,
Its keeper stretched on the ground.
. . . . . (5) . . .
Had I raised my voice at that time,
To save me from the pain I am in!
Lo, the private chamber, its books are stolen,
The secrets in it are laid bare.
Lo, magic spells are divulged,
Spells are made worthless through being repeated by people.
Lo, offices are opened,
Their records stolen,
The serf becomes an owner of serfs.
Lo, [scribes] are slain,
Their writings stolen,
Woe is me for the grief of this time!
Lo, the scribes of the land-register,
Their books are destroyed,
The grain of Egypt is "I go-get-it."
Lo, the laws (10) of the chamber are thrown out,
Men walk on them in the streets,
Beggars tear them up in the alleys.
Lo, the beggar comes to the place of the Nine Gods,
The procedure of the House of Thirty is laid bare.
Lo, the great council chamber is invaded,
Beggars come and go in the great mansions.
Lo, there is much hatred in the streets,
The wise says, "Yes," the fool says, "No,"
The ignorant is satisfied.[13]
Lo, those who were entombed are cast on high ground,
Embalmers' secrets are thrown away.

(7, 1) See now, fire has leaped high,
Its flame will attack the land's foes!
See now, things are done that never were before,
The king has been robbed by beggars.

See, one buried as hawk is . . .
What the pyramid hid is empty.
See now, the land is deprived of kingship
By a few people who ignore custom.
See now, men rebel against the Serpent,
[Stolen] is the crown of Re, who pacifies the Two Lands.
See, the secret of the land, its limits are unknown,
If the residence is stripped, it will collapse in a moment.[14]
See, Egypt has fallen to (5) pouring water,[15]
He who poured water on the ground seizes the mighty in misery.
See, the Serpent is taken from its hole,[16]
The secrets of Egypt's kings are bared.
See, the residence is fearful from want,
Men stir up strife unopposed.
See, the land is tied up in gangs,
The coward is emboldened to seize his goods.[17]
See, the Serpent ––– the dead,
He who could not make a coffin owns a tomb.
See, those who owned tombs are cast on high ground,
He who could not make a grave owns a treasury.

See now, the transformations of people,[18]
He who did not build a hut is an owner of coffers.
See the judges of the land are driven from the land,
⟨The nobles⟩ are expelled from the royal (10) mansions.
See, noble ladies are on boards,
Princes in the workhouse,
He who did not sleep on a box owns a bed.
See, the man of wealth lies thirsting,
He who begged dregs has overflowing bowls.
See, those who owned robes are in rags,
He who did not weave for himself owns fine linen.
See, he who did not build a boat for himself owns ships,
Their owner looks at them: they are not his.
See, he who lacked shelter has shelter,
Those who had shelter are in the dark of the storm.
See, he who did not know a lyre owns a harp,
He who did not sing extols the goddess.[19]
See, those who owned offering-tables of bronze,
Not one of their vessels is garlanded.

See, he who slept (8, 1) wifeless found a noblewoman,[20]
He who ⌐was not seen⌐ stands . . .
See, he who had nothing is a man of wealth,
The nobleman sings his praise.
See, the poor of the land have become rich,
The man of property is a pauper.
See, cooks have become masters of butlers,
He who was a messenger sends someone else.
See, he who had no loaf owns a barn,
His storeroom is filled with another's goods.
See, the baldhead who lacked oil
Has become owner of jars of sweet myrrh.
(5) See, she who lacked a box has furniture,
She who saw her face in the water owns a mirror.
See now –––.

Lo, a man is happy eating his food. Consume your goods in gladness, while there is none to hinder you. It is good for a man to eat his food. God ordains it for him whom he favors.

⟨See now⟩, he who ignored his god
Offers him another's incense
–––––––
See, great ladies who owned wealth give their children for beds.
See, a man who ––––––
––– a lady as wife
. . . . . .
See, the children of magistrates are –––––– (10)
The calves of their herds ––– to robbers.
See, the serfs eat beef,[21]
The paupers ––––––
See, he who did not slaughter for himself slaughters bulls,
He who did not know carving sees [⌐meat cuts⌐] of all kinds.
See, the serfs eat geese,
Offered ⟨to⟩ the gods in place of cattle.
See, maidservants –––––– offer ducks,
Noblewomen ––––––
See, noblewomen flee ––––––
–––––– cast down in fear of death.
⟨See⟩, the chiefs of the land flee,
They have no purpose because of want –––

[See], (9, 1) those who owned beds are on the ground,
He who lay in the dirt spreads a rug.
See, noblewomen go hungry,
And serfs are sated with what was made for them.
See, all the ranks, they are not in their place,
Like a herd that roams without a herdsman.
See, cattle stray with none to bring them back,
Everyone fetches for himself and brands with his name.
See, a man is slain by the side of his brother,
Who abandons him to save himself.
See, he who lacked a team owns herds,
He who could not find plow-oxen owns cattle.
See, he who lacked grain owns granaries,
(5) He who fetched grain on loan issues it.
See, he who lacked dependents owns serfs,
He who was a ⟨magnate⟩ does his own errands.
See, the mighty of the land are not reported to,
The affairs of the people have gone to ruin.
See, all the craftsmen, they do not work,
The land's foes have despoiled its craftsmen.
[See, he who recorded] the harvest knows nothing about it,
He who did not plow [for himself] –––.
–––––– it is not reported,
The scribe ––– his hands [⌜idle⌝] in it.

Destroyed is –––––– in their time,
A man sees ––––––
–––––– brings coolness ––––––
–––––– (10) ––––––

Destroyed is ––––––. Their food [is taken] from them. ––––––
fear of his terror. The citizen begs ––––––. –––––– messenger,
but not –––––– time. He is seized loaded with his goods, taken
––––––. –––––– pass by his door –––––– ... rooms filled with
falcons ––––––. As to the citizen, when he wakes, (10, 1) day dawns
on him without his being ready. One runs ...... ⌜tents⌝ are what
they make, like foreigners.

Destroyed is the doing of errands[22] by attendants in the service of
their masters. They are not ready. Though there are five of them,
they say: "Go you on that road; we have just come."

Lower Egypt weeps. The king's storehouse is "I go-get-it," for everyone, and the whole palace is without its revenues. It should have emmer, barley, fowl, and fish; it should have white cloth, fine linen, copper, and oil. (5) It should have carpet and mat –––, all good woven products. ......

Destroy the foes of the noble residence, resplendent in courtiers, –––––––. The mayor of the city goes unescorted.
Destroy [the foes of the noble residence], resplendent –––––––.
[Destroy the foes of] the noble residence, rich in laws, –––––––.
[Destroy the foes of] (10) that noble [residence] –––––––.
Destroy the foes of that [noble] residence –––––––.
None can stand –––––––.
[Destroy the foes of] that noble [residence], rich in offices. Lo, –––––––.
Remember the immersing –––––––.[23]
––––––– the sickness of his body. –––––––.
Remember (11, 1) ... , fumigating with incense, libating from a jar at dawn.
Remember ⟨bringing⟩ fat *ro*-geese, *terep*-geese, *set*-geese, and making divine offerings to the gods.
Remember chewing natron, preparing white bread, ⌐as done⌐ by a man on the day of ...
Remember the erecting of flagstaffs, the carving of offering stones; the priest cleansing the chapels, the temple whitewashed like milk; sweetening the fragrance of the sanctuary, setting up the bread-offerings.
Remember the observing of rules, the adjusting of dates, removing one who enters (5) the priestly service unclean; for to do this is wrong, ... –––––––.
Remember the slaughtering of oxen –––––––.
Remember going out ––– ... ––––––– (10) –––––––.

Lo, why does he seek to fashion ⟨men⟩, when the timid is not distinguished from the violent?[24] If he would bring coolness upon the heat, (12, 1) one would say: "He is the herdsman of all; there is no evil in his heart. His herds are few, but he spends the day herding them." There is fire in their hearts! If only he had perceived their nature in the first generation! Then he would have smitten the evil, stretched out his arm against it, would have destroyed their seed and their heirs! But since giving birth is desired, grief has come and misery is everywhere. So it is and will not pass, while these gods are

in their midst. Seed comes forth from mortal women; it is not found
on the road. Fighting has come, (5) and the punisher of crimes
commits them! There is no pilot in their hour. Where is he today?
Is he asleep? Lo, his power is not seen!

If we had been ⌐fed⌐, I would not have found you, one would not
have summoned me . . . . . . –––––– . . . . . .²⁵

Authority, Knowledge, and Truth²⁶ are with you—turmoil is what
you let happen in the land, and the noise of strife. Lo, one man
assaults another, and one transgresses²⁷ what you commanded. When
three men travel on the road, only two are found. For the greater
number kills the lesser. Is there a herdsman who loves death? Then
you could order it done.²⁸ (13, 1) It means the replacement of love:
one man hates another. It means reducing their numbers everywhere.
Is it your doing that brought this about? Do you speak falsely?

The land is a weed that kills people. One does not expect to live.
All these years there is strife. A man is killed on his roof. He must
keep watch in his gatehouse. If he is brave he may save himself. Such
is his life!

When a ⌐servant⌐ is sent to citizens, he walks on the road until he
sees the flood. If the road is washed out, (5) he halts distressed. Then
he is robbed, attacked with blows of the stick, and criminally slain.

If only you would taste a little of these miseries! Then you would
say ––––––.

> [It is however] good when ships sail upstream,
> –––––– (10) ––––––.
> It is however good ––––––.
> It is however good when the net is drawn in.
> And birds are tied up ––––––.
> It is however good ––––––,
> And the roads are made for walking.
> It is however good when men's hands build tombs,
> When ponds are dug and orchards made for the gods.
> It is however good when people get drunk,
> When they drink *miyet* with happy hearts.
> It is however good when mouths shout for joy,
> When the nome-lords watch the shouting(14, 1)from their houses,
> When one is clothed in clean robes . . .
> It is however good when beds are readied,
> The masters' headrests safely secured;

When every man's need is filled by a mat in the shade,
And a door shut on him who slept in the bushes.
It is however good when fine linen is spread on New Year's Day,
–––––– fine linen is spread, robes are laid out. ––––––
(5) ––––––

–––––– (10) ––– in their [midst] like Asiatics ––––––.[29] None
are found who would stand up to protect them. –––––– Every man
fights for his sisters and protects himself. Is it Nubians? Then we
will protect ourselves. There are plenty of fighters to repel the
Bowmen. Is it Libyans? Then we will turn them back. The Medjai
are content with Egypt.

How then does every man kill his brother? The troops (15, 1)
we raised for ourselves have become Bowmen bent on destroying!
What has come from it is to let the Asiatics know the state of the land.
Yet every foreigner fears it.[30] The experience of the people is that they
say: "Egypt will not be given over ⟨to⟩ sand!" ––––––. (5) ––––––.

What Ipuwer said when he answered the majesty of the All-Lord:
–––––. It pleases the heart to ignore it. You have done what pleases
their hearts. You have sustained people among them. Yet they cover
(16, 1) their faces in fear of tomorrow.

There was an old man who was about to die, while his son was a
child without knowledge. ––––––

NOTES

1. "People" = "Egyptians."
2. *Ḏriwt*, "coffers, chests," in accordance with Vandier's discussion
of *ḏrit* in *Moʿalla*, pp. 208-211.
3. *Špsswt*, "noblewomen," rather than "good things."
4. Contrary to Goedicke's rendering in *JARCE*, 6 (1967), 93, I take
the two sentences, as those preceding it, to be descriptions of the reversal
of fortune, i.e., variations on the theme "the first will be the last".
5. I retain the traditional rendering of the passage. A different one was
proposed by Goedicke, *loc. cit.*
6. I read *mꜣʿw*, "gifts, ribute," rather than *mꜣʿwt*, "truth." The text
abounds in corruptions. But the feminine form, *mꜣʿwt*, for the word
"gifts" is attested for the Late Period; hence the writing may be correct.
7. The meaning of the metaphor *mw·n pw*, "this is our water," is
uncertain. Faulkner took it to mean "bad luck" and the sentence to be
ironic. I take it to be "good luck," "success," parallel to *wꜣḏ*, "fortune."
8. Reading *iwty*, as suggested by Posener, *RdE*, 5 (1946), 254.
9. A rather obscure section which is thought to mean that the Delta
is overrun by Asiatics. In the choice between *dgi*, "hide," and *dgi*, "see,"
I have preferred the latter.

10. *Šdw* is an object on which one can lie down and on which a load can be placed; hence "board" seems to me more suitable than "raft."

11. Emending *ḏd·i* to *ḏd·s*; ladies are made to labor and no longer have the use of their palanquins, or the service of their butlers.

12. *Ḥsꜣ*, "unanointed," rather than Gardiner's restored *ḥsꜣt*, "spices(?)".

13. The passage recurs in the *Instruction of Amenemhet*; see there n. 12.

14. This passage has always been rendered: "The secret of the land whose limits were unknown is divulged, and the Residence is thrown down in a moment," But the first sentence, besides being overlong, has an abnormal word order. Moreover, the sense is poor; for the text nowhere implies that the residence is threatened. I divide: *sštꜣ n tꜣ ḫmm ḏrw·f/ sḥꜣw ḫnw ḥn·f n wnwt.*

15. On *sti mw* see *Amenemhet*, n. 6.

16. The *ḳrḥt*-serpent was a guardian spirit.

17. I.e., to acquire goods for himself by robbing.

18. There is no need to emend the text when *ḫprw* is understood as "transformations, changes," as in *Khakheperre-sonb, recto* 10.

19. Meret, the goddess of song, as in 4, 13.

20. Again reading *špsst*, "noblewoman," rather than *špsswt*, "riches"; see above, n. 3.

21. This sentence has been misunderstood by all translators. Gardiner read it as: *Mtn nswtyw ḥr ḳnḳn m iḥw mꜣ[rw] – – – ḥꜣkyw*, and rendered, "Behold, butchers transgress(?) with the cattle of the poor ...... plunderers," a rendering that all have retained with minor variations. It should be observed that, first, *mꜣrw* is the subject of the second sentence; second, that "poor people" do not own cattle; third, that *nswtyw*, which stands in parallelism with *mꜣrw*, means "serfs," or the like (see S. Wenig, *ZÄS*, 88 (1962), 67-69, and P. Kaplony, *ZÄS*, 88 (1962), 73-74), and last, that *ḳnḳn* is a spelling of *wnm*, "to eat." The preposition *m*, unintelligible after *ḳnḳn*, is in perfect order after *wnm*. In 8, 12, the *nswtyw* eat geese, and in 9, 1-2, they have appropriated the food destined for noblewomen.

22. *Hꜣb·tw ḥr·s* looks like an idiom for "errand, commission."

23. *Contra* Gardiner and Faulkner, Wilson was surely right in taking this section not as "exhortations to pious conduct," but as a recalling of the past when the right order prevailed.

24. This section is interesting for being a criticism of the sun-god, the creator of gods and men, who is chided for passively permitting people to kill each other, instead of intervening. It also offers confirmation for the point of view expressed in CT 1130: the evil in men's natures is not the work of the creator.

25. This section appears to be an address to the king, rather than to the sun-god.

26. Hu, Sia, and Maat.

27. *Sni*, "overstep," rather than *sni*, "imitate." Ipuwer is not reproaching the king with committing crimes but with allowing them to happen.

28. I divide: *ḥr kꜣ wḏ·k ir·tw/ šb n mrwt is pw/ w꜄ msd ky. Šbi* = "change, exchange."

29. The king is now speaking. What is left of his speech indicates that he places the blame for the disorders on the people themselves and maintains that Egypt has nothing to fear from foreigners.

30. The *f* of *snḏ·f* can only refer to "the land." J. Van Seters, *The Hyksos* (New Haven, 1966), p. 117, saw in the passage a reference to

"a new independent power in the Delta," i.e., the Hyksos. When the sentence is correctly translated, however, it contains nothing to promote that conclusion. Van Seters's attempt to date the *Admonitions* to the Hyksos period is based on historical and archaeological considerations which are, however, inconclusive.

THE DISPUTE BETWEEN A MAN AND HIS BA

Papyrus Berlin 3024

This famous text is preserved in a single manuscript which dates from the Twelfth Dynasty. The first portion is missing. In its present form it consists of 155 vertical columns, broken by a number of lacunae. An exceedingly difficult and intriguing work, it has engendered a great deal of controversy. In translating it for this anthology I had two choices: to provide sentence-by-sentence summaries and discussions of the widely diverging translations and interpretations—this would have required may pages of annotations—or to dispense with notes altogether. I have chosen the latter course. Scholars familiar with the text know its problems. Those unfamiliar with it who wish to study it in detail are advised to consult all translations and commentaires.

My translation owes much to that of Faulkner, though I differ from him on a number of points, especially on the rendering of the crucial word *íhm*, where I hold with those scholars who take it to mean "lead toward," not "hold back from."

Given the great variety of interpretations, I also refrain from a general discussion of the meaning of the work and content myself with a bald and brief sketch of what I believe to be its *plot*.

A man who suffers from life longs for death. Angered by his complaints, his *ba* threatens to leave him. This threat fills the man with horror, for to be abandoned by his *ba* would mean total annihilation, instead of the resurrection and immortal bliss that he envisages. He therefore implores his *ba* to remain with him, and not to oppose him in his longing for death, a death that he does not appear to contemplate as a suicide but rather as a natural, though greatly welcomed, death, to be followed by a traditional burial. The *ba* counters his pleas by telling him that death is a sad business, and that those who have fine tombs are no better off than those who have none. It urges him to stop complaining and to enjoy life. And it tells two parables designed to drive home the point that life is worth living. The man's final answer is delivered through four exquisite poems, in which he deplores the miseries of life and exalts death and resurrection. In a brief concluding speech the *ba* agrees to remain with him.

As I see it, the work is composed of a mixture of the three main styles of Egyptian literature: prose, symmetrically structured speech, and lyric poetry.

Publication: A. Erman, *Gespräch eines Lebensmüden mit seiner Seele*, APAW (Berlin, 1896). R. O. Faulkner, *JEA*, 42 (1956), 21-40. W. Barta, *Das Gespräch eines Mannes mit seinem Ba*; Münchner ägyptologische Studien, 18 (Berlin, 1969). H. Goedicke, *The Report about the Dispute of a Man with His Ba* (Baltimore, 1970).

Translation: Erman, *Literature*, pp. 86-92. J. A. Wilson in *ANET*, pp. 405-407. Bissing, *Lebensweisheit*, pp. 124-128.

Commentaries and comments: A. Scharff, *SBAW*, 1937, Phil.-hist. Abt., Heft 9 (Munich, 1937).   A. Hermann, *OLZ*, 42 (1939), 141-153. A. de Buck, *Ex Oriente Lux*, 7 (1947), 19-32.   R. Weill, *BIFAO*, 45 (1947), 89-154.   H. Junker, *AOAW*, Phil.-hist. Kl., 1948, No. 17 (Vienna, 1949).   H. Jacobsohn, in *Zeitlose Dokumente der Seele*, Studien aus dem C. G. Jung Institut, Zürich, vol. 3 (Zurich, 1952), pp. 1-48.   S. Herrmann, *Untersuchungen*, pp. 62-79.   G. Thausing, *MDIK*, 15 (1957), 262-267.   R. Williams, *JEA*, 48 (1962), 49-56.   E. Brunner-Traut, *ZÄS*, 94 (1967), 6-15. Additional references will be found in the works cited.

—————— (1) your ——— in order to say —————— [their tongue] is not partial —————— payment; their tongue is not partial.

I opened my mouth to my *ba*, to answer what it had said:
(5) This is too great for me today,
My *ba* will not converse with me!
It is too great for exaggeration,
It is like deserting me!
My *ba* shall not go,
It shall attend to me in this!

——————

——— in my body with a net of cord.
(10) It shall not be able to flee on the day of pain!
Look, my *ba* misleads me—I do not listen to it—
Drags me toward death before ⟨I⟩ come to it,
Casts ⟨me⟩ on fire so as to burn me!

——————

(15) It shall be near me on the day of pain!
It shall stand on that side as does a . . .
It is he who comes forth,
⌈He has brought himself.⌉
My *ba*, too ignorant to still pain in life,
Leads me toward death before I come to it!
Sweeten (20) the West for me!
Is that difficult?
Life is a passage; trees fall.
Tread on the evil, put down my misery!
May Thoth judge me, he who appeases the gods!
May Khons defend me, (25) he who writes truly!
May Re hear my speech, he who calms the sun-bark!
May Isdes defend me in the sacred hall!

For my suffering is ⌐too heavy a burden to be borne by me⌐. May it please that the gods (30) repel my body's secrets!

What my *ba* said to me: "Are you not a man? Are you not alive? What do you gain by complaining about life like a man of wealth?" I said: "I will not go as long as this is neglected. Surely, if you run away, you will not (35) be cared for. Every criminal says: "I shall seize you." Though you are dead, your name lives. Yonder is the place of rest, the heart's goal. The West is a dwelling place, a voyage ------.

If my *ba* listens to me ⌐without (40) malice⌐, its heart in accord with me, it shall be happy. I shall make it reach the West like one who is in his tomb, whose burial a survivor tends. I shall make a ⌐shelter⌐ over your corpse, so that you will make envious another *ba* (45) in weariness. I shall make a ⌐shelter⌐—it shall not be freezing—so that you will make envious another *ba* which is hot. I shall drink water at the pond over which I made shade, so that you will make envious another *ba* that hungers.

But if you lead (50) me toward death in this manner, you will not find a place on which to rest in the West. Be patient, my *ba*, my brother, until my heir comes, one who will make offerings, who will stand at the tomb on the day of burial, having prepared the bier (55) of the graveyard.

My *ba* opened its mouth to me, to answer what I had said: If you think of burial, it is heartbreak. It is the gift of tears by aggrieving a man. It is taking a man from his house, casting (him) on high ground. You will not go up to see (60) the sun. Those who built in granite, who erected halls in excellent tombs of excellent construction—when the builders have become gods, their offering-stones are desolate, as if they were the dead who died on the riverbank for lack of a survivor. (65) The flood takes its toll, the sun also. The fishes at the water's edge talk to them. Listen to me! It is good for people to listen. Follow the feast day, forget worry!

A man plowed his plot. He loaded his harvest into (70) a boat. He towed the freight. As his feast day approached, he saw rising the darkness of a north wind. Watching in the boat, as the sun went down, (he) came out with his wife and children and foundered on the lake infested at (75) night with crocodiles. When at last he sat down, he broke out saying: "I do not weep for that mother, for whom there is no coming from the West for another being-on-earth. I grieve for her children broken in the egg, who have seen the face of the Crocodile (80) before they have lived."

A man asked for an early meal. His wife said: "It is for supper."
He went outdoors to ... a while. When he came back to the house
he was like another (person). His wife beseeches him and he does not
listen to her. He ... (85) heedless of the household.

I opened my mouth to my *ba*, to answer what it had said:

I

Lo, my name reeks
Lo, more than carrion smell
On summer days of burning sky.

Lo, my name reeks
Lo, more than a catch of fish
(90) On fishing days of burning sky.

Lo, my name reeks
Lo, more than ducks smell,
More than reed-coverts full of waterfowl.

Lo, my name reeks
Lo, more than fishermen smell,
More than the (95) marsh-pools where they fish.

Lo, my name reeks
Lo, more than crocodiles smell,
More than a shore-site full of crocodiles.

Lo, my name reeks
Lo, more than that of a wife
About whom lies are told to the husband.

Lo, my name (100) reeks
Lo, more than that of a sturdy child
Who is said to belong to one who rejects him.

Lo, my name reeks
Lo, more than a king's town
That utters sedition behind his back.

II

To whom shall I speak today?
Brothers are mean,
The friends of today do not love.

To whom (105) shall I speak today?
Hearts are greedy,
Everyone robs his comrade's goods.

⟨To whom shall I speak today?⟩
Kindness has perished,
Insolence assaults everyone.

To whom shall I speak today?
One is content with evil,
Goodness is cast to the ground everywhere.

To whom shall I speak (110) today?
He who should enrage men by his crimes—
He makes everyone laugh ⟨at⟩ his evildoing.

To whom shall I speak today?
Men plunder,
Everyone robs his comrade.

To whom shall I speak today?
The criminal is one's intimate,
The brother with whom one dealt is (115) a foe.

To whom shall I speak today?
The past is not remembered,
Now one does not help him who helped.

To whom shall I speak today?
Brothers are mean,
One goes to strangers for affection.

To whom shall I speak today?
Faces are blank,
Everyone turns his face from (120) his brothers.

To whom shall I speak today?
Hearts are greedy,
No man's heart can be relied on.

To whom shall I speak today?
None are righteous,
The land is left to evildoers.

To whom shall I speak today?
One lacks an intimate,
One resorts to an unknown (125) to complain.

To whom shall I speak today?
No one is cheerful,
He with whom one walked is no more.

To whom shall I speak today?
I am burdened with grief
For lack of an intimate.

To whom shall I speak today?
Wrong roams the earth,
(130) And ends not.

III

Death is before me today
⟨Like⟩ a sick man's recovery,
Like going outdoors after confinement.

Death is before me today
Like the fragrance of myrrh,
Like sitting under sail on breeze day.

Death is before me today
(135) Like the fragrance of lotus,
Like sitting on the shore of drunkenness.

Death is before me today
Like a well-trodden way,
Like a man's coming home from warfare.

Death is before me today
Like the clearing of the sky,
As when a man discovers (140) what he ignored.

Death is before me today
Like a man's longing to see his home
When he has spent many years in captivity.

IV

Truly, he who is yonder will be a living god,
Punishing the evildoer's crime.

Truly, he who is yonder will stand in the sun-bark,
Making its bounty flow (145) to the temples.

Truly, he who is yonder will be a wise man,
Not barred from appealing to Re when he speaks.

What my *ba* said to me: "Now throw complaint on the ⌜wood-pile⌝, you my comrade, my brother! Whether you offer on the brazier, (150) whether you bear down on life, as you say, love me here when you have set aside the West! But when it is wished that you attain the West, that your body joins the earth, I shall alight after you have become weary, and then we shall dwell together!"

Colophon: It is finished (155) from beginning to end, as it was found in writing.

THE ELOQUENT PEASANT

This long work is preserved in four papyrus copies, all dating from the Middle Kingdom. The individual copies are incomplete, but together they yield the full text, which comprises 430 lines. The three principal copies are P. Berlin 3023 (Bl), P. Berlin 3025 (B2), and P. Berlin 10499 (R); the fourth is P. Butler 527 = P. British Museum 10274.

The text consists of a narrative frame and nine poetic speeches. It is both a serious disquisition on the need for justice, and a parable on the utility of fine speech. The connection between the two themes is achieved by means of an ironic device in the narrative frame: after the peasant has been robbed and has laid his complaint before the magistrate in a stirring plea, the latter is so delighted with this unlearned man's eloquence that he reports it to the king; and on the king's orders the magistrate goads the peasant to continue pleading until the poor man is completely exhausted. Only then does he receive justice and ample rewards.

The tension between the studied silence of the magistrate and the increasingly despairing speeches of the peasant is the operative principle that moves the action forward. And the mixture of seriousness and irony, the intertwining of a plea for justice with a demonstration of the value of rhetoric, is the very essense of the work.

Publication: F. Vogelsang and A. H. Gardiner, *Die Klagen des Bauern*, Literarische Texte des Mittleren Reiches, I (Berlin, 1908).   F. Vogelsang, *Kommentar zu den Klagen des Bauern*, Untersuchungen, 6 (Leipzig, 1913; reprint, Hildesheim, 1964).

Excerpts: de Buck, *Readingbook*, pp. 88-99.   Sethe, *Lesestücke*, pp. 17-25.   *Idem, Erl.*, pp. 21-32.

Translation: A. H. Gardiner, *JEA*, 9 (1923), 5-25.   Erman, *Literature*, pp. 116-131.   F. Lexa, *Arch. Or.*, 7 (1935), 372-383.   Lefebvre, *Romans*, pp. 41-69.   J. A. Wilson in *ANET*, pp. 407-410 (excerpts). Bissing, *Lebensweisheit*, pp. 155-170.

Comments: F. Lexa, *RT*, 34 (1912), 218-231.   A. H. Gardiner, *PSBA*, 35 (1913), 264-276.   E. Suys, *Étude sur le conte du fellah plaideur*

(Rome, 1933).   A. M. Blackman, *JEA*, 20 (1934), 218-219.   S. Herrmann, *Untersuchungen*, pp. 79-98.   *Idem*, *ZÄS*, 80 (1955), 34-39, and *ZÄS*, 82 (1958), 55-57.   G. Lanczkowski, *Altägyptischer Prophetismus* (Wiesbaden, 1960).

(R1) There was a man named Khun-Anup, a peasant of Salt-Field.[1] He had a wife whose name was [Ma]rye. This peasant said to his wife: "Look here, I am going down to Egypt to bring food from there for my children. Go, measure for me the barley which is in the barn, what is left of [last year's] barley." Then she measured for him [twenty-six] gallons of barley. (5) This peasant said to his wife: "Look, you have twenty gallons of barley as food for you and your children. Now make for me these six gallons of barley into bread and beer for every day in which [I shall travel]."

This peasant went down to Egypt. He had loaded his donkeys with rushes, *rdmt*-grass, (10) natron, salt, sticks of –––, staves from Cattle-Country,[2] leopard skins, (15) wolf skins, *ns3*-plants, *'nw*-stones, *tnm*-plants, *ḥprwr*-plants, (20) *s3hwt*, *s3skwt*, *miswt*-plants, *snt*-stones, *'b3w*-stones, (25) *ibs3*-plants, *inbi*-plants, pidgeons, *n'rw*-birds, *wgs*-birds, (30) *wbn*-plants, *tbsw*-plants, *gngnt*, earth-hair, and *inst*; (35) in sum, all the good products of Salt-Field. This peasant went south toward Hnes.[3] He arrived in the district of Perfefi, north of Medenyt. There he met a man standing on the riverbank whose name was Nemtynakht.[4] He was the son of a man (40) named Isri and a subordinate of the high steward Rensi, the son of Meru.

This Nemtynakht said, when he saw this peasant's donkeys which tempted his heart: "If only I had a potent divine image through which I could seize this peasant's goods!" Now the house of this Nemtynakht was at the beginning (45) of a path[5] which was narrow, not so wide as to exceed the width of a shawl. And one side of it was under water, the other under barley. This Nemtynakht said to his servant: "Go, bring me a sheet from my house." It was brought to him straightway. He spread it out on the beginning of the path, (50) so that its fringe touched the water, its hem the barley.

Now this peasant came along the public road. (B1, 1) Then this Nemtynakht said: "Be careful, peasant; don't step on my clothes!" This peasant said: "I'll do as you wish, my course is a good one." So he went up higher. This Nemtynakht said: (5) "Will you have my barley for a path?" This peasant said: "My course is a good one. The riverbank is steep and our way is under barley, for you block the path with your clothes. Will you then not let us pass on the road?"

Just then one of the donkeys filled (10) its mouth with a wisp of barley. This Nemtynakht said: "Now I shall seize your donkey, peasant, for eating my barley. It shall tread out grain for its offense!" This peasant said: "My course is a good one. Only one (wisp) is destroyed. Could I buy my donkey for its value, if you seize it (15) for filling its mouth with a wisp of barley?[6] But I know the lord of this domain; it belongs to the high steward Rensi, the son of Meru. He punishes every robber in this whole land. Shall I be robbed in his domain?" This Nemtynakht said: "Is this the saying people say: (20) 'A poor man's name is pronounced for his master's sake.' It is I who speak to you, and you invoke the high steward!"

Then he took a stick of green tamarisk to him and thrashed all his limbs with it, seized his donkeys, drove them to his domain. Then this peasant (25) wept very loudly for the pain of that which was done to him. This Nemtynakht said: "Don't raise your voice, peasant. Look, you are bound for the abode of the Lord of Silence!"[7] This peasant said: "You beat me, you steal my goods, and now you take the complaint from my mouth! O Lord of Silence, give me back (30) my things, so that I can stop crying to your dreadedness!"[8]

This peasant spent the time of ten days appealing to this Nemtynakht who paid no attention to it. So this peasant proceeded southward to Hnes, in order to appeal to the high steward Rensi, the son of Meru. He found him coming out of the door (35) of his house, to go down to his courthouse barge. This peasant said: "May I be allowed to acquaint you with this complaint? Might a servant of your choice be sent to me, through whom I could inform you of it?" So the high steward Rensi, the son of Meru, (40) sent a servant of his choice ahead of him, and this peasant informed him of the matter in all its aspects.

Then the high steward Rensi, the son of Meru, denounced this Nemtynakht to the magistrates who were with him. Then they said to him: "Surely it is a peasant of his who has gone to someone else beside him. (45) That is what they do to peasants of theirs who go to others beside them.[9] That is what they do. Is there cause for punishing this Nemtynakht for a trifle of natron and a trifle of salt? If he is ordered to replace it, he will replace it." Then the high steward Rensi, the son of Meru, (50) fell silent. He did not reply to these magistrates, nor did he reply to this peasant.

First Petition

Now this peasant came to appeal to the high steward Rensi, the son of Meru. He said: "O high steward, my lord, greatest of the great, leader of all!

When you go down to the sea of (55) justice
And sail on it with a fair wind,[10]
No squall shall strip away your sail,
Nor will your boat be idle.
No accident will affect your mast,
Your yards will not break.
You will not founder when you touch land,
No flood will carry you away.
You will not taste the river's (60) evils,
You will not see a frightened face.
Fish will come darting to you,
Fatted fowl surround you.
For you are father to the orphan,
Husband to the widow,
Brother to the rejected woman,
Apron to the motherless.

Let me make your name in (65) this land according to all the good rules:[11]

Leader free of greed,
Great man free of baseness,
Destroyer of falsehood,
Creator of rightness,
Who comes at the voice of the caller!
When I speak, may you hear!
Do justice, O praised one,
Who is praised by the praised;
Remove (70) my grief, I am burdened,
Examine me, I am in need!"

Now this peasant made this speech in the time of the majesty of King Nebkaure, the justified. Then the high steward Rensi, the son of Meru, went before his majesty and said: "My lord, (75) I have found one among those peasants whose speech is truly beautiful. Robbed of his goods by a man who is in my service, he has come to petition me about it." Said his majesty: "As truly as you wish to see me in health, you shall detain him here, without answering whatever he says. In order to keep him (80) talking, be silent. Then have it brought to us in writing, that we may hear it. But provide for his wife and his children. For one of those peasants comes here (only) just before his house is empty. Provide also for this peasant himself. You shall let food be given him without letting him know that it is you who gives it to him."

So they gave him ten loaves of bread and two jugs of beer (85) every day. It was the high steward Rensi, the son of Meru, who gave it. He gave it to a friend of his, and he gave it to him. Then the high steward Rensi, the son of Meru, wrote to the mayor of Salt-Field about providing food for this peasant's wife, a total of three bushels of grain every day.

Second Petition

Now this peasant came to petition him a second time. He said: "O high steward, my lord, greatest of the great, richest of the rich, truly greater that his great ones, richer than his (90) rich ones!

> Rudder of heaven, beam of earth,
> Plumb-line that carries the weight!
> Rudder, drift not,
> Beam, tilt not,
> Plumb-line, swing not awry!

A great lord taking a share of that which is (now) ownerless; stealing from a lonely man? Your portion is in your house: a jug of beer and three loaves. What is that you expend to satisfy your (95) clients? A mortal man dies along with his underlings; shall you be a man of eternity?

> Is it not wrong, a balance that tilts,
> A plummet that strays,
> The straight becoming crooked?
> Lo, justice flees from you,
> Expelled from its seat!
> The magistrates do wrong,
> Right-dealing is bent sideways,
> The judges snatch what has been stolen.
> He who trims a matter's rightness (100) makes it swing awry:
> The breath-giver chokes him who is down,

He who should refresh makes pant.
The arbitrator is a robber,
The remover of need orders its creation.
The town is a floodwater,
The punisher of evil commits crimes!"

Said the high steward Rensi, the son of Meru: "Are your belongings
a greater concern to you than that my servant might seize you?"[12]
This peasant said:

"The measurer of (105) grain-heaps trims for himself,
He who fills for another shaves the other's share;
He who should rule by law commands theft,
Who then will punish crime?
The straightener of another's crookedness
Supports another's crime.
Do you find here something for you?
Redress is short, misfortune long,
A good deed is remembered.
This is the precept:
Do to the doer (110) to make him do.[13]
It is thanking a man for what he does,
Parrying a blow before it strikes,
Giving a commission to one who is skillful.

Oh for a moment of destruction, havoc in your vineyard, loss among
your birds, damage to your water birds!

A man who saw has turned blind,
A hearer deaf,
A leader now leads astray!

(115) ...... You are strong and mighty. Your arm is active,
your heart greedy, mercy has passed you by. How miserable is the
wretch whom you have destroyed! You are like a messenger of the
Crocodile; you surpass (120) the Lady of Pestilence![14] If you have
nothing, she has nothing. If there's nothing against her, there's
nothing against you. If you don't act, she does not act. The wealthy
should be merciful; violence is for the criminal; robbing suits him who
has nothing. The stealing done by the robber is the misdeed of one
who is poor.[15] One can't reproach him; he merely seeks for himself.
But you are sated (125) with your bread, drunken with your beer,
rich in all kinds of [treasures].

Though the face of the steersman is forward, the boat drifts as it pleases. Though the king is in the palace, though the rudder is in your hand, wrong is done around you. Long is my plea, heavy my task. "What is the matter with him?" people ask.

> Be a shelter, (130) make safe your shore,
> See how your quay is infested with crocodiles!
> Straighten your tongue, let it not stray,
> A serpent is this limb of man.
> Don't tell lies, warn the magistrates,
> Greasy baskets are the judges,
> Telling lies is their herbage,
> It weighs lightly on them.
> Knower of (135) all men's ways:
> Do you ignore my case?
> Savior from all water's harm:
> See I have a course without a ship!
> Guider to port of all who founder:
> Rescue the drowning!
> . . . . . . "

Third Petition

Then this peasant came to petition him a third time; he said:

> (14) "High steward, my lord,
> You are Re, lord of sky, with your courtiers,
> Men's sustenance is from you as from the flood,
> You are Hapy who makes green the fields,
> Revives the wastelands.
> Punish the robber, save the sufferer,
> Be not (145) a flood against the pleader!
> Heed eternity's coming,
> Desire to last, as is said:
> Doing justice is breath for the nose.
> Punish him who should be punished,
> And none will equal your rectitude.
> Does the hand-balance deflect?
> Does the stand-balance tilt?
> Does Thoth (150) show favor
> So that you may do wrong?
> Be the equal of these three:

If the three show favor,
Then may you show favor!
Answer not good with evil,
Put not one thing in place of another!

My speech grows more than *snmyt*-weed, to assault[16] the smell with its answers. Misfortune pours water (155) till cloth will grow! Three times now to make him act![17]

By the sail-wind should you steer,
Control the waves to sail aright;
Guard from landing by the helm-rope,
Earth's rightness lies in justice!
Speak not falsely—you are great,
Act not lightly—(160) you are weighty;
Speak not falsely—you are the balance,
Do not swerve—you are the norm!
You are one with the balance,
If it tilts you may tilt.
Do not drift, steer, hold the helm-rope!
Rob not, act against the robber,
(165) Not great is one who is great in greed.
Your tongue is the plummet,
Your heart the weight,
Your two lips are its arms.
If you avert your face from violence,
Who then shall punish wrongdoing?
Lo, you are a wretch of a washerman,
A greedy one who harms (170) a friend,
One who forsakes his friend for his client,
His brother is he who comes with gifts.
Lo, you are a ferryman who ferries him who pays,
A straight one whose straightness is splintered,
A storekeeper who does not let a poor man pass,
Lo, you are (175) a hawk to the little people,
One who lives on the poorest of the birds.
Lo, you are a butcher whose joy is slaughter,
The carnage is nothing to him.
You are a herdsman . . . . . .
. . . . . .

(180) Hearer, you hear not! Why do you not hear? Now I have subdued the savage; the crocodile retreats! What is your gain? When the secret of truth is found, falsehood is thrown on its back on the ground. Trust not the morrow before it has come; none knows the trouble in it."[18]

Now this peasant had made this speech (185) to the high steward Rensi, the son of Meru, at the entrance to the courthouse. Then he had two guards go to him with whips, and they thrashed all his limbs.

This peasant said: "The son of Meru goes on erring. His face is blind to what he sees, deaf to what he hears; his heart strays from what is recalled to him.

> You are like a town[19] (190) without a mayor,
> Like a troop without a leader,
> Like a ship without a captain,
> A company without a chief.
> You are a sheriff who steals,
> A mayor who pockets,
> A district prosecutor of crime
> Who is the model for the (evil)-doer!"

Fourth Petition

Now this peasant came to petition him a fourth time. Finding him (195) coming out of the gate of the temple of Harsaphes, he said: "O praised one, may Harsaphes praise you, from whose temple you have come!

> Goodness is destroyed, none adhere to it,
> To fling falsehood's back to the ground.
> If the ferry is grounded, wherewith does one cross? . . . . . .

Is crossing (200) the river on sandals a good crossing? No! Who now sleeps till daybreak? Gone is walking by night, travel by day, and letting a man defend his own good cause. But it is no use to tell you this; mercy has passed you by. How miserable is the wretch (205) whom you have destroyed!

> Lo, you are a hunter who takes his fill,[20]
> Bent on doing what he pleases;
> Spearing hippopotami, shooting bulls,
> Catching fish, snaring birds.
> (But) none quick to speak is free from haste,

None light of heart is weighty in conduct.
Be patient (210) so as to learn justice,
Restrain your [˹anger˺] for the good of the humble seeker.[21]
No hasty man attains excellence,
No impatient man is leaned upon.

Let the eyes see, let the heart take notice. Be not harsh in your power, lest trouble befall you. (215) Pass over a matter, it becomes two. He who eats tastes; one addressed answers. It is the sleeper who sees the dream; and a judge who deserves punishment is a model for the (evil)doer. Fool, you are attacked! Ignorant man, you are (220) questioned! Spouter of water, you are attained!

Steersman, let not drift your boat,
Life-sustainer, let not die,
Provider, let not perish,[22]
Shade, let one not dry out,[23]
Shelter, let not the crocodile snatch!
The fourth time I petition you! (225) Shall I go on all day?"

Fifth Petition

Now this peasant came to petition him a fifth time; he said:
"O high steward, my lord! The fisher of ḥwdw-fish ------, the --- slays the iy-fish; the spearer of fish pierces the ʿwbb-fish; the dзbḥw-fisher (230) attacks the pʿḥr-fish; and the catcher of wḥʿ-fish ravages the river.[24] Now you are like them! Rob not a poor man of his goods, a humble man whom you know! Breath to the poor are his belongings; he who takes them stops up his nose. It is to hear cases that you were installed, to judge between two, (235) to punish the robber. But what you do is to uphold the thief! One puts one's trust in you, but you have become a transgressor! You were placed as a dam for the poor lest he drown, but you have become a swift current to him!

Sixth Petition

Now this peasant came (240) to petition him a sixth time; he said: "O high steward, my lord![25]

He who lessens falsehood fosters truth,
He who fosters the good reduces ⟨evil⟩,
As satiety's coming removes hunger,

Clothing removes nakedness;
As the sky is serene after a (245) storm,
Warming all who shiver;
As fire cooks what is raw,
As water quenches thirst.
Now see for yourself:
The arbitrator is a robber,
The peacemaker makes grief,
He who should soothe (250) makes sore.
But he who cheats diminishes justice!
Rightly filled justice neither falls short nor brims over.

If you acquire, give to your fellow; gobbling up is dishonest. But my grief will lead to (255) parting; my accusation brings departure. The heart's intent cannot be known. Don't delay! Act on the charge! If you sever, who shall join? The sounding pole is in your hand; sound! The water is shallow![26] If the boat enters and is grounded, its cargo perishes (260) on the shore.

You are learned, skilled, accomplished,
But not in order to plunder!
You should be the model for all men,
But your affairs are crooked!
The standard for all men cheats the whole land!
The vintner of evil waters his plot with crimes,
Until his plot sprouts (265) falsehood,
His estate flows with crimes!"

Seventh Petition

Now this peasant came to petition him a seventh time; he said: "O high steward, my lord!

You are the whole land's rudder,
The land sails by your bidding;
You are the peer of Thoth,
The judge who is not partial.

My lord, be patient, so that a man may invoke you (270) about his rightful cause. Don't be angry; it is not for you. The long-faced becomes short-tempered. Don't brood on what has not yet come, nor rejoice at what has not yet happened. The patient man prolongs friendship; he who destroys a case will not be trusted.[27] If law is laid waste and order destroyed, no poor man can (275) survive: when he is robbed, justice does not address him.

My body was full, my heart burdened. Now therefore it has come from my body. As a dam is breached and water escapes, so my mouth opened to speak. I plied my sounding pole, I bailed out my water; I have emptied what was in my body; I have washed my soiled linen. (280) My speech is done. My grief is all before you. What do you want? But your laziness leads you astray; your greed makes you dumb; your gluttony makes enemies for you. But will you find another peasant like me? Is there an idler at whose house door a petitioner will stand?

> (285) There is no silent man whom you gave speech,
> No sleeper whom you have wakened,
> None downcast whom you have roused,
> None whose shut mouth you have opened,
> None ignorant whom you gave knowledge,
> None foolish whom you have taught.
> (Yet) magistrates are dispellers of evil,
> Masters of the good,
> Craftsmen who create what is,
> Joiners of the severed head!"

Eighth Petition

Now this peasant (290) came to petition him an eighth time; he said: "O high steward, my lord! Men fall low through greed. The rapacious man lacks success; his success is loss. Though you are greedy it does nothing for you. Though you steal you do not profit. Let a man defend his rightful cause!

Your portion is in your house; your belly is full. The grain-bin brims over; shake it, (295) its overflow spoils on the ground. Thief, robber, plunderer! Magistrates are appointed to suppress crime. Magistrates are shelters against the aggressor. Magistrates are appointed to fight falsehood!

No fear of you makes me petition you; you do not know my heart. A humble man who comes back to reproach you is not afraid of him with whom he pleads. (300) The like of him will not be brought you from the street!

You have your plot of ground in the country, your estate in the district, your income in the storehouse. Yet the magistrates give to you and you take! Are you then a robber? Does one give to you and the troop with you at the division of plots?

Do justice for the Lord of Justice
The justice of whose justice is real!
(305) Pen, papyrus, palette of Thoth,
Keep away from wrongdoing!
When goodness is good it is truly good,
For justice is for eternity:
It enters the graveyard with its doer.
When he is buried and earth enfolds him,
His name (310) does not pass from the earth;
He is remembered because of goodness,
That is the rule of god's command.

The hand-balance—it tilts not; the stand-balance—it leans not to one side. Whether I come, whether another comes, speak! (315) Do not answer with the answer of silence! Do not attack one who does not attack you. You have no pity, you are not troubled, you are not disturbed! You do not repay my good speech which comes from the mouth of Re himself!

Speak justice, do justice,
For it is mighty;
It is great, it endures,
Its worth is tried,[28]
It leads one to reveredness.

Does the hand-balance tilt? Then it is its scales which carry things. The standard has no fault. Crime does not attain its goal; he who is helpful[29] reaches land."

Ninth Petition

(B2, 91) Now this peasant came to petition him a ninth time; he said: "O high steward, my lord! The tongue is men's stand-balance. It is the balance that detects deficiency. Punish him who should be punished, and ⟨none⟩ shall equal your rectitude. (95) --- . . . . . . When falsehood walks it goes astray. It does not cross in the ferry; it does not ⌐progress⌐. (100) He who is enriched by it has no children, has no heirs on earth. He who sails with it does not reach land; his boat does not moor at its landing place.

Be not heavy, nor yet light,
Do not tarry, nor yet hurry,
Be not partial, nor listen to (105) desire.

Do not avert your face from one you know,
Be not blind to one you have seen,
Do not rebuff one who beseeches you.
Abandon this slackness,
Let your speech be heard.
Act for him who would act for you,
Do not listen to everyone,
Summon a man to his rightful cause!

A sluggard has no yesterday;[30] (110) one deaf to justice has no friend; the greedy has no holiday. When the accuser is a wretch, and the wretch becomes a pleader, his opponent is a killer. Here I have been pleading with you, and you have not listened to it. I shall go and plead (115) about you to Anubis!"

Conclusion

Then the high steward Rensi, the son of Meru, sent two guards to bring him back. Then this peasant was fearful, thinking it was done so as to punish him for this speech he had made. This peasant said: "A thirsty man's approach to water, an infant's mouth (120) reaching for milk, thus is a longed-for death seen coming, thus does his death arrive at last." Said the high steward Rensi, the son of Meru: "Don't be afraid, peasant; be ready to deal with me!" Said this peasant: (125) "By my life! Shall I eat your bread and drink your beer forever?" Said the high steward Rensi, the son of Meru: "Now wait here and hear your petitions!" Then he had them read from a new papyrus roll, each petition in its turn. (130) The high steward Rensi, the son of Meru, presented them to the majesty of King Nebkaure, the justified. They pleased his majesty's heart more than anything in the whole land. His majesty said: "Give judgment yourself, son of Meru!"

Then the high steward Rensi, the son of Meru, sent two guards [to bring Nemtynakht]. (135) He was brought and a report was made of [all his property] —————— his wheat, his barley, his donkeys, ———, his pigs, his small cattle ———————. ——— of this Nemtynakht [was given] to this peasant ——————.

Colophon: It is finished ——————.

NOTES

1. The Wadi Natrun.
2. The Farafra Oasis.

3. Heracleopolis Magna (Ahnas), the metropolis of the twentieth nome of Upper Egypt and the capital of the Ninth/Tenth Dynasty.

4. So rather than Thutnakht, as shown by O. Berlev, *Vestnik Drevnei Istorii*, 1 (107) (1969), 3-30 (pointed out to me by K. Baer).

5. *Sm3-t3 n r3-w3t* was rendered "riverside path" by Gardiner, but this is a rather free rendering which hardly accounts for the term or for the situation. The text says that the house was *hr sm3-t3*, but it could not have stood *on* the path. The implied situation is that the house stood at the side of a narrow path which at this point merged with the "public road" on which the peasant was approaching. Hence I take *sm3-t3* to mean the "beginning", or similar, of the path.

6. The meaning of the passage was established by E. Wente in *JNES*, 24 (1965), 105-109, where he rendered: "Only one (wisp) has been destroyed. It is for its (i.e., the wisp's) price that I will buy back my donkey if you seize possession of it for a (mere) filling of its mouth with a wisp of Upper Egyptian barley," and explained it as a quick-witted response. I differ only in taking it as a rhetorical question rather than an assertion.

7. The god Osiris, who had a sanctuary in the neighborhood.

8. Among the epithets of Osiris are "lord of fear," "lord of awe."

9. The magistrates exculpate Nemtynakht by surmising that the peasant was a serf of his who had tried to do business with another landlord and was being punished for it.

10. Wordplay on *m3't*, "justice" and *m3'w*, "fair wind." The poetic speeches contain numerous wordplays and assonances. Where possible I have tried to imitate them, as in rendering *nn iwt iyt m ht·k* as "no accident will affect your mast," rather than "no mishap will befall your mast," or the like.

11. As Ranke explained in *ZÄS*, 79 (1954), 72, the peasant makes for the high steward a titulary of five great names in analogy with the five great names of the royal titulary.

12. In order to goad the peasant to further speeches, the high steward threatens him with a beating.

13. The peasant quotes a proverb that embodies the *do ut des* principle.

14. The goddess Sakhmet.

15. I emend *iwty* to *nty*.

16. *Dmi* here, as in the *Dispute between a Man and His Ba*, line 150, cannot mean "cling to," but rather "press against," "attack."

17. I.e., this is the peasant's third plea.

18. A proverb similar to *Ptahhotep*, line 343: "Though one plans the morrow one knows not what will be."

19. Reading *mi* instead of *m*; the speeches of the peasant by and large make a clear distinction between the two. The high steward is *identified* with individual characters or things (steersman, balance, etc.) and is *likened* to larger entities, such as a troop without leader, etc.

20. Literally, "washes his heart." In *Ptahhotep*, lines 79 and 152, *i'-ib* is an "outburst of anger." See there n. 9.

21. *Bss grw*, "he who enters humbly." Here and in B 1, 298 *grw* is "humble", not "silent."

22. A wordplay on *htm*, "to provide," and *htm*, "to destroy."

23. *Šwyt m ir m šw* is not: "Shade, act not as the sunheat," but rather: "Shade, don't make one into one who is *šw*," i.e., "dry."

24. *Wh'* is the *synodontis schall*; the other fishes are unidentified.

25. If the scribe skipped a line here, as Gardiner assumed, the omitted sentence ended with the second *nb*. But perhaps *nb* is a dittography and nothing is missing.

26. *Sp n mw* seems to mean "remnant of water," i.e., "shallow water." The garbled *sḫpr sp mw*(?) in B1, 199 probably contained the same expression. If so, the passage there would mean: "If the water is shallow and one crosses the river on sandals, is that a good crossing?"

27. Literally, "becomes one-does-not-know-what-is-in-the-heart."

28. *Gmi*, "to find useful."

29. I take *ḫry s3*, "under the back," to mean "to support the back" similar to *tsw psd* in *Merikare*, P 136.

30. I.e., is not remembered; a wordplay on *sf* and *wsf*.

THE SATIRE OF THE TRADES

Like the other Instructions, this work has a prologue and an epilogue which frame the actual teaching and set its stage. A father conducts his young son to the residence in order to place him in school, and during the journey he instructs him in the duties and rewards of the scribal profession. In order to stress the amenities and advantages that accrue to the successful scribe, he contrasts the scribal career with the hardships of other trades and professions, eighteen of which are described in the most unflattering terms.

Ever since Maspero called this Instruction "Satire des Métiers," scholars have understood it to be a satire, that is to say, a deliberately derisive characterization of all trades other than the scribal profession. Helck, however, in his new edition of the text has denied its satiric character and has claimed it to be a wholly serious, non-humorous work. I continue to think of it as a satire. What are the stylistic means of satire? Exaggeration and a lightness of tone designed to induce laughter and a mild contempt. Our text achieves its satirical effects by exaggerating the true hardships of the professions described, and by suppressing all their positive and rewarding aspects.

If it were argued that the exaggerations were meant to be taken seriously, we would have to conclude that the scribal profession practiced deliberate deception out of a contempt for manual labor so profound as to be unrelieved by humor. Such a conclusion is, however, belied by all the literary and pictorial evidence. For tomb reliefs and texts alike breathe joy and pride in the accomplishments of labor. Moreover, the principal didactic works, such as *Ptahhotep* and the *Eloquent Peasant*, teach respect for all labor.

In short, the unrelievedly negative descriptions of the laboring professions are examples of humor in the service of literary satire. The result is obtained through unflattering comparisons and through exaggerations that rise to outright fabrications. What if not a fabrication for the sake of caricature is a bird-catcher who does not have a net—the very tool of his trade? What if not a caricature is a potter who is compared to a grubbing pig, a cobbler whose hides are termed "corpses," a courier terrorized out of his wits by the dangers of the road, and a fisherman blinded by his fear of crocodiles?

The text is preserved entirely in P. Sallier II, and partially in P. Anastasi

VII (both in the British Museum), both of which were written by the same Nineteenth Dynasty scribe. Small portions are preserved on an Eighteenth Dynasty writing board in the Louvre, the Eighteenth Dynasty P. Amherst in the Pierpont Morgan Library, P. Chester Beatty XIX of the British Museum, and numerous, mostly Ramesside, ostraca.

Though ample, the textual transmission is exceedingly corrupt. Helck's comprehensive new edition has advanced the understanding considerably. But the corruptions are so numerous and so extreme that there remains much room for differing conjectures and interpretations.

Publication: Budge, *Facsimiles*, pls. 65-73. H. Brunner, *Die Lehre des Cheti, Sohnes des Duauf*, Ägyptologische Forschungen, 13 (Glückstadt, 1944). W. Helck, *Die Lehre des Dwꜣ-Ḫtjj* (Wiesbaden, 1970).

Translation: Erman, *Literature*, pp. 67-72. B. Van de Walle, *CdE*, 24 (1949), 244-256. J. A. Wilson in *ANET*, pp. 432-434.

Comments: A. Piankoff, *RdE*, 1 (1933), 51-74 (the Louvre Tablet). A. Théodoridès, *Bruxelles Annuaire*, 15 (1958-60), 39-69. B. Van de Walle, *CdE*, 22 (1947), 50-72. Idem, *L'Humour dans la littérature et dans l'art de l'ancienne Egypte*, Scholae Adriani de Buck memoriae dicatae, 4 (Leiden, 1969), p. 11. Seibert, *Charakteristik*, pp. 99-192.

(3, 9) Beginning of the Intruction made by the man of Sile,[1] whose name is ⌈Dua-khety⌉,[2] for his son, called Pepi, as he journeyed south (4, 1) to the residence, to place him in the school for scribes, among the sons of magistrates, with the elite of the residence. He said to him:

I have seen many beatings—
Set your heart on books!
I watched those seized for labor—
There's nothing better than books!
It's like a boat on water.

Read the end of the *Kemit*-Book,[3]
You'll find this saying there:
A scribe at whatever post in town,
He will not suffer in it;
As he fills another's need,
He will ⌈not lack rewards⌉.
I don't see a calling like it
Of which this saying could be (5) said.

I'll make you love scribedom more than your mother,
I'll make its beauties stand before you;
It's the greatest of all callings,
There's none like it in the land.

Barely grown, still a child,
He is greeted, sent on errands,
Hardly returned he wears a gown.
I never saw a sculptor as envoy,
Nor is a goldsmith ever sent;
But I have seen the smith at work
At the opening of his furnace;
With fingers like claws of a crocodile
He stinks more than fish roe.

The carpenter who wields an adze,
He is wearier than a field-laborer;
His field is the timber, his hoe the adze.
There is no end to his labor,
He does more (5, 1) than his arms can do,
Yet at night he kindles light.
The jewel-maker bores with his chisel[4]
In hard stone of all kinds;
When he has finished the inlay of the eye,
His arms are spent, he's weary;
Sitting down when the sun goes down,
His knees and back are cramped.

The barber barbers till nightfall,
He betakes himself to town,[5]
He sets himself up in his corner,
He moves from street to street,
Looking for someone to barber.
He strains his arms to fill his belly,
(5) Like the bee that eats as it works.

The reed-cutter travels to the Delta to get arrows;
When he has done more than his arms can do,
Mosquitoes have slain him,
Gnats have slaughtered him,
He is quite worn out.

The potter is under the soil,
Though as yet among the living;
He grubs in the mud more than a pig,
In order to fire his pots.
His clothes are stiff with clay,

His girdle is in shreds;
If air enters his nose,
It comes straight from the fire.
He makes a pounding with his feet,
And is himself crushed;[6]
He grubs the yard of every house
And roams the public places.

(6, 1) I'll describe to you also the mason:
His loins give him pain;
Though he is out in the wind,
He works without a cloak;
His loincloth is a twisted rope
And a string in the rear.[7]
His arms are spent from exertion,
Having mixed all kinds of dirt;
When he eats bread [with] his fingers,
⌐He has washed at the same time⌐.

The carpenter also suffers much[8]
. . . . . .
The room measures ten by six cubits.
A month passes after the beams are laid,
. . . . . .
And all its work is done.
(5) The food which he gives to his household,
It does not ⌐suffice⌐ for his children.

The gardener carries a yoke,
His shoulders are bent as with age;
There's a swelling on his neck
And it festers.
In the morning he waters vegetables,
The evening he spends with the herbs,[9]
While at noon he has toiled in the orchard.
He works himself to death
More than all other professions.

The farmer wails more than the guinea fowl,
His voice is louder than a raven's;
His fingers are swollen
And stink to excess.

He is weary . . . . . .
. . . (7, 1) . . .
He is well if one's well among lions.[10]
. . . . . .
When he reaches home at night,
The march has worn him out.

The weaver[11] in the workshop,
He is worse off than a woman;
With knees against his chest,
He cannot breathe air.
If he skips a day of weaving,
He is beaten fifty strokes;
He gives food to the doorkeeper,
To let him see the light of day.

The arrow-maker suffers much
As he goes out (5) to the desert;
More is what he gives his donkey
Than the work it does for him.
Much is what he gives the herdsmen,
So they'll put him on his way.
When he reaches home at night,
The march has worn him out.

The courier[12] goes into the desert,
Leaving his goods to his children;
Fearful of lions and Asiatics,
He knows himself (only) when he's in Egypt.
When he reaches home at night,
The march has worn him out;
Be his home of cloth or brick,
His return is joyless.[13]

The ⌜stoker⌝, his fingers are foul,
Their smell is that of corpses;
His eyes are inflamed by much smoke,
(8, 1) He cannot get rid of his dirt.
He spends the day cutting reeds,
His clothes are loathsome to him.

The cobbler suffers much
Among his vats of oil;

He is well if one's well with corpses,
What he bites is leather.

The washerman washes on the shore
With the crocodile as neighbor;
⌜"Father, leave the flowing water,"⌝
Say his son, his daughter,
⌜It is not a job that satisfies⌝
. . . . . .
His food is mixed with dirt,
No limb of his is clean
⌜He is given⌝ (5) women's clothes,
. . . . . .
He weeps as he spends the day at his washboard
. . . . . .
One says to him, "Soiled linen for you,"
. . . . . .

The bird-catcher suffers much
As he watches out for birds;
When the swarms pass over him,
He keeps saying, "had I a net!"
But the god grants it not,
And he's angry with his lot.

I'll speak of the fisherman also,
His is the worst of all the jobs;
He labors on the river,
Mingling with crocodiles.
When the time of reckoning comes,
He is full of lamentations;
He does not say, "There's a (9, 1) crocodile,"
Fear has made him blind.
⌜Coming from⌝ the flowing water
He says, "Mighty god!"

See, there's no profession without a boss,
Except for the scribe; he is the boss.
Hence if you know writing,
It will do better for you
Than those professions I've set before you,
Each more wretched than the other.[14]

A peasant is not called a man,
Beware of it!

Lo, what I do in journeying to the residence,
Lo,[15] I do it for love of you.
The day in school will profit you
Its works are for ever . . .
. . . (5) . . .
. . . . . .
I'll tell you also other things,
So as to teach you knowledge.
Such as: if a quarrel breaks out,
Do not approach the contenders!
If you are chided . . . . . .
And don't know how to repel the heat,
⌐Call the listeners to witness¬,
And delay the answer.

When you walk behind officials,
Follow at a proper distance.
When you enter a man's house,
And he's busy with someone before you,
Sit with your hand over your mouth.
Do not ask him for anything,
Only do as he tells you,
Beware of rushing to the table!

Be weighty and very dignified,
Do not speak of (10, 1) secret things,
Who hides his thought[16] shields himself.
Do not say things recklessly,
When you sit with one who's hostile.
If you leave the schoolhouse
When midday is called,
And go roaming in the streets,
⌐All will scold you in the end¬.[17]
When an official sends you with a message,
Tell it as he told it,
Don't omit, don't add to it.[18]
He who neglects to praise,
His name will not endure;
He who is skilled in all his conduct,

From him nothing is hidden,
He is not ⌐opposed¬ anywhere.

Do not tell lies (5) against your mother,
The magistrates abhor it.
The descendant who does what is good,
His actions all emulate the past.
Do not consort with a rowdy,
It harms you when one hears of it.
If you have eaten three loaves,
Drunk two jugs of beer,
And the belly is not sated, restrain it!
When another eats, don't stand there,
Beware of rushing to the table!
It is good if you are sent out often,
And hear the magistrates speak.
You should acquire the manner of the wellborn,[19]
As you follow in their steps.
The scribe is regarded as one who hears,
For the hearer becomes a doer.
You should rise when you are addressed,
Your feet should hurry when you go;
⌐Do not¬ (11, 1) ⌐trust¬.
Associate with men of distinction,
Befriend a man of your generation.

Lo, I have set you on god's path,
A scribe's Renenet[20] is on his shoulder
On the day he is born.
When he attains the council chamber,
The court . . . . . .
Lo, no scribe is short of food
And of riches from the palace.
The Meskhenet assigned to the scribe,
She promotes him in the council.
Praise god for your father, your mother,
Who set you on the path of life!
This is what I put before you,
Your children and their children.

Colophon: (5) It has come to a happy conclusion.

NOTES

1. *Ṯзrt*, or *Ṯзrw*, i.e., Sile, the border fortress in the eastern Delta.

2. Three manuscripts write the name as "Khety, son of Duauf," two write "Dua-Khety"; a sixth gives yet another form. Helck has adopted Seibert's preference for "Dua-Khety." Brunner, in *BiOr*, 26 (1969), 71, has reaffirmed his support for "Khety, son of Duauf."

3. A book of Instructions, the fragments of which were published by Posener, *Ostr. hiér.*, II, pls. 1-25; see also Posener, *Littérature*, pp. 4-6.

4. *Ms-ʿзt:* Brunner, "Steinmetz," Wilson, "fashioner of costly stones," Seibert, "Schmuckarbeiter," and Helck, "Juwelier." The activity of this craftsman is described by the verb *whb* in *DeM* 1014, which means "to bore." The conjecture that *mnḥ* means "to string beads" lacks support, for in *Admonitions*, 3, 3 Gardiner merely took it to mean "to fasten."

5. Emending *ʿmʿyt* to *dmyt*, as proposed by Vandier, *BiOr*, 6 (1949), 15.

6. The pounding with the feet that occurred in pottery making was in the initial molding of the clay prior to its being shaped by hand. I see no occasion for the conjectured pounding tools.

7. This seems to refer to the narrow strip of cloth tied in front, with its ends hanging down to cover the genitals, which was worn by some laborers. The dangling ends were sometimes tucked into the waistband or turned to the back. The resulting nudity may have aroused the derision of the well-dressed scribes.

8. As Helck pointed out, this section deals with the carpenter. Unfortunately it is very obscure.

9. A meaning broader than "coriander" is indicated for *šзw*. In the sun-temple of Ni-user-re, *šзw* is a water plant eaten by fish; see Edel, *Inschriften*, p. 217.

10. This rendering, which is Brunner's, was rejected by Seibert and Helck but seems to me the right one. The sentences following it are extremely obscure.

11. Or specifically, the "mat-weaver."

12. *Šḥзḥзty:* Brunner, "Eilbote," Helck, " ̣arawanenträger." A member of a caravan would have much less reason to be frightened than a lone courier.

13. This was Brunner's tentative rendering and seems to me the best guess.

14. I emend to: *mk ky ỉry ḥwrw r ỉryf.*

15. Connective iterated *mk*, as also in the first poem of the *Dispute between a Man and His Ba*, and in the *Prophecies of Neferti* (see there n. 2).

16. Literally, "his belly."

17. In this garbled passage I chose the reading of *DeM* (= ODM) 1039, emending only *bw nk* to *bw nb.*

18. Compare the eighth maxim of the *Instruction of Ptahhotep.*

19. Literally, "the children of people," which is the plural counterpart of the term *sз s*, "son of man."

20. Renenet (Thermuthis) was a goddess of ̣ounty and good luck. She was frequently associated with the goddess Meskhenet who presided over births.

IV. Songs and Hymns

While the distinction between poems and songs is sometimes uncertain, we may first claim as songs those poems that are indicated as being recited to the accompaniment of a musical instrument. Second, it is customary to treat as religious songs, i.e., hymns, those poems that show a clear connection with the temple cult and with festivals. Third, we may class as songs the short pieces of poetry carved above scenes of labor depicted in tomb reliefs. Such workmen's songs are in fact comparable to songs sung by Egyptian workmen to this day.

The few snatches of workmen's songs that have survived—they are not included in this anthology—are the only truly secular songs that can be identified for the periods of the Old and Middle Kingdoms. All other songs come from the cultic sphere, the cult of the dead, and the cult of gods and kings.

The instrument that accompanied the songs sung to the dead was almost always the harp; hence these compositions are known as *Harper's Songs*. Carved on tomb walls and on mortuary stelae, Harper's Songs are part of the mortuary repertoire, albeit a very special part. Their theme was death. But they were reflections on death, and not ritual texts required in the ceremonies of burial and revivification. Hence their authors were free to pursue the theme of death in an imaginative way. Their main approach was to sing a praise of death and of the tomb, and to reassure the owner of the tomb about his fate. But their freedom from ritual requirements produced an unexpected and startling innovation: a song that lamented the passing of life and urged enjoyment of life while it lasts! This song, the famous *Harper's Song from the Tomb of King Intef*, went so far as to cast doubt on the reality of the afterlife and on the usefulness of tombs. Once this note of hedonism coupled with skepticism had been sounded, it continued to occupy the minds and to be reflected both in Harpers' Songs and in other compositions—notably in the *Dispute between a Man and His Ba*, in which the *ba* voices precisely the same opinion.

Songs and hymns were functional compositions, designed to serve in a particular setting. At the same time they could become literature in the narrow sense of writings transmitted on papyrus and appreciated as works of imaginative art. This was the fate of the *Harper's Song from the Tomb of King Intef*, and of some of the hymns to gods and kings. In some cases, notably in the *Hymn to the Nile*, the literary character is so dominant that one may doubt whether it ever had a cultic function.

THREE HARPERS' SONGS

Funerary Stela of Iki

Leiden V 68

A stela in door form which is divided into three registers. On the left side of the upper register, the deceased Iki is seated at the offering-table while his wife stands behind him. Before him squats a very fat harper. Eight columns of text above the couple contain the prayer for offerings. In front of the harper is his song in four short columns. In the two lower registers, the deceased and several of his children receive offerings. In this song as in a number of others, the harper identifies himself by name, thus reflecting his personal relation to the tomb-owner, as well as his own professional identity. The harper Neferhotep of this stela had a memorial stela of his own, also preserved in the Leiden Museum (V 75). Both memorial stelae were the work of the same sculptor, who signed his name on the latter monument.

Publication: Holwerda-Boeser, *Beschreibung*, Vol. II, pl. 9.   G. Steindorff, *ZÄS*, 32 (1894), 123-126.   Sethe, *Lesestücke*, p. 87.

Translation and study: M. Lichtheim, *JNES*, 4 (1945), 189.

This is the song:

O Tomb, you were built for festivity,
You were founded for happiness!
The singer Neferhotep, born of Henu.

Stela of Nebankh from Abydos

Cairo Museum

The Harper's Song, in eight horizontal lines, fills the upper portion of the round-topped stela. In the lower left corner, the deceased is seated at the offering-table, and the harper squats before him.

Publication: *Cemeteries of Abydos*, II, pl. xxiii, 5.   Sethe, *Lesestücke*, p. 87.

Translation and study: M. Lichtheim, *JNES*, 4 (1945), 188-189.

(1) The singer Tjeniaa says:
How firm you are in your seat of eternity,
Your monument of everlastingness!
It is filled with offerings of food,
It contains every good thing.
Your *ka* is with you,
It does not leave you,
O Royal Seal-bearer, Great Steward, (5) Nebankh!
Yours is the sweet breath of the northwind!
So says his singer who keeps his name alive,
The honorable singer Tjeniaa, whom he loved,
Who sings to his *ka* every day.

The Song from the Tomb of King Intef

The song is preserved in two New Kingdom copies. First, on pages vi, 2-vii, 3, of the Ramesside Papyrus Harris 500 (= P. British Museum 10060); and, second, carved on a wall of the tomb of Paatenemheb from

Saqqara, now in Leiden, which dates from the reign of Amenhotep IV (Akhenaten). The latter copy, which is incomplete, is written above the heads of a group of four musicians led by a blind harpist. The song's introductory line states that it reproduces a song inscribed in the tomb of a King Intef—a name that was borne by a number of kings of the Eleventh and of the Seventeenth Dynasties. Since the two New Kingdom copies reproduce a genuinely Middle Egyptian text, we need not doubt that an original text, carved in a royal tomb of the Middle Kingdom, existed.

The phrase "make holiday" (*ir hrw nfr*), which the singer of the *Intef Song* addresses to the audience, was a term employed in situations of daily life as well as in reference to death and the afterlife. Furthermore, it is known that funerary banquets were held in the cemeteries on feast days. It is thus quite possible that Harpers' Songs were sung at such funerary banquets, and that they employed the "make holiday" theme in its multiple meanings. In the context of the funerary banquet the various meanings would blend into one.

The theme of sorrow over death properly belonged to the Laments on Death which were an integral part of the burial ceremony. What is noteworthy is that these laments juxtapose sorrow and joy in a manner similar to the *Intef Song* and subsequent Harpers' Songs, and move rapidly back and forth between grief and joy:

I have wept, I have mourned!
O all people, remember getting drunk on wine,
With wreaths and perfume on your heads![1]

The dead too had joy: "How good is this which happens to him!"[2]

Given the multiple meanings of the "make holiday" theme, it follows that it was not the use of this theme which made the *Intef Song* so startling, but rather its skepticism concerning the reality of the afterlife and the effectiveness of tomb-building. It was this skepticism which injected a strident note of discord into a class of songs that had been designed to praise and reassure. The incongruity is of the same order as that which one observes in the *Dispute between a Man and His Ba*. For there the *ba*, though itself the guarantor of immortality, is given the role of denigrating death and immortality, denying the worth of tombs, and counseling enjoyment of life. The incongruity was not lost on the Egyptians, as the subsequent development of Harpers' Songs reveals. The Harpers' Songs of the New Kingdom show two responses to the *Intef Song:* an outright rejection of its "impious" thoughts, and a toning down of its skepticism so as to remove the sting. Both solutions are found side by side in two Harpers' Songs carved on the walls of the New Kingdom tomb of a priest Nefer-hotep.[3]

The objection to the skeptic-hedonistic message is phrased thus:

I have heard those songs that are in the tombs of old,
And what they relate in extolling life on earth,
And in belittling the land of the dead.
Why is this done to the land of eternity,
The just and fair that holds no terror?

There follows the praise of eternal life.

The toning down of the skeptical approach took various forms, and resulted in Harpers' Songs that were eclectic and lacked unity. But though toned down, the note of skepticism could be heard, sometimes faintly, sometimes clearly, in Harpers' Songs and in other compositions, as a haunting suspicion that the struggle to win immortality was at best beset by uncertainties and at worst, futile.

Publication: Budge, *Facsimiles*, pls. xlv-xlvi and pp. 23-24.   Müller, *Liebespoesie*, pls. xii-xvi and pp. 29-30.   Holwerda-Boeser, *Beschreibung*, Vol. IV, pl. 6 (the tomb copy).

Translation: Erman, *Literature*, pp. 133-134.   J. H. Breasted, *The Dawn of Conscience* (New York, 1933), pp. 163-164.   M. Lichtheim, *JNES*, 4 (1945), 192-193.   J. A. Wilson in *ANET*, pp. 467-468. F. Daumas, *La civilisation de l'Egypte pharaonique* (Paris, 1965), pp. 404-405.

(vi, 2) Song which is in the tomb of King Intef, the justified, in front of the singer with the harp.

He is happy, this good prince!
⌐Death is a kindly fate⌐.[4]
A generation passes,
Another stays,
Since the time of the ancestors.
The gods who were before rest in their tombs,
Blessed (5) nobles too are buried in their tombs.
(Yet) those who built tombs,
Their places are gone,
What has become of them?
I have heard the words of Imhotep and Hardedef,[5]
Whose sayings are recited whole.
What of their places?
Their walls have crumbled,
Their places are gone,
As though they had never been!
None comes from there,
To tell of their state,
To tell of their needs,
To calm our hearts,
Until we go where they have gone!

Hence rejoice in your heart!
Forgetfulness profits you,[6]
Follow your heart as long as you live!
(10) Put myrrh on your head,
Dress in fine linen,

Anoint yourself with oils fit for a god.[7]
Heap up your joys,
Let your heart not sink!
Follow your heart and your happiness,
Do your things on earth as your heart commands!
When there comes to you that day of mourning,
The Weary-hearted[8] hears not their mourning,
Wailing saves no man from the pit!

Refrain (vii, 2): Make holiday,
Do not weary of it!
Lo, none is allowed to take his goods with him,
Lo, none who departs comes back again!

NOTES

1. See Lüddeckens, *Totenklagen*, pp. 149-150; the passage is from a Saqqara tomb in Leiden (Holwerda-Boeser, *Beschreibung*, Vol. IV, pl. 15.)

2. Lüddeckens, *op. cit.*, p. 100: *wꜣḏ wy nn ḫpr n·f*, from Theban tomb no. 49.

3. Theban tomb no. 50; see Lichtheim, *JNES*, 4 (1945), 178 ff.

4. *Šꜣw nfr ḥḏy* has been variously interpreted. In *ibid.*, p. 192, I emended *ḥḏy* to *ḫpr* in accordance with the parallel introductory phrase in the first Harper's Song of the Tomb of Neferhotep. In *JNES* 5 (1946), 259, Federn proposed a different division of the sentences: *wꜣḏ pw sr pn/ nfr šꜣw/ nfr ḥḏy*, and rendered, "A happy one is this prince; good is the destiny; good is the injury." In *ANET*, p. 467, Wilson retained the earlier division and translated: "Prosperous is he, this good prince/ Even though good fortune may suffer harm." In addition, some have wanted to read *wḏ* rather than *wꜣḏ*. But *wꜣḏ* is strongly supported by the parallel phrases in the *Totenklagen*. The sentence *wꜣḏ wy nn ḫpr n·f* from Theban tomb no. 49 recurs in Theban tomb no. 106 in the form of a quotation (See Lüddeckens, *op. cit.*, pp. 100-101), thereby showing that it was the proper thing to say at a funeral.

I now attempt yet another rendering, in which *ḥḏy* is taken to be a noun denoting destruction, i.e., death, and *šꜣw nfr*, though undoubtedly a euphemism for death, is retained in its literal meaning, the whole being a nominal sentence without *pw*.

The new interpretation of the whole song which D. Lorton tried in *JARCE*, 7 (1968), 45 ff., is entirely mistaken.

5. The two famous sages of the Old Kingdom, who were worshiped as gods. An Instruction ascribed to Imhotep, the vizier of King Djoser, has not come to light.

6. Contrary to my earlier rendering I now divide *wḏꜣ·k ib·k rs/ mhꜣ ib ḥr sꜣḥ n·k*; for I have become convinced that any overlong and unbalanced sentence in a poetic text is the result of wrong division and mistranslation.

7. Literally, "with the genuine marvels that belong to a god."

8. The god Osiris.

A CYCLE OF HYMNS TO KING SESOSTRIS III

The six hymns are written on the recto of a single large sheet of papyrus which measures 114 × 30 cm and dates from the Middle Kingdom. Starting from the right side, the scribe wrote the first hymn in eleven vertical columns. Next to it, in the center of the page, he wrote the second and third hymns in horizontal lines. Hymns 4-6, also written horizontally, occupy the left side. The last two hymns have been reduced to fragments and are omitted here.

Hymns 2-4 have anaphoric patterns which the scribe underlined by stichic writing. He wrote the anaphoric phrase only once, at the beginning of each hymn, and indented all lines after the first by the length of the anaphora, thereby showing that the phrase was to be repeated. Each anaphoric sentence is followed by a complementary statement, and together they form a verse which is written as a single line, not divided into its two hemistichs, as we are accustomed to do. The hymns may have been sung on the occasion of the king's ceremonial visit to an Upper Egyptian town.

Publication: F. Ll. Griffith, *Hieratic Papyri from Kahun and Gurob* (London, 1898), pls. i-iii and pp. 1-3.   Möller, *Lesestücke*, I, pls. 4-5. Sethe, *Lesestücke*, pp. 65-67.

Translation and study: H. Grapow, "Liederkranz," *MIO*, I (1953), 189-209.

Translation: Erman, *Literature*, pp. 134-137.   H. Goedicke, *JARCE*, 7 (1968), 23-26.

Comments: Posener, *Littérature*, pp. 128-130.

I

(1) Horus: Divine of Form; the Two Ladies: Divine of Birth; Gold-Horus: Being; the King of Upper and Lower Egypt: *Khakaure*; the Son of Re: *Sesostris*—he has seized the Two Lands in triumph.

Hail to you, *Khakaure*, our Horus, Divine of Form!
Land's protector who widens its borders,
Who smites foreign countries with his crown.
Who holds the Two Lands in his arms' embrace,
[Who subdues foreign] lands by a motion of his hands.
Who slays Bowmen without a blow of the club,
Shoots the arrow (5) without drawing the string.
Whose terror strikes the Bowmen in their land,
Fear of whom smites the Nine Bows.
Whose slaughter brought death to thousands of Bowmen,
[Who had come] to invade his borders.
Who shoots the arrow as does Sakhmet,
When he felled thousands who ignored his might.
His majesty's tongue restrains Nubia,
His utterances make Asiatics flee.

Unique youth who fights for his frontiers,
Not letting his subjects weary themselves.
Who lets the people[1] (10) sleep till daylight,
The youths may slumber, his heart protects them.
Whose commands made his borders,
Whose words joined the Two Shores!

II

(1) How [the gods] rejoice:
   you have strengthened their offerings!
How your [⌜people⌝] rejoice:
   you have made their frontiers!
How your forbears rejoice:
   you have enriched their portions!
How Egypt rejoices in your strength:
   you have protected its customs!
(5) How the people rejoice in your guidance:
   your might has won increase [for them]!
How the Two Shores rejoice in your dreadedness:
   You have enlarged their holdings!
How the youths whom you levied rejoice:
   you have made them prosper!
How your elders rejoice:
   you have made them youthful!
How the Two Lands rejoice in your power:
   you have protected their walls!

⌜Chorus⌝:[2] Horus, extender of his borders, may you repeat eternity!

III

(1) How great is the lord of his city:
   he is Re[3], little are a thousand other men!
How great is the lord of his city:
   [4]he is a canal that restrains the river's flood water!
How great is the lord of his city:
   he is a cool room that lets a man sleep till dawn!
How great is the lord of his city:
   he is a walled rampart of copper of Sinai!
(5) How great is the lord of his city:
   he is a shelter whose hold does not fail!

How great is the lord of his city:
  he is a fort that shields the timid from his foe!
How great is the lord of his city:
  he is an overflowing shade, cool in summertime!
How great is the lord of his city:
  he is a warm corner, dry in wintertime!
How great is the lord of his city:
  he is a mountain that blocks the storm when the sky rages!
(10) How great is the lord of his city:
  he is Sakhmet to foes who tread on his frontier!

IV

(1) He came to us[5] to take the Southland:
  the Double-Crown was fastened to his head!
He came and gathered the Two Lands:
  he joined the Sedge to the Bee!
He came and ruled the Black Land:[6]
  he took the Red Land to himself!
He came and guarded the Two Lands:
  he gave peace to the Two Shores!
(5) He came and nourished the Black Land:
  he removed its needs!
He came and nourished the people:
  he gave breath to his subjects' throats!
He came and trampled foreign lands,
  he smote the Bowmen who ignored his terror!
He came and fought [on] his frontier:
  he rescued him who had been robbed!
He came and [⌈showed the power⌉] of his arms:
  glorying in what his might had brought!
(10) He came [to let us raise] our youths:
  inter our old ones [⌈by his will⌉].

NOTES

1. One of several terms denoting "the people," the word *p't* appears to have had the connotation "patricians, nobility," and is sometimes so rendered; but here and elsewhere I have preferred the translation, "people."
2. The meaning of the term *inyt* is unknown; it is guessed to mean "refrain," "tune,", or the like. It appears to be a direction addressed to the singers, similar to the term *mȝwt* in the *Intef Song*.

3. I have adopted Goedicke's suggestion (*loc. cit.*, p. 24) to read *r⁽ pw* instead of *w⁽ ḥḥ pw*. The second sentence I read as *nḏs pw kwy ḥꜣ n rmṯ*.

4. The non-enclitic particle *isw*, "lo," is written under the anaphora at the beginning of each line.

5. As Grapow observed, the anaphora consists only of the word *ty·n·f*, "he came," and the *n·n*, "to us," belongs only to the first verse. The repetition of the *n·n* in Sethe's *Lesestücke* is an error.

6. The contrast with "Red Land" makes it desirable to translate *kmt* as "Black Land," rather than the conventional "Egypt."

A HYMN TO THE RED CROWN

This hymn to the red crown of Lower Egypt comes from a cycle of ten hymns addressed to the crowns of Upper and Lower Egypt. The crowns are here not associated with a king but rather with the crocodile-god Sobk, the lord of the Fayyum town of Shedyt (Crocodilopolis). The papyrus, P. Golenischeff, dates from the Hyksos Period.

Each hymn is introduced by a phrase that identifies the crown. In this case the phrase is "Adoration of *Nt*," the word *nt* being one of several names designating the crown of Lower Egypt.

The god Sobk is addressed as "Sobk of Shedyt, Horus in Shedyt," that is to say, he is viewed as a manifestation of Horus, the god most closely identified with the kingship of Egypt. In the translation I have shortened the god's name to "Sobk-Horus of Shedyt."

Publication: A. Erman, *Hymnen an das Diadem der Pharaonen*, APAW, Phil.-hist. Kl. 1911, no. 1 (Berlin, 1911). The hymn here translated is no. f, pp. 46-47.

Two other hymns from this cycle are translated in Erman, *Literature*, pp. 11-12.

Adoration of *Net*:

Shining is *Net* upon you—Sobk-Horus of Shedyt,
    You are shielded!
Tall is *Net* upon you,
    You are shielded!
Coiled upon your brow,[1]
    You are shielded!
Slung about your temples,
    You are shielded!
All you gods of the South, North, West, East,
All Nine Gods who follow Sobk-Horus of Shedyt,
Let your *kas* rejoice over this king—Sobk-Horus of Shedyt,
As Isis rejoiced over her son Horus,
When he was a child in Chemmis.

Subscription: To be said four times.

NOTES

1. The words that I rendered as "coiled" and "slung" are in fact two nouns in the plural, ḥȝbwt and wȝbwt, which designate parts of the crown. The hymn is compactly and symmetrically phrased through parallelisms, repetitions, and assonances.

A HYMN TO OSIRIS AND A HYMN TO MIN

On the Stela of Sobk-iry
Louvre C 30

The recto of the stela is inscribed with a hymn to Osiris, the verso with a hymn to Min. Both are recited by the official Sobk-iry and are preceded by the prayer for offerings.

Hymns to Egyptian gods consist largely of enumerations of the gods' powers, attributes, and cult centers. And since Egyptian theology associated and equated the gods with one another, their hymns too were similar. Yet each god retained some distinctive traits that are reflected in the hymns. As to Osiris, his personality remained sharply etched, owing to the singular fate he had suffered: his death at the hands of Seth. Thus all hymns tc Osiris allude to some of the features of his myth.

This particular hymn to Osiris was very popular, as is shown by its numerous copies, embodying some variations, which occur on private stelae of the Middle and New Kingdoms.

As was pointed out by Grapow, the central portion of the hymn consists of twelve sentences which are grouped together by a particular stylistic device: a rising and descending pattern. The first six sentences begin with the words kmȝ, rdi, ʿȝ, nb, ʿȝ, nb, respectively, while the next six begin with the same words in reverse order: nb, ʿȝ, nb, ʿȝ, rdi, kmȝ. (In the translation these lines have been designated by marginal letters.) The device is interesting as a principle of organization. It has not been extended to the whole hymn, however, nor has it been preserved in the many variants of the hymn. Its value to us lies in its providing some evidence on the nature of Egyptian metrics. For it shows what constituted a metrical line in this text, and thus makes possible a metrical reading of the hymn as a whole which is not mere guesswork. As usual, the actual writing of the hymn on the stone surface utilizes the space in complete disregard of the poetic form. Thus the eighteen horizontal lines in which the text is written contain approximately thirty metrical lines.

In the brief hymn on the verso, the god Min is equated with Horus, an identification often made in the Middle Kingdom, which we have encountered in the text of the *Rock Stela of Mentuhotep IV*.

Publication: P. Pierret, *Recueil d'inscriptions inédites du musée égyptien du Louvre* (Paris, 1874-1878), II, 59-60.   A. Gayet, *Musée du Louvre: Stèles de la xiie dynastie*, Bibliothèque de l'École des Hautes Études, 68 (Paris, 1886), pls. xlvii and liii.   L. Speleers, *RT*, 39 (1921), 117-127. S. Hassan, *Hymnes religieux du moyen empire* (Cairo, 1930), pp. 5-84 (Osiris) 140-148 (Min).   Sethe, *Lesestücke*, pp. 64-65.

Variants of the Osiris Hymn: P. C. Smither and A. N. Dakin, *JEA*, 25 (1939), 157-159.   P. Munro, *ZÄS*, 85 (1960), 58-63.

Poetic form: H. Grapow, *ZÄS*, 79 (1954), 20-21.

Translation: Erman, *Literature*, pp. 137-138 (Min) and 145 (Osiris).

Recto: Hymn to Osiris

(1) Recitation. The Deputy-treasurer Sobk-iry, born of the lady Senu, the justified, says:

> Hail, Osiris, son of Nut!
> Two-horned, tall of crown,
> Given crown and joy before the Nine Gods.
> *a* Whose awe Atum set in the heart of men, gods, spirits, and dead,
> *b* Whom rulership was given in On;
> *c* Great of presence in Djedu,
> *d* Lord of fear in Two-Mounds;[1]
> *e* Great of terror in Rostau,[2]
> *f* Lord of awe in Hnes.
> *f* Lord of power in Tenent,[3]
> *e* Great of love upon earth;
> *d* Lord of fame in the palace,
> *c* Great of glory in Abydos;
> *b* Whom triumph was given before the assembled Nine Gods,
> *a* For whom slaughter was made in Herwer's great hall.
> Whom the great powers (10) fear,
> For whom the great rise from their mats;
> Fear of whom Shu has made,
> Awe of whom Tefnut fashioned,
> To whom the Two Assemblies come bowing down,[4]
> For great is fear of him,
> Strong is awe of him.
>
> Such is Osiris, king of gods,
> Great power of heaven,
> Ruler of the living,
> King of those beyond!
> Whom thousands bless (15) in Kher-aha,[5]
> Whom mankind extols in On;
> Who owns the choice cuts in Houses-on-High,[6]
> For whom sacrifice is made in Memphis.

> *The text of the stela of Sobk-iry ends here.*
> *Other variants of the hymn add:* ˏ

> For whom a night's feast is made in Sekhem.[7]
> Whom the gods, when they see him, worship,
> Whom the spirits, when they see him, adore,

Who is mourned by multitudes in This,[8]
Who is hailed by those below!

Verso: Hymn to Min

(1) Recitation. The Deputy-treasurer Sobk-iry, born of the lady
Senu, the justified, speaks as one clean and pure:

I worship Min, I extol arm-raising Horus:
Hail to you, Min in his procession!
Tall-plumed, son of Osiris,
Born of divine Isis.
Great in Senut, mighty in Ipu,[9]
You of Coptus, Horus (5) strong-armed,
Lord of awe who silences pride,
Sovereign of all the gods!
Fragrance laden when he comes from Medja-land,
Awe inspiring in Nubia,
You of Utent, hail and praise![10]

NOTES

1. Two-Mounds" is probably a place name, rather than a term for
Upper and Lower Egypt.
2. The necropolis of Giza.
3. Name of a sanctuary near Memphis.
4. The assembled sanctuaries of Upper and Lower Egypt.
5. A locality south of Heliopolis which in Ptolemaic times became
known as "Babylon."
6. Another place near Heliopolis.
7. Letopolis, on the west bank, opposite Heliopolis.
8. The hymn ends with a reference to the god's tomb and temple at
Abydos.
9. *Snwt* designated a sanctuary of Min situated in the ninth nome of
Upper Egypt, and *'Ipw* was a name for the nome-capital—Panopolis =
Akhmim. It was one of the two principal cult centers of Min, the other
being Coptus, the metropolis of the fifth nome.
10. Utent was a region to the south or southeast of Egypt which has
not been precisely localized. The words *i3 ḥsw*, hitherto left untranslated,
I take to be two words for "praise"; *i3* as short form of *i3w* is not uncommon.

THE HYMN TO HAPY

Hapy, the personified inundating Nile, aroused feelings of thankful
exuberance which inspired some fine poetry. Pyramid Text 581 speaks of
the "meadows laughing when the riverbanks are flooded," and the great
hymn before us has woven the reactions of the people to the annual
miracle of the inundation into a highly effective composition, which was
much admired by the Egyptians, as the numerous text copies attest, and
which we too can appreciate. The god Hapy did not have a regular temple-

cult. But there were festivals in his honor, at which hymns were undoubtedly sung. By its very length and complexity, however, the great hymn
gives the impression of being a specifically literary composition.

The work undoubtedly dates from the Middle Kingdom, but none of
the surviving manuscripts are older than the Eighteenth Dynasty. In the
New Kingdom, the hymn served as a classical text copied in schools.
Unfortunately, the aspiring scribes, sometimes writing from dictation or
from memory, produced copies incredibly garbled and corrupt. Only the
Eighteenth Dynasty manuscripts are reasonably good. But for the bulk
of the text we possess only Ramesside papyri and ostraca with their
abundance of errors.

The two complete copies, in P. Sallier II and P. Anastasi VII, are the
most corrupt. Better but fragmentary is P. Chester Beatty V. Good but
extant only in a few fragments is the copy of a papyrus in Turin which has
not yet been fully published. Portions of the text are preserved on numerous
ostraca. The most important of these is Ostr. Golenischeff, of the eighteenth
Dynasty, which contains slightly less than the first third of the hymn. The
large Ramesside ostracon ODM 1176, which gives a text similar to that
of P. Chester Beatty V, provides some useful readings. This translation
is based on a combination of Ostr. Golenischeff, P. Sallier II, P. Anastasi
VII, P. Chester Beatty V, ODM 1176, and the published fragments of
P. Turin. The line numbering is according to P. Sallier II.

Publication: Maspero, *Hymne au Nil* (= P. Sallier II, P. Anastasi VII,
Ostr. Golenischeff, and one fragment of P. Turin).   Gardiner, *Hieratic
Papyri*, pls. 23-24 (= P. Chester Beatty V).   H. Grapow, *ZÄS*, 52
(1914), 103-106 (= two fragments of P. Turin).   A. Hermann, *ZÄS*,
85 (1960), 35-42 (study of final portion according to P. Turin).   E.
Bacchi, *L'Inno al Nilo* (Turin, n.d.) (a composite text which integrates the
fragments of P. Turin but fails to identify them).   Posener, *Ostraca
hiératiques*, Vols. I-II (= ODM 1027, 1028, 1033, 1034, 1051, 1052, 1053,
and especially 1176 in Vol. II, pls. 27-31).   A list of the manuscripts
known till 1948 was given by Posener as *Annexe* III to Van de Walle,
Transmission.

Addendum: The new edition by W. Helck, *Der Text des "Nilhymnus"*
(Wiesbaden, 1972) came too late to be utilized.

Translation: Erman, *Literature*, pp. 146-149.   Roeder, *Kulte*,
pp. 332-339.   J. A. Wilson in *ANET*, pp. 372-373.

(xi, 6) Adoration of Hapy:
Hail to you, Hapy,
Sprung from earth,
Come to nourish Egypt!
Of secret ways,
A darkness by day,
To whom his followers sing!
Who floods the fields that Re has made,
To nourish all who thirst;
Lets drink the waterless desert,
His dew descending from the sky.

Friend of Geb, lord of Nepri,
Promoter of the arts of Ptah.
Lord of the fishes,
He makes fowl stream south,
No bird falling down from heat.
Maker of barley, creator of emmer,
He lets the temples celebrate.

When he is sluggish (xii, 1) noses clog,
Everyone is poor;
As the sacred loaves are pared,
A million perish among men.
When he plunders, the whole land rages,
Great and small roar;
People change according to his coming,
When Khnum has fashioned him.[1]
When he floods, earth rejoices,
Every belly jubilates,
Every jawbone takes on laughter,
Every tooth is bared.[2]

Food provider, bounty maker,
Who creates all that is good!
Lord of awe, sweetly fragrant,
Gracious when he comes.
Who makes herbage for the herds,
Gives (5) sacrifice for every god.
Dwelling in the netherworld,
He controls both sky and earth.
Conqueror of the Two Lands,
He fills the stores,
Makes bulge the barns,
Gives bounty to the poor.

Grower of all delightful trees—
He has no revenue;
Barges[3] exist by his might—
He is not hewn in stone.
Mountains cleave[4] by his surge—
One sees no workmen, no leader,
He carries off in secrecy.

No one knows the place he's in,
His cavern is not found in books.
He has no shrines, no portions,
No service of his choice;
But youths, his children, hail him,
One greets him like a king.
Lawful, timely, he comes forth,
Filling Egypt, South and North;
(xiii, 1) As one drinks, all eyes are on him,
Who makes his bounty overflow.

He who grieved goes out in joy,
Every heart rejoices;
Sobk, Neith's child, bares his teeth,
˹The Nine Gods exult˺.
As he spouts, makes drink the fields,
Everyone grows vigorous.
Rich because another toils,[5]
One has no quarrel with him;
Maker of food he's not defied,
One sets no limits for him.

Light-maker who comes from dark,
Fattener of herds,
Might that fashions all,
None can live without him.
People are clothed (5) with the flax of his fields,
For he made Hedj-hotep[6] serve him;
He made anointing with his unguents,
For he is the like of Ptah.
All kinds of crafts exist through him,
All books of godly words,
His produce from the sedges.[7]

Entering the cavern,
Coming out above,
He wants his coming secret.
If he is heavy,[8] the people dwindle,
A year's food supply is lost.
The rich man looks concerned,
Everyone is seen with weapons,

Friend does not attend to friend.
Cloth is wanting for one's clothes,
Noble children lack their finery;
There's no eye-paint to be had,[9]
No one is anointed.

This truth is fixed in people's hearts:
Want is followed by deceit.[10]
He who consorts with the sea,
Does not (xiv, 1) harvest grain.
Though one praises all the gods,
Birds will not come down to deserts.
No one beats his hand with gold,
No man can get drunk on silver,
One can not eat lapis lazuli,
Barley is foremost and strong!

Songs to the harp are made for you,
One sings to you with clapping hands;
The youths, your children hail you,
Crowds adorn themselves for you,
Who comes with riches, decks the land,
Makes flourish every body;
Sustains the pregnant woman's heart,
And loves a multitude of herds.

When he rises at the residence,
Men feast on the meadows' gifts,
(5) Decked with lotus for the nose,
And all the things that sprout from earth.
Children's hands are filled with herbs,
They forget to eat.
Good things are strewn about the houses,
The whole land leaps for joy.[11]

When you overflow, O Hapy,
Sacrifice is made for you;
Oxen are slaughtered for you,
A great oblation is made to you.
Fowl is fattened for you,
Desert game snared for you,
As one repays your bounty.

One offers to all the gods
Of that which Hapy has provided,
Choice incense, oxen, goats,
And birds in holocaust.

Mighty is Hapy in his cavern,[12]
His name unknown to those below,
For the gods do not reveal it.[13]
You people who extol the gods,
Respect the awe his son has made,
The All-Lord who sustains the shores!
    Oh joy when you come![14]
    Oh joy when you come, O Hapy,
    Oh joy when you come!
    You who feed men and herds
    With your meadow gifts!
    Oh joy when you come!
    Oh joy when you come, O Hapy,
    Oh joy when you come!

NOTES

1. Taking *ḳd·n sw Ḫnmw* as a temporal clause implies that Khnum creates a new Hapy each year.

2. In the *Wilson Festschrift*, pp. 66-68, I pointed out that the hymn describes the *three* modes of the inundation: the sluggish, insufficient rise, which brings hunger; the excessive flood, which brings destruction and turmoil; and the flood in right measure, which creates abundance and joy. What I there, in conformity with older translations, termed the "second and third stanzas" I have here unified into a single stanza. Only P. Chester Beatty V divides the hymn into stanzas; what remains of these dividing marks shows that the stanzas averaged ten to twelve sentences and clauses.

3. Though all copies write *imw*, "barges, boats," the reading is dubious.

4. Bacchi gives [*š*]*d·tw dww*; from P. Turin?

5. Reading *swsr wꜥ m irt·n ky*.

6. The weaver-god; this reading is preserved in P. Chester Beatty V and several ostraca.

7. The papyrus plant from which books were made.

8. I.e., if his rise is sluggish and insufficient.

9. In P. Sallier II and Anastasi VII the sentence is completely garbled, but P. Chester Beatty V and ODM 1176 have preserved *nn msdmt*, "there is no eye-paint."

10. Introduced as a "saying" by means of *m-dd*, this sentence may be added to our meager store of Egyptian proverbs. The text is that of P. Chester Beatty V and the literal rendering is "deceit after want." The sentences that follow are generalizations on the theme "man lives by bread."

11. Reading *p3 t3 r-3w ḥr ftft*, with ODM 1176.

12. Reading *Ḥ'py m tpḥt:f wsr*, with P. Chester Beatty V and ODM 1176. The version of Sallier and Anastasi, "Hapy has made his cavern at Thebes," makes poor sense, after it has been said that the location of his cavern is unknown.

13. Reading *nn pr ntrw ḥr:f*, with P. Turin *apud* Grapow, *loc. cit.*, p. 104. Note the idiomatic *pri ḥr*, "to come out with," for "to reveal."

14. As was pointed out by Hermann in *ZÄS*, 85 (1960), 35 ff., this concluding song is correctly preserved only in P. Turin and reads *w3ḏ k3 iw·k, w3ḏ k3 iw·k Ḥ'py*, etc., which all other manuscripts have corrupted to *w3ḏ k3 pw*.

V. Prose Tales

Perhaps more than any other genre of Egyptian literature, these few surviving prose tales speak to the modern reader, for they are creations of the universal storytelling impulse, and of an imagination that roamed and played upon experience, unfettered by the functional orientation of most Egyptian literary works. It would be a mistake, however, to think of these tales as being folklore, as being simply and artlessly told. Like all Egyptian writings, the tales come from the sphere of the educated scribes and from the ambience of the court. It is true that the style of the *Shipwrecked Sailor* is considerably simpler than that of *Sinuhe*. It is nevertheless written in a literary style that is quite distinct from the colloquial language one finds in the private letters.

The *Tale of the Shipwrecked Sailor*, and the *Tales from Papyrus Westcar* share the quality of fairy tales. They are tales of wonder, of miraculous events in which human beings encounter the supernatural. The *Story of Sinuhe*, on the other hand, is the story of a life as it could have been lived. In fact it may be a true story. It is told in the form of the autobiography composed for the tomb, and at least one scholar has voiced the hope that the original tomb-text may yet be found. Whether or not it relates the actual experience of an individual, the story reflects a true historical situation—the death of Amenemhet I and the reign of Sesostris I. But to the Egyptians it was above all a tale magnificently told, which, using all the modes of a rich and refined literary art, created a character whose actions, sorrows, and joys enthralled the listeners. It became a classic, endlessly recopied, and it can still fascinate today.

THE TALE OF THE SHIPWRECKED SAILOR

The only preserved papyrus copy of the tale was discovered by Golenischeff in the Imperial Museum of St. Petersburg. Nothing is known about its original provenience. The papyrus, called P. Leningrad 1115, is now in Moscow. The work, and the papyrus copy, date from the Middle Kingdom.

The tale is set in a narrative frame. A high official is returning from an expedition that apparently failed in its objective, for he is despondent and fearful of the reception awaiting him at court. One of his attendants exhorts him to take courage, and as an example of how a disaster may turn into a success, tells him a marvelous adventure that happened to him years ago. At the end of his tale, however, the official is still despondent.

Publication: W. Golenischeff, *Papyrus hiératiques*, pls. 1-8.   A. Erman, *ZÄS*, 43 (1906), 1-26.   W. Golenischeff, *Le conte du naufragé*, Bibliothèque d'étude, 2 (Cairo, 1912).   A. M. Blackman, *Middle Egyptian Stories*, Bibliotheca Aegyptiaca, II (Brussels, 1932), pp. 41-48.

Translation: Erman, *Literature*, pp. 29-35.   Lefebvre, *Romans*, pp. 29-40.   Brunner-Traut, *Märchen*, pp. 5-10. For additional references see Lefebvre, *op. cit.*, p. 32.

(1) The worthy attendant said: Take heart, my lord! We have reached home. The mallet has been seized, the mooring-post staked, the prow-rope placed (5) on land. Praise is given, god is thanked, everyone embraces his fellow. Our crew has returned safely; our troops have had no loss. We have left Wawat behind, we have passed (10) Senmut; we have returned in safety, we have reached our land. Now listen to me, my lord! I am not exaggerating. Wash yourself, pour water over your fingers. You must answer (15) when questioned. You must speak to the king with presence of mind. You must answer without stammering! A man's mouth can save him. His speech makes one forgive him. (20) But do as you like! It is tiresome to talk to you.

But I shall tell you something like it that happened to me. I had set out to the king's mines, and had gone (25) to sea in a ship of a hundred and twenty cubits in length and forty cubits in width. One hundred and twenty sailors were in it of the pick of Egypt. Looked they at sky, looked they at land, their hearts were stouter (30) than lions. They could foretell a storm before it came, a tempest before it broke.

A storm came up while we were at sea, before we could reach land. As we sailed (35) it made a ⌈swell⌉, and in it a wave eight cubits tall. The mast—it (the wave) struck (it).[1] Then the ship died. Of those in it not one remained. I was cast (40) on an island by a wave of the sea. I spent three days alone, with my heart as companion. Lying in the shelter of trees I hugged (45) the shade.

Then I stretched my legs to discover what I might put in my mouth. I found figs and grapes there, all sorts of fine vegetables, sycamore figs, unnotched and notched,[2] (50) and cucumbers that were as if tended. Fish were there and fowl; there is nothing that was not there. I stuffed myself and put some down, because I had too much in my arms. Then I cut a fire drill, (55) made a fire and gave a burnt offering to the gods.

Then I heard a thundering noise and thought, "It is a wave of the sea." Trees splintered, (60) the ground trembled. Uncovering my face, I found it was a snake that was coming. He was of thirty cubits; his beard was over two cubits long. His body was overlaid (65) with gold; his eyebrows were of real lapis lazuli. He was bent up in front.

Then he opened his mouth to me, while I was on my belly before him. He said to me: "Who brought you, who brought you, fellow, (70) who brought you? If you delay telling me who brought you to this island, I shall make you find yourself reduced to ashes, becoming like a thing unseen." ⟨I said⟩: "Though you speak to me, I do not hear (75) it; I am before you without knowing myself." Then he took me in his mouth, carried me to the place where he lived, and set me down unhurt, (80) I being whole with nothing taken from me.

Then he opened his mouth to me, while I was on my belly before him. He said to me: "Who brought you, who brought you, fellow, who brought you to this island (85) of the sea, whose two sides are in water?" Then I answered him, my arms bent before him. I said to him: "I had set out (90) to the mines on a mission of the king in a ship of a hundred and twenty cubits in length and forty cubits in width. One hundred and twenty sailors were in it of the pick of Egypt. (95) Looked they at sky, looked they at land, their hearts were stouter than lions. They could foretell a storm before it came, a tempest before it struck. Each of them—his heart was stouter, (100) his arm stronger than his mate's. There was no fool among them. A storm came up while we were at sea, before we could reach land. As we sailed it made a ⌈swell⌉, and in it a wave (105) eight cubits tall. The mast—it struck (it). Then the ship died. Of those in it not one remained, except myself who is here with you. I was brought to this island (110) by a wave of the sea."

Then he said to me: "Don't be afraid, don't be afraid, fellow; don't be pale-faced, now that you have come to me. It is god who has let you live and brought you to this island of the ka.[3] (115) There is nothing that is not in it; it is full of all good things. You shall pass month upon month until you have completed four months in this island. Then (120) a ship will come from home with sailors in it whom you know. You shall go home with them, you shall die in your town.

"How happy is he who tells what he has tasted,[4] when the calamity has passed. (125) I shall tell you something similar that happened on this island. I was here with my brothers and there were children with them. In all we were seventy-five serpents, children and brothers, without mentioning a little daughter whom I had obtained through prayer. Then a star (130) fell, and they went up in flames through it. It so happened that I was not with them in the fire, I was not among them. I could have died for their sake when I found them as one heap of corpses.

"If you are brave and control your heart, you shall embrace your children, you shall kiss your wife, you shall see your home. It is better than everything else. (135) You shall reach home, you shall be there among your brothers."

Stretched out on my belly I touched the ground before him;then I said to him: "I shall speak of your power to the king, I shall let him know (140) of your greatness. I shall send you *ibi* and *ḥknw* oils, laudanum, *ḥsyt*-spice, and the incense of the temples which pleases all the gods. I shall tell what happened to me, what I saw of your power. One will praise god for you in the city before the councillors of the whole land. I shall slaughter (145) oxen for you as burnt offering; I shall sacrifice geese to you. I shall send you ships loaded with all the treasures of Egypt, as is done for a god who befriends people in a distant land not known to the people."

Then he laughed at me for the things I had said, which seemed foolish to him. (150) He said to me: "You are not rich in myrrh and all kinds of incense. But I am the lord of Punt, and myrrh is my very own. That *ḥknw*-oil you spoke of sending, it abounds on this island. Moreover, when you have left this place, you will not see this island again; it will have become water."

Then the ship (155) came, as he had foretold. I went and placed myself on a tall tree, I recognized those that were in it. When I went to report it, I found that he knew it. He said to me: "In health, in health, fellow, to your home, that you may see your children! Make me a good name in your town; that is what I ask (160) of you." I put myself on my belly, my arms bent before him. Then he gave me a load of myrrh, *ḥknw*-oil, laudanum, *ḥsyt*-spice, *tišpss*-spice, perfume, eye-paint, giraffe's tails, great lumps of incense, (165) elephant's tusks, greyhounds, long-tailed monkeys, baboons, and all kinds of precious things.

I loaded them on the ship. Then I put myself on my belly to thank him and he said to me: "You will reach home in two months. You will embrace your children. You will flourish at home, you will be buried."[5]

I went down to the shore (170) near the ship; I hailed the crew which was in the ship. I gave praise on the shore to the lord of the island, those in the ship did the same. We sailed north to the king's residence. We reached the residence in two months, all as he had said. I went in to the king; (175) I presented to him the gifts I had brought from the island. He praised god for me in the presence of the councillors of the whole land. I was made an attendant and endowed with serfs of his.

See me after (180) I had reached land, after I saw what I had tasted! Listen to me! It is good for people to listen.

He said to me: "Don't make an effort, my friend. Who would give water at dawn (185) to a goose that will be slaughtered in the morning ?"

Colophon: It is done from beginning to end as it was found in writing, by the scribe with skilled fingers, Imenaa, son of Imeny—life, prosperity, health!

NOTES

1. The sentence has been read as: *in ḥt ḥw n·i s(t)*, and rendered as "the mast (or, a piece of wood) struck the wave for me," thereby flattening it and thus helping the sailor, while the ship nevertheless sank. But the sense is poor, for the context leads one to expect that the wave hit the ship and sank it. I believe that the element *ni* is not the preposition with suffix but rather the common graphic peculiarity of the spelling of *ḥwi*, "to strike," and also of *ḥwi*, "to flood," with an intrusive *ni* (see *Wb.*, III, 49). I also take the *s* to be the suffix referring to the wave; and the dependent pronoun *sw* needs to be added as the object. This admittedly imperfect solution is presented largely in order to emphasize that the passage remains problematic.

2. I.e., unripe and ripe figs; the ripe ones were notched, as was explained by L. Keimer, *Acta Or.*, 6 (1928), 288 ff., and *idem, BIFAO*, 28 (1928), 50 ff.

3. The expression "island of the *ka*" is curious. In *ZÄS*, 45 (1908), 65, Gardiner rendered it as "phantom island."

4. Egyptian says "to taste" for "to experience."

5. This has been the usual rendering of *rnpy·k m ḥnw ḳrst·k*, in which *ḥnw* was taken to mean "home," as it does elsewhere in the tale, and *ḳrst·k* to stand for *ḳrs·tw·k*. Brunner-Traut, *Märchen*, p. 9, now renders: "und wirst dich in deinem Grabe verjüngen." This is grammatically perfect, but I find the older rendering more plausible, since the emphasis of the tale is on the "return home."

THREE TALES OF WONDER

From Papyrus Westcar (= P. Berlin 3033)

This important papyrus, the beginning of which is lost, contains a series of tales woven together by a narrative frame. The whole cycle consisted of at least five tales. Of the first, only the last words are preserved. The second has large lacunae, while the third, fourth, and fifth are complete except for the abrupt ending of the fifth tale. The three complete tales are translated here. The works are written in classical Middle Egyptian; the papyrus dates from the Hyksos period.

The setting of the tales is the Old Kingdom, specifically the time of the Fourth Dynasty: King Khufu is being entertained by his sons. First each son in turn tells a marvelous event that happened in the past. Then, when it is the turn of Prince Hardedef, instead of telling a story of past wonders, he asks permission to introduce a living magician. When the magician is brought to the court, he impresses everyone by his wonders, and, in conversation with the king, proceeds to prophecy the wondrous birth of the kings who were to found the next dynasty. This shift of focus from the present to the future provides the transition to the last tale, which describes the wondrous birth of the triplets who were to be the first three kings of the Fifth Dynasty.

Publication: Erman, *Papyrus Westcar.*   Sethe, *Lesestücke*, pp. 26-36. *Idem, Erl.*, pp. 32-45.

Translation: Erman, *Literature*, pp. 36-47.   Lefebvre, *Romans*, pp. 70-90.   Schott, *Liebeslieder*, pp. 176-187.   Brunner-Traut, *Märchen*, pp. 11-24.   For additional references see Lefebvre, *op. cit.*, p. 73. The third tale begins on p. 4, line 17 of the papyrus.

The Boating Party

(4, 17) Baufre stood up to speak, he said: "I shall let your majesty hear a wonder that happened in the time of your father Snefru, the justified, a deed of the chief lector-priest (20) Djadja-em-ankh, [a thing] that illuminates the past —————— which had never happened before ——————.

["One day King Snefru wandered through all the rooms] of the palace in search of [relaxation and found none. Then he said]: 'Go, bring me the chief lector-priest, the scribe of books, Djadja-em-ankh!' He was brought to him straightway. His majesty said to him: ['I have gone through all the rooms] of the palace in search of (5, 1) relaxation and found none.' Djadja-em-ankh said to him: 'May your majesty proceed to the lake of the palace. Fill a boat with all the beautiful girls of your palace. Your majesty's heart will be refreshed by seeing them row, a rowing up and down. (5) As you observe the fine nesting places of your lake, as you observe its beautiful fields and shores, your heart will be refreshed by it.'

"Said his majesty: 'Indeed, I shall go boating! Let there be brought to me twenty oars of ebony plated with gold, their handles of sandal-wood plated with electrum. Let there be brought to me twenty women (10) with the shapeliest bodies, breasts, and braids, who have not yet given birth. Also let there be brought to me twenty nets and give these nets to these women in place of their clothes!'[1] All was done as his majesty commanded.

"They rowed up and down, and his majesty's heart was happy (15) seeing them row. Then the one who was at the stroke oar fingered her braids, and a pendant of new turquoise fell into the water. Then she stopped rowing, and her side of women stopped rowing. Said his majesty: 'Why don't you row?' Said they: 'Our leader (20) has stopped

rowing.' Said his majesty to her: 'Why have you stopped rowing?'
Said she: 'Because the pendant of new turquoise fell into the water.'
[Then his majesty said to her: 'Row! I shall replace it for you!']
Said she: 'I prefer my thing to one like it.' Said [his majesty: 'Go,
bring me the chief] lector-priest [Djadja-em-ankh!' He was brought
to him straightway].

   "Said (6, 1) his majesty: 'Djadja-em-ankh, my brother, I did as
you had said. My majesty's heart was refreshed seeing them row.
Then a pendant of new turquoise of one of the leaders fell into the
water. She stopped rowing and thereby spoiled her side. I said to her:
(5) "Why have you stopped rowing?" She said to me: "Because the
pendant of new turquoise fell into the water." I said to her: "Row!
I shall replace it for you!" She said to me: "I prefer my thing to one
like it." '

   "Then the chief lector-priest Djadja-em-ankh said his say of magic.
He placed one side of the lake's water upon the other; and he found the
pendant (10) lying on a shard. He brought it and gave it to its owner.
Now the water that had been twelve cubits deep across[2] had become
twenty four cubits when it was turned back. Then he said his say of
magic and returned the waters of the lake to their place. His majesty
spent the day feasting with the entire palace. Then he rewarded the
chief lector-priest (15) Djadja-emankh with all good things.

   "This is the wonder that happened in the time of your father, King
Snefru, the justified, the deed of the chief lector-priest and scribe of
books, Djadja-em-ankh."

   Said the majesty of King Khufu: "Let there be given an offering
of a thousand loaves, a hundred jars of beer, an ox, and two measures
of incense to the majesty of King Snefru, the justified. (20) And let
there be given one loaf, one jug of beer, and one measure of incense
to the chief lector-priest and scribe of books, Djadja-em-ankh, for I
have seen his display of skill." One did according to his majesty's
command.

The Magician Djedi

Now Prince Hardedef[3] stood up to speak and said: ["So far you have
heard examples] of the skills of those who have passed away, and one
cannot tell truth from falsehood. [But there is a subject] of your
majesty in your own time, (25) unknown to you [who is a great magician."] Said his majesty: "What is this about, Har[dedef, my son?"]
[Said Prince Har]dedef: "There is a man (7, 1) named Djedi who lives

in Djed-Snefru. He is a man of a hundred and ten years who eats five hundred loaves of bread, half an ox for meat, and drinks one hundred jugs of beer to this very day. He can join a severed head. He can make a lion (5) walk behind him, its leash on the ground. And he knows the number of the secret chambers of the sanctuary of Thoth."

Now the majesty of King Khufu had been spending time searching for the secret chambers of the sanctuary of Thoth in order to copy them for his temple. Said his majesty: "You yourself, Hardedef, my son, shall bring him to me!"

Ships were made ready for Prince Hardedef. He journeyed (10) upstream to Djed-Snefru. After the ships had been moored to the shore, he traveled overland seated in a carrying chair of ebony, the poles of which were of *ssndm*-wood plated with gold.

Now when he had reached Djedi, the carrying chair was set down. Having got up to greet him, he found (15) him lying on a mat in the courtyard of his house, with a servant beside him anointing him and another rubbing his feet. Said Prince Hardedef: "Your condition is like that of one who lives above age—for old age is the time for death, enwrapping, and burial—one who sleeps till daytime free of illness, without a hacking cough. Thus greetings (20) to a venerable one! I have come here to summon you, commissioned by my father Khufu. You shall eat the delicacies that the king gives, the food of those who are in his service. He will convey you in good time to your fathers who are in the necropolis."

Said this Djedi: "In peace, in peace, Hardedef, king's son, beloved of his father! May your father, King Khufu, praise you. May he advance (25) you to rank among the elders. May your *ka* prevail over your enemy. May your *ba* know the way that leads to the portal that conceals the dead. Thus greetings (8, 1) to a prince!"

Then Prince Hardedef held out his hands to him and helped him up. He proceeded with him to the shore, holding his arm. Then Djedi said: "Let me have a barge to bring me my children and my books." Then two vessels and their crews were put in his service. Djedi journeyed (5) downstream in the ship in which Prince Hardedef was.

After he had reached the residence, Prince Hardedef entered in to report to the majesty of King Khufu. Said Prince Hardedef: "O king, my lord, I have brought Djedi." Said his majesty: "Go, bring him to me!" His majesty proceeded to the great hall of the (10) palace. When Djedi had been ushered in to him, his majesty said: "How is it, Djedi, that I never got to see you?" Said Djedi: "He who is summoned comes, O king, my lord. I was summoned, and I have come."

His majesty said: "Is it true, what they say, that you can join a severed head?" Said Djedi: "Yes, I can, O king, my lord." (15) Said his majesty: "Have brought to me a prisoner from the prison, that he be executed." Said Djedi: "But not to a human being, O king, my lord! Surely, it is not permitted to do such a thing to the noble cattle!"[4]

A goose was brought him and its head cut off. The goose was placed on the west side of the great hall, its head on the east (20) side of the great hall. Djedi said his say of magic: the goose stood up and waddled, its head also. When one had reached the other, the goose stood cackling. He had a "long-leg"-bird brought him, and the same was done to it. His majesty had an ox brought to him, (25) and its head was cut off. Djedi said his say of magic, and the ox stood up. ------[5]

(9, 1) Then the majesty of King Khufu said: "It was also said that you know the number of the secret chambers of the sanctuary of Thoth." Said Djedi: "Please, I do not know their number, O king, my lord. But I know the place where it is." Said his majesty: "Where is that?" Said this Djedi: "There is a chest (5) of flint in the building called 'Inventory' in On. It is in that chest." Said his majesty: ["Go, bring it to me!"] Said Djedi: "O king, my lord, it is not I who shall bring it to you." Said his majesty: "Who then will bring it to me?" Said Djedi: "It is the eldest of the three children who are in the womb of Ruddedet who will bring it to you." Said his majesty: "I want it; but say: who is this Ruddedet?" Said Djedi: "She is the wife of a priest of Re, lord of Sakhbu, (10) who is pregnant with three children of Re, lord of Sakhbu.[6] He has said concerning them that they will assume this beneficent office in this whole land, and the eldest of them will be high priest in On."

His majesty's heart grew sad at this. Said Djedi: "What is this mood, O king, my lord? Is it because of those three children? I say: first your son, then his son, then one of them." Said his majesty: (15) "When will Ruddedet give birth?" [Said Djedi]: "She will give birth on the fifteenth day of the first winter month." Said his majesty: "Just when the sandbanks of the Two-Fish Channel are dry! I would have crossed over myself, so as to see the temple of Re, lord of Sakhbu." Said Djedi: "Then I shall make four cubits of water over the sandbanks of the Two-Fish Channel."

His majesty went into his palace. His majesty said: "Let Djedi be assigned to the house of Prince Hardedef, to live (20) with him. Make his rations a thousand loaves of bread, a hundred jugs of beer, one ox, and a hundred bundles of vegetables." One did all that his majesty commanded.

The Birth of the Royal Children

On one of those days Ruddedet felt the pangs and her labor was difficult. Then said the majesty of Re, lord of Sakhbu, to Isis, Nephthys, Meskhenet, Heket, and Khnum: "Please go, deliver Ruddedet of the three children who are in her womb, who will assume (25) this beneficent office in this whole land. They will build your temples. They will supply your altars. They will furnish your libations. They will make your offerings abundant!"

These gods set out, having changed their appearance (10, 1) to dancing girls, with Khnum as their porter. When they reached the house of Rawoser, they found him standing with his loincloth upside down. They held out to him their necklaces and sistra. He said to them: "My ladies, look, it is the woman who is in pain; her labor is difficult." They said: (5) "Let us see her. We understand childbirth." He said to them: "Come in!" They went in to Ruddedet. They locked the room behind themselves and her.

Isis placed herself before her, Nephthys behind her, Heket hastened the birth. Isis said: "Don't be so mighty in her womb, you whose name is 'Mighty.'[7] The child (10) slid into her arms, a child of one cubit, strong boned, his limbs overlaid with gold, his headdress of true lapis lazuli. They washed him, having cut his navel cord, and laid him on a pillow of cloth. Then Meskhenet approached him and said: "A king who will assume the kingship in this whole land." And Khnum gave health to his body.

Isis placed herself before (15) her, Nephthys behind her, Heket hastened the birth. Isis said: "Don't tread in her womb, you whose name is 'Tread-of-Re'!" The child slid into her arms, a child of one cubit, strong boned, his limbs overlaid with gold, his headdress of true lapis lazuli. They washed him, having cut his navel cord, and laid him on (20) a pillow of cloth. Then Meskhenet approached him and said: "A king who will assume the kingship in this whole land." And Khnum gave health to his body.

Isis placed herself before her, Nephthys behind her, Heket hastened the birth. Isis said: "Don't be so dark in her womb, you whose name is 'Dark'!" The child slid into (25) her arms, a child of one cubit, strong boned, his limbs overlaid with gold, his headdress of true lapis lazuli. They washed him, having cut his navel cord, and laid him on a pillow of cloth. Then Meskhenet approached him (11, 1) and said: "A king who will assume the kingship in the whole land." And Khnum gave health to his body.

These gods came out, having delivered Ruddedet of the three children. (5) They said: "Rejoice, Rawoser! Three children are born to you." He said to them: "My ladies, what can I do for you? Please give this sack of barley to your porter and take it as payment for beer." Then Khnum loaded himself with the sack of barley. They proceeded toward the place (10) they had come from. Then Isis said to these gods: "What is it we came for if not to do wonders for those three children, to report to their father who made us come?" So they made three royal crowns and placed them in the sack of barley. Then they let a sky of storm and rain come up (15) and they returned to the house. They said: "Please put the sack of barley here in a sealed room, until we come back from dancing in the north." Then they put the sack of barley in a sealed room.

Ruddedet cleansed herself in a cleansing of fourteen days. She said to her maid: "Has the house (20) been made ready?" She said: "It is ready with everything good except beer jugs. They were not brought." Said Ruddedet: "Why have the beer jugs not been brought?" Said the maid: "There is nothing here for making (it) except the sack of barley of those dancers, which is in the room under their seal." Said Ruddedet: (25) "Go down, bring some of it. Rawoser shall give them its equivalent when he comes." The maid went, (12, 1) opened the room, and heard the sound of singing, music, dancing, and shouting—all that is done for a king—in the room. She went and told all that she had heard to Ruddedet. She then went around in the room without finding the spot in which it was done. Then she laid her cheek against the sack of barley and found it was done inside it. Then she put it (5) in a box, placed it in another container, bound it with a leather strap, placed it in a room containing her belongings, and locked it up. When Rawoser came, returning from the field, Ruddedet told him the matter. Then his heart was happy beyond everything, and they sat down to a day of feasting.

Now after days had passed, Ruddedet had a quarrel with her maid, (10) and had her punished with a beating. Then the maid said to the people in the house: "How could she do this? She has born three kings! I will go tell it to the majesty of King Khufu!" She went and found her older half-brother binding bundles of flax on the threshing floor. He said to her: "Whereto, little girl?" (15) Then she told him the matter. Her brother then said to her: "Is this a thing to do, to come to me, so as to involve me in your tattle?" He tore off a strand of flax and dealt her a bad blow. Off went the maid to draw a bucket of water, and a crocodile snatched her.

Now her brother went to tell it to Ruddedet. (20) He found Ruddedet sitting, her head on her knee, her heart sore beyond anything. He said to her: "My lady, why is your heart thus?" She said: "It is the little girl who grew up in the house. Just now she went off saying, 'I will go tell.' " Then he hung his head and said: "My lady, she did in fact come to tell me about it. (25) As she stood beside me I dealt her a bad blow. She went off to draw a little water, and a crocodile snatched her. ------

NOTES

1. These were nets made of pearls which ladies liked to wear over their dresses. Here they are to be worn in place of dresses. On these pearl-nets see E. Staehelin, *Untersuchungen zur ägyptischen Tracht im alten Reich*, Münchner ägyptologische Studien, 8 (Berlin, 1966), p. 169.

2. The expression *ḥr ỉst·f*, "on its back," has been rendered as "in its middle." I translate it as "across," and mean to show elsewhere that this is its true meaning.

3. Prince Hardedef is of course the famous sage and author of an Instruction. In P. Westcar and in the *Intef Song* the name is written as Hardedef, rather than Hardjedef. The actual reading may have been Djedef-Hor. It is an open question how names of this type are to be read; there are good arguments for either reading.

4. The "noble cattle" is mankind. See the hymn to the creator in the *Instruction to Merikare*, line 131.

5. The sentence "his leash trailing on the ground," which follows here, probably belonged to the demonstration of taming a lion which the scribe of P. Westcar omitted.

6. The location of the town of Sakhbu was discussed by S. Sauneron in *Kemi*, 11 (1950), 63-72; see *Merikare*, n. 10.

7. The triplets whom the goddesses deliver are the kings Userkaf, Sahure, and Neferirkare, the first three kings of the Fifth Dynasty. The words that Isis addresses to them are wordplays on their names.

THE STORY OF SINUHE

The numerous, if fragmentary, copies of this work testify to its great popularity, and it is justly considered the most accomplished piece of Middle Kingdom prose literature.

The two principal manuscripts are: (1) P. Berlin 3022 (abbr. B) which dates from the Twelfth Dynasty. In its present state, it lacks the beginning of the story and contains a total of 311 lines; (2) P. Berlin 10499 (abbr. R) which contains 203 lines and includes the beginning. It dates to the end of the Middle Kingdom.

A third major copy is on a large ostracon in the Ashmolean Museum, Oxford, which gives 130, partly incomplete, lines. It is, however, an inferior copy, dating to the Nineteenth Dynasty. Its principal value lies in the detailed commentary of its editor, J. Barns. In addition, small portions of the text are preserved on papyrus fragments and on numerous ostraca.

The present translation uses as principal manuscripts the text of R for the beginning and of B for the bulk, and incorporates an occasional variant from other manuscripts.

The list of publications, translations, and studies given below, while ample, is not comprehensive.

Publication: A. H. Gardiner, *Die Erzählung des Sinuhe und die Hirtengeschichte*, in A. Erman, *Literarische Texte des mittleren Reiches*, Hieratische Papyrus aus den königlichen Museen zu Berlin, Bd. V/2 (Leipzig, 1909). A. M. Blackman, *The Story of Sinuhe*, Bibliotheca Aegyptiaca, II (Brussels, 1932), pp. 1-41. J. W. B. Barns, *The Ashmolean Ostracon of Sinuhe* (London, 1952). Sethe, *Lesestücke*, pp. 3-17 (abridged). *Idem, Erl.*, pp. 5-21.

Translation with commentary: A. H. Gardiner, *Notes on the Story of Sinuhe* (Paris, 1916) (an expansion of Gardiner's articles in *RT*, Vols. 32-34, 36). H. Grapow, *Der stilistische Bau der Geschichte des Sinuhe*, Untersuchungen zur ägyptischen Stilistik, I (Berlin, 1952).

Translation: Erman, *Literature*, pp. 14-29. Lefebvre, *Romans*, pp. 1-25. J. A. Wilson in *ANET*, pp. 18-22 (abridged). E. Edel in *Textbuch zur Geschichte Israels*, ed. K. Galling, 2. Aufl. (Tübingen, 1968), pp. 1-12 (slightly abridged).

Analysis and evaluation: Posener, *Littérature*, pp. 87-115.

Comments (selection): A. Alt, *ZÄS*, 58 (1923), 48-50. *Idem, PJ*, 37 (1941), 19 ff. A. M. Blackman, *JEA*, 16 (1930), 63-65. *Idem, JEA*, 22 (1936), 35-40. A. de Buck, *Griffith Studies*, pp. 57-60. J. Clère, *JEA*, 25 (1939), 16-29. *Idem, Mélanges Dussaud*, II, 829 ff. H. Brunner, *ZÄS* 80 (1955), 5-11. *Idem, ZÄS*, 91 (1964), 139-140. H. Goedicke, *JEA*, 43 (1957), 77-85. *Idem, JEA*, 51 (1965), 29-47. J. Yoyotte, *Kemi*, 17 (1964), 69-73. G. Lanczkowski, *MDIK*, 16 (1958), 214-218. J. W. B. Barns, *JEA*, 53 (1967), 6-14. W. Westendorf, *Schott Festschrift*, pp. 125-131.

(R, 1) The Prince, Count, Governor of the domains of the sovereign in the lands of the Asiatics, true and beloved Friend of the King, the Attendant Sinuhe, says:

I was an attendant who attended his lord, a servant of the royal harem, waiting on the Princess, the highly praised Royal Wife of King Sesostris in Khenemsut, the daughter of King Amenemhet in Kanefru, Nefru, the revered.[1]

Year 30, third month of the inundation, day 7: the god ascended to his horizon. The King of Upper and Lower Egypt, *Sehetepibre*, flew to heaven and united with the sun-disk, the divine body merging with its maker. Then the residence was hushed; hearts grieved;

the great portals were shut; (10) the courtiers were head-on-knee; the people moaned.

His majesty, however, had despatched an army to the land of the Tjemeh, with his eldest son as its commander, the good god Sesostris. He had been sent to smite the foreign lands and to punish those of Tjehenu.[2] (15) Now he was returning, bringing captives of the Tjehenu and cattle of all kinds beyond number. The officials of the palace sent to the western border to let the king's son know the event that had occurred at the court. The messengers met him on the road, (20) reaching him at night. Not a moment did he delay. The falcon flew with his attendants, without letting his army know it.

But the royal sons who had been with him on this expedition had also been sent for. (B, 1) One of them was summoned while I was standing (there). I heard his voice, as he spoke, while I was in the near distance. My heart fluttered, my arms spread out, a trembling befell all my limbs. I removed myself in leaps, to seek a hiding place. I put (5) myself between two bushes, so as to leave the road to its traveler.

I set out southward. I did not plan to go to the residence. I believed there would be turmoil and did not expect to survive it. I crossed Maaty near Sycamore; I reached Isle-of-Snefru.[3] I spent the day there at the edge (10) of the cultivation. Departing at dawn I encountered a man who stood on the road. He saluted me while I was afraid of him. At dinner time I reached "Cattle-Quay." I crossed in a barge without a rudder, by the force of the westwind. I passed to the east of the quarry, (15) at the height of "Mistress of the Red Mountain." Then I made my way northward. I reached the "Walls of the Ruler," which were made to repel the Asiatics and to crush the Sand-farers. I crouched in a bush for fear of being seen by the guard on duty upon the wall.

I set out (20) at night. At dawn I reached Peten. I halted at "Isle-of-Kem-Wer." An attack of thirst overtook me; I was parched, my throat burned. I said, "This is the taste of death." I raised my heart and collected myself when I heard the lowing sound of cattle (25) and saw Asiatics. One of their leaders, who had been in Egypt, recognized me. He gave me water and boiled milk for me. I went with him to his tribe. What they did for me was good.

Land gave me to land. I traveled to Byblos; I returned to Qedem. I spent (30) a year and a half there. Then Ammunenshi,[4] the ruler of Upper Retenu, took me to him, saying to me: "You will be happy with me; you will hear the language of Egypt." He said this because he knew my character and had heard of my skill, Egyptians who were with him having borne witness for me. He said to me: "Why (35) have you come here? Has something happened at the residence?" I said to him: "King Sehetepibre departed to the horizon, and one did not know the circumstances." But I spoke in half-truths:[5] "When I returned from the expedition to the land of the Tjemeh, it was reported to me and my heart grew faint. It carried (40) me away on the path of flight, though I had not been talked about; no one had spat in my face; I had not heard a reproach; my name had not been heard in the mouth of the herald. I do not know what brought me to this country; it is as if planned by god. As if a Delta-man saw himself in Yebu, a marsh-man in Nubia."

Then he said to me: "How then is that land without that excellent god, fear of whom was throughout (45) the lands like Sakhmet in a year of plague?" I said to him in reply: "Of course his son has entered into the palace, having taken his father's heritage.

He is a god without peer,
No other comes before him;
He is lord of knowledge, wise planner, skilled leader,
One goes and comes by (50) his will.

He was the smiter of foreign lands,
While his father stayed in the palace,
He reported to him on commands carried out.

He is a champion who acts with his arm,
A fighter who has no equal,
When seen engaged in archery,
When joining the melee.

Horn-curber who makes hands turn weak,
His foes (55) can not close ranks;
Keen-sighted he smashes foreheads,
None can withstand his presence.

Wide-striding he smites the fleeing,
No retreat for him who turns him his back;
Steadfast in time of attack,
He makes turn back and turns not his back.

Stouthearted when he sees the mass,
He lets not slackness fill his heart;

(60) Eager at the sight of combat,
Joyful when he works his bow.

Clasping his shield he treads under foot,
No second blow needed to kill;
None can escape his arrow,
None turn aside his bow.

The Bowmen flee before him,
As before the might of the goddess;
As he fights he plans the goal,
(65) Unconcerned about all else.

Lord of grace, rich in kindness,
He has conquered through affection;
His city loves him more than itself,
Acclaims him more than its own god.

Men outdo women in hailing him,
Now that he is king;
Victor while yet in the egg,
Set to be ruler since his birth.

Augmenter of those born with him,
(70) He is unique, god-given;
Happy the land that he rules!

Enlarger of frontiers,
He will conquer southern lands,
While ignoring northern lands,
Though made to smite Asiatics and tread on Sand-farers!

"Send to him! Let him know your name as one who inquires while being far from his majesty. He will not fail to do (75) good to a land that will be loyal to him."

He said to me: "Well then, Egypt is happy knowing that he is strong. But you are here. You shall stay with me. What I shall do for you is good."

He set me at the head of his children. He married me to his eldest daughter. He let me choose for myself of his land, (80) of the best that was his, on his border with another land. It was a good land called Yaa. Figs were in it and grapes. It had more wine than water. Abundant was its honey, plentiful its oil. All kinds of fruit were on its trees. Barley was there and emmer, and no end of cattle of all kinds.

(85) Much also came to me because of the love of me; for he had made me chief of a tribe in the best part of his land. Loaves were made for me daily,[6] and wine as daily fare, cooked meat, roast fowl, as well as desert game. (90) For they snared for me and laid it before me, in addition to the catch of my hounds. Many sweets were made for me, and milk dishes of all kinds.

I passed many years, my children becoming strong men, each a master of his tribe. The envoy who came north or went south to the residence (95) stayed with me. I let everyone stay with me. I gave water to the thirsty; I showed the way to him who had strayed; I rescued him who had been robbed. When Asiatics conspired to attack the Rulers of Hill-Countries,[7] I opposed their movements. For this ruler of (100) Retenu made me carry out numerous missions as commander of his troops. Every hill tribe against which I marched I vanquished, so that it was driven from the pasture of its wells. I plundered its cattle, carried off its families, seized their food, and killed people (105) by my strong arm, by my bow, by my movements and my skillful plans. I won his heart and he loved me, for he recognized my valor. He set me at the head of his children, for he saw the strength of my arms.

> There came a hero of Retenu,[8]
> To challenge me (110) in my tent.
> A champion was he without peer,
> He had subdued it all.
> He said he would fight with me,
> He planned to plunder me,
> He meant to seize my cattle
> At the behest of his tribe.

The ruler conferred with me and I said: "I do not know him; I am not his ally, (115) that I could walk about in his camp. Have I ever opened his back rooms or climbed over his fence? It is envy, because he sees me doing your commissions. I am indeed like a stray bull in a strange herd, whom the bull of the herd charges, (120) whom the longhorn attacks. Is an inferior beloved when he becomes a superior? No Asiatic makes friends with a Delta-man. And what would make papyrus cleave to the mountain? If a bull loves combat, should a champion bull retreat for fear of being equaled? (125) If he wishes to fight, let him declare his wish. Is there a god who does not know what he has ordained, and a man who knows how it will be?"

At night I strung my bow, sorted my arrows, practiced with my dagger, polished my weapons. When it dawned Retenu came. (130) It had assembled its tribes; it had gathered its neighboring peoples; it was intent on this combat.

He came toward me while I waited, having placed myself near him. Every heart burned for me; the women jabbered. All hearts ached for me thinking: "Is there another champion who could fight him?" He ⟨raised⟩ his battle-axe and shield,[9] (135) while his armful of missiles fell toward me. When I had made his weapons attack me, I let his arrows pass me by without effect, one following the other. Then, when he charged me, I shot him, my arrow sticking in his neck. He screamed; he fell on his nose; (140) I slew him with his axe. I raised my war cry over his back, while every Asiatic shouted. I gave praise to Mont, while his people mourned him. The ruler Ammunenshi took me in his arms.

Then I carried off his goods; I plundered his cattle. What he had meant to do (145) to me I did to him. I took what was in his tent; I stripped his camp. Thus I became great, wealthy in goods, rich in herds. It was the god who acted, so as to show mercy to one with whom he had been angry, whom he had made stray abroad. For today his heart is appeased.

> A fugitive fled (150) his surroundings—[10]
>   I am famed at home.
> A laggard lagged from hunger—
>   I give bread to my neighbor.
> A man left his land in nakedness—
>   I have bright clothes, fine linen.
> A man ran for lack of one to send—
>   I am (155) rich in servants.
> My house is fine, my dwelling spacious—
>   My thoughts are at the palace!

Whichever god decreed this flight, have mercy, bring me home! Surely you will let me see the place in which my heart dwells! What is more important than that my corpse be buried in the land (160) in which I was born! Come to my aid! What if the happy event should occur![11] May god pity me! May he act so as to make happy the end of one whom he punished! May his heart ache for one whom he forced to live abroad! If he is truly appeased today, may he hearken to the prayer of one far away! May he return one whom he made roam the earth to the place from which he carried him off!

(165) May Egypt's king have mercy on me, that I may live by his mercy! May I greet the mistress of the land who is in the palace! May I hear the commands of her children! Would that my body were young again! For old age has come; feebleness has overtaken me. My eyes are heavy, my arms weak; (170) my legs fail to follow. The heart is weary; death is near. May I be conducted to the city of eternity! May I serve the Mistress of All! May she speak well of me to her children; may she spend eternity above me![12]

Now when the majesty of King Kheperkare was told of the condition in which I was, his majesty sent word (175) to me with royal gifts, in order to gladden the heart of this servant like that of a foreign ruler. And the royal children who were in his palace sent me their messages. Copy of the decree brought to this servant concerning his return to Egypt:

Horus: Living in Births; the Two Ladies: Living in Births; the King of Upper and Lower Egypt: *Kheperkare*; the Son of Re: (180) *Sesostris*, who lives forever. Royal decree to the Attendant Sinuhe:

This decree of the King if brought to you to let you know: That you circled the foreign countries, going from Qedem to Retenu, land giving you to land, was the counsel of your own heart. What had you done that one should act against you? You had not cursed, so that your speech would be reproved. You had not spoken against the counsel of the nobles, that your words should have been rejected. (185) This matter—it carried away your heart. It was not in my heart against you. This your heaven in the palace lives and prospers to this day.[13] Her head is adorned with the kingship of the land; her children are in the palace. You will store riches which they give you; you will live on their bounty. Come back to Egypt! See the residence in which you lived! Kiss the ground at the great portals, mingle with the courtiers! For today (190) you have begun to age. You have lost a man's strength. Think of the day of burial, the passing into reveredness.

A night is made for you with ointments and wrappings from the hand of Tait. A funeral procession is made for you on the day of burial; the mummy case is of gold, its head of lapis lazuli. The sky is above you as you lie in the hearse, oxen drawing you, musicians going before you. The dance of (195) the *mww*-dancers is done at the door of your tomb; the offering-list is read to you; sacrifice is made before your offering-stone. Your tomb-pillars, made of white stone, are among (those of) the royal children. You shall not die abroad! Not shall Asiatics inter you. You shall not be wrapped in the skin of a ram to serve as your coffin.[14] Too long a roaming of the earth! Think of your corpse, come back!

This decree reached me while I was standing (200) in the midst of my tribe. When it had been read to me, I threw myself on my belly. Having touched the soil, I spread it on my chest.[15] I strode around my camp shouting: "What compares with this which is done to a servant whom his heart led astray to alien lands? Truly good is the kindness that saves me from death! Your *ka* will grant me to reach my end, my body being at home!"

Copy of the reply to this decree:

The servant of the Palace, Sinuhe, (205) says:[16] In very good peace! Regarding the matter of this flight which this servant did in his ignorance. It is your *ka*, O good god, lord of the Two Lands, which Re loves and which Mont lord of Thebes favors; and Amun lord of Thrones-of-the-Two-Lands, and Sobk-Re lord of Sumenu, and Horus, Hathor, Atum with his Ennead, and Sopdu-Neferbau-Semseru the Eastern Horus, and the Lady of Yemet—may she enfold your head—and the conclave upon the flood, and Min-Horus of the hill-countries, and Wereret lady of (210) Punt, Nut, Haroeris-Re, and all the gods of Egypt and the isles of the sea—may they give life and joy to your nostrils, may they endue you with their bounty, may they give you eternity without limit, infinity without bounds! May the fear of you resound in lowlands and highlands, for you have subdued all that the sun encircles! This is the prayer of this servant for his lord who saves from the West.

The lord of knowledge who knows people knew (215) in the majesty of the palace that this servant was afraid to say it. It is like a thing too great to repeat. The great god, the peer of Re, knows the heart of one who has served him willingly. This servant is in the hand of one who thinks about him. He is placed under his care. Your Majesty is the conquering Horus; your arms vanquish all lands. May then your Majesty command to have brought to you the prince of Meki from Qedem, (220) the mountain chiefs from Keshu, and the prince of Menus from the lands of the Fenkhu. They are rulers of renown who have grown up in the love of you. I do not mention Retenu—it belongs to you like your hounds.

Lo, this flight which the servant made—I did not plan it. It was not in my heart; I did not devise it. I do not know what removed me from my place. It was like (225) a dream. As if a Delta-man saw himself in Yebu, a marsh-man in Nubia. I was not afraid; no one ran after me. I had not heard a reproach; my name was not heard in the mouth of the herald. Yet my flesh crept, my feet hurried, my heart drove me; the god who had willed this flight (230) dragged me away. Nor am I a haughty man. He who knows his land respects men. Re has set the fear of you throughout the land, the dread of you in every foreign country. Whether I am at the residence, whether I am in this place, it is you who covers this horizon.[17] The sun rises at your pleasure. The water in the river is drunk when you wish. The air of heaven is breathed at your bidding. This servant will hand over (235) to the brood[18] which this servant begot in this place. This servant has been sent for! Your Majesty will do as he wishes! One lives by the breath which you give. As Re, Horus, and Hathor love your august nose, may Mont lord of Thebes wish it to live forever!

I was allowed to spend one more day in Yaa, handing over my possessions to my children, my eldest son taking charge of my tribe; (240) all my possessions became his—my serfs, my herds, my fruit, my fruit trees. This servant departed southward. I halted at Horus-ways. The commander in charge of the garrison sent a message to the residence to let it be known. Then his majesty sent a trusted overseer of the royal domains with whom were loaded ships, (245) bearing royal gifts for the Asiatics who had come with me to escort me to Horusways. I called each one by his name, while every butler was at his task. When I had started and set sail, there was kneading and straining beside me, until I reached the city of Itj-tawy.

When it dawned, very early, they came to summon me. Ten men came and ten men went to usher me into the palace. My forehead touched the ground between the sphinxes, (250) and the royal children stood in the gateway to meet me. The courtiers who usher through the forecourt set me on the way to the audience-hall. I found his majesty on the great throne in a kiosk of gold.[19] Stretched out on my belly, I did not know myself before him, while this god greeted me pleasantly. I was like a man seized by darkness. (255) My *ba* was gone, my limbs trembled; my heart was not in my body, I did not know life from death.

His majesty said to one of the courtiers: "Lift him up, let him speak to me." Then his majesty said: "Now you have come, after having roamed foreign lands. Flight has taken its toll of you. You have aged, have reached old age. It is no small matter that your corpse will be interred without being escorted by Bowmen. But don't act thus, don't act thus, speechless (260) though your name was called!" Fearful of punishment[20] I answered with the answer of a frightened man: "What has my lord said to me, that I might answer it? It is not disrespect to the god![21] It is the terror which is in my body, like that which caused the fateful flight! Here I am before you. Life is yours. May your Majesty do as he wishes!"

Then the royal daughters were brought in, and his majesty said to the queen: "Here is Sinuhe, (265) come as an Asiatic, a product of nomads!" She uttered a very great cry, and the royal daughters shrieked all together. They said to his majesty: "Is it really he, O king, our lord?" Said his majesty: "It is really he!" Now having brought with them their necklaces, rattles, and sistra, they held them out to his majesty:[22]

> Your hands (270) upon the radiance, eternal king,
> Jewels of heaven's mistress!
> The Gold[23] gives life to your nostrils,
> The Lady of Stars enfolds you!
>
> Southcrown fared north, northcrown south,
> Joined, united by your majesty's word.
> While the Cobra decks your brow,
> You deliver the poor from harm.
> Peace to you from Re, Lord of Lands!
> Hail to you and the Mistress of All!
>
> Slacken your bow, lay down your arrow,
> (275) Give breath to him who gasps for breath!
> Give us our good gift on this good day,[24]
> Grant us the son of northwind, Bowman born in Egypt!
>
> He made the flight in fear of you,
> He left the land in dread of you!
> A face that sees you shall not pale,
> Eyes that see you shall not fear!

His majesty said: "He shall not fear, he shall not (280) dread!" He shall be a Companion among the nobles. He shall be among the courtiers. Proceed to the robing-room to wait on him!"

I left the audience-hall, the royal daughters giving me their hands. (285) We went through the great portals, and I was put in the house of a prince. In it were luxuries: a bathroom and mirrors.[25] In it were riches from the treasury; clothes of royal linen, myrrh, and the choice perfume of the king and of his favorite courtiers were in every (290) room. Every servant was at his task. Years were removed from my body. I was shaved; my hair was combed. Thus was my squalor returned to the foreign land, my dress to the Sand-farers. I was clothed in fine linen; I was anointed with fine oil. I slept on a bed. I had returned the sand to those who dwell in it, (295) the tree-oil to those who grease themselves with it.

I was given a house and garden that had belonged to a courtier. Many craftsmen rebuilt it, and all its woodwork was made anew. Meals were brought to me from the palace three times, four times a day, apart from what the royal children gave without a moment's pause.

(300) A stone pyramid was built for me in the midst of the pyramids. The masons who build tombs constructed it. A master draughtsman designed in it. A master sculptor carved in it. The overseers of construction in the necropolis busied themselves with it. All the equipment that is placed in (305) a tomb-shaft was supplied. Mortuary priests were given me. A funerary domain was made for me. It had fields and a garden in the right place, as is done for a Companion of the first rank. My statue was overlaid with gold, its skirt with electrum. It was his majesty who ordered it made. There is no commoner for whom the like has been done. I was in (310) the favor of the king, until the day of landing[26] came.

Colophon: It is done from beginning to end as it was found in writing.

NOTES

1. Sinuhe was specifically in the service of Princess Nefru, the wife of Sesostris I, the latter being co-regent at the time of his father's death. Khenemsut and Kanefru are the names of the pyramids of Sesostris I and Amenemhet I.

2. Tjemeh and Tjehenu designated two distinct Libyan peoples who merged in the course of time. In this story the terms are used interchangeably.

3. Goedicke, *JEA*, 43 (1957), 77-85, has made it plausible that *Mꜣꜥty* was not a lake but a name for the Giza region (see also Gauthier, *DG*, IV, 218 on a town *mꜣꜥty*), and that Isle-of-Snefru and Isle-of-Kem-Wer were not islands. Sinuhe is traveling south along the edge of the western desert, until he crosses the Nile at a spot the name of which Goedicke explained as "Cattle-Quay." He landed in the vicinity of the "Red Mountain" (today's Gebel al-Ahmar), and only then did he decide to flee the country and hence turned northward.

4. K. Baer would read the name as Amorite 'Ammulanasi, "God is verily (my) prince." On the name pattern see H. Huffmon, *Amorite Personal Names in the Mari Texts* (Baltimore, 1965), pp. 223 and 240. I retain the reading "Ammunenshi" largely because I adhere to the method of transliterating the Egyptian consonantal script with a minimum of vocalization and without regard for actual pronunciation.

5. Some scholars have adopted the rendering, "It was told to me incorrectly" (see Barns, *AO*, p. 5 n. 23). I do not find this convincing. Sinuhe's "half-truths" consist in pretending that the death of the old king was reported to him when in fact he had only overheard a conspiratorial message, and in disclaiming any knowledge of the circumstances.

6. Or: "supplies of *mint*-drink;" see Barns, *AO*, p. 9 n. 38.

7. Sinuhe is on the side of the *ḥḳꜣw ḫꜣswt*, the "rulers of mountainlands," the term from which the name "Hyksos" was derived.

8. In this passage Sinuhe's prose assumes the symmetrical rhythm of poetry.

9. The insertion of a verb still seems to me the best solution for this much debated passage. Weapons, including a shield, do not simply "fall" from a fighter. Only missiles, whether arrows or javelins, "fall." An alternative might be to take *'ḥ·n* not as the auxiliary but as the verb "to stand" referring to shield and axe. The champion held his shield and axe in readiness while shooting his missiles.

10. In *Schott Festschrift*, p. 128, Westendorf gave a new analysis and translation of this beautiful poem which climaxes the account of Sinuhe's career abroad. While it is true that the preposition *n* in all four occurrences here has the meaning "because of," to translate it thus would destroy the attempt to render the poem as a poem. The change of mood, from Sinuhe's exultation over his success to his intense longing for the lost homeland, occurs in the last distich (as Westendorf suggested), and provides the transition to the prayers for return.

11. I.e., "what if death should occur while I am still abroad?" So with Westendorf, *loc. cit.*, pp. 129-130.

12. In this context the "Mistress of All" could be either the queen or the goddess Nut. The latter interpretation was preferred by C. E. Sander-Hansen, *Acta Or.*, 22 (1955-1957), 147.

13. The queen is meant.

14. *AO*, 2, 48, has *n ir·tw ḏri·k*, and Barns, *ibid.*, p. 21 n. 18, suggests to read *nn ir·tw ḏri·k*. But since elsewhere *ḏrit* means "container," "coffin," I assume the same word here and, following the text of B, take it to mean that the ram's skin will not be Sinuhe's coffin.

15. As a gesture of humility.

16. This translation of Sinuhe's reply to the king's letter follows in essentials that of Barns in *JEA*, 53 (1967), 6-14.

17. Or: yours is all that the horizon covers.

18. Taking *ṯꜣt* to mean "progeny, brood," as proposed by Barns, *AO*, p. 26 n. 36.

19. There is no need to transpose the word before *nt ḏ'm* if it is read as *wmt·t* (not *wmt*), this being the word for "enclosure" (see *Wb.*, I, 307). I take it to refer to the light, kiosk type of structure which was built over the dais on which the throne stood, and surrounded the throne on three sides.

20. *AO*'s version (2, 49): "fear your punishment," seems to me inferior.

21. Read: *n ḥr-ʿ n ntr ìs pw*, and see Barns's note on *ḥr-ʿ*, "shortcoming," in *AO*, pp. 30-32 n. 50.

22. The princesses hold out the emblems sacred to Hathor and perform a ceremonial dance and a song in which they beg a full pardon for Sinuhe. The song was studied by H. Brunner in *ZÄS*, 80 (1955), 5-11.

23. Epithet of Hathor.

24. Reading *ìmì n·n ḫnt·n nfr m hrw pn nfr*, according to *AO*, 2, 58, and see Barns, *ibid.*, p. 33 n. 58.

25. Following C. E. Sander-Hansen, *Acta Or.*, 22 (1955-1957), 149, in taking *ʿḥmw nw ȝḥt* to mean 'mirrors.''

26. The day of death. Through its beginning and its ending, the story is given the form of the tomb-autobiography in which the narrator looks back on his completed life.

Indexes

Indexes

I. DIVINITIES

239

II. KINGS AND QUEENS

III. PERSONAL NAMES

IV. GEOGRAPHICAL AND ETHNICAL TERMS

V. EGYPTIAN WORDS

VI. SOME MAJOR CONCEPTS